Changing the Wor(l)d

Changing the Wor(l)d

Discourse, Politics,
and the Feminist Movement

Stacey Young

ROUTLEDGE
New York   London

Published in 1997 by

Routledge
29 West 35th Street
New York, NY 10001

Published in Great Britain by

Routledge
11 New Fetter Lane
London EC4P 4EE

Catologuing-in-Publication Data is available from the Library of Congress.

For Joan Rulison Young, my mother
and
For Margaret Bailey Denio, my great-aunt

Contents

Acknowledgments

This work has been encouraged, refined, and sustained by colleagues and friends too numerous to mention but nonetheless indispensable to it. Special thanks, however, go to Lauren Pinsley, Kim Christensen, Shane Phelan, Linda Nicholson, Rosemary Nossiff, Verónica Frenkel, Trevor Hope, Kris Miller, Michael Busch, Jal Mistry, and Cecelia Cancellaro. Heartfelt thanks also to my family.

Susan Buck-Morss, Biddy Martin, Mary Katzenstein, and Bud Kenworthy shepherded this project through its dissertation stage. That dissertation and this book have gained immeasurably from their incisive critiques, their enthusiasm for the project, and their irreverence for disciplinary boundaries and for the mainstream of political science. This book would not have been possible without them.

Nor would it have been possible without the generous and patient participation of Nancy Bereano of Firebrand Books, Dionne Brooks of South End Press, Barbara Grier of Naiad Books, Andrea Lockett of Kitchen Table: Women of Color Press, Cynthia Peters of South End Press, Joan Pinkvoss of Aunt Lute Books, Karin San Juan of South End Press, Carol Seajay of *Feminist Bookstore News,* and Barbara Smith of Kitchen Table: Women of Color Press. These publishers shared their time and insights freely and thoughtfully. The work they do is tremendously important; I hope that my own work facilitates theirs in some small way.

Deep appreciation and thanks go to Beverly McIntyre, for sublime companionship and so much more, including motorcycles, Africa, and the time and support to complete this work. Here's to the optimists.

Introduction 1

Women have come a long way. I turned on the preliminary hear-
ings for the O. J. Simpson trial and saw a woman magistrate and a
woman prosecutor. How can you complain?
> —Harriet Woods, President of the National Women's
> Political Caucus, in an address to the City Club
> of Cleveland, aired July 21, 1995

The Grammar Of Liberalism

Ben Anderson[1] has argued that nationalism is the "grammar" through
which people make sense of their places in the world in the current
historical period. His point is that nationalism is much more fundamental even than perspective, as it is the medium through which we formulate, express, promote, or alter perspectives. Nationalism, he argues, is the very
structure through which we see, think about, and make sense of the world.

Yet nationalism is not the only grammar that defines American society;
liberalism is equally salient (and, of course, not unrelated to nationalism). It
structures how we define well-being, what we think about individuality and
the citizen's relationship to the state, the nature of power, democracy, freedom,
and equality—and, more fundamentally, that we think in these terms at all.
Liberalism structures how we identify abuses and imbalances of power, how
we respond (or fail to respond) to those abuses and imbalances, and what kinds
of responses we deem appropriate and "successful."

In the United States over the last fifty years, several challenges to liberal notions of power, abuse, and redress have emerged in connection with mass movements for social change. The two most fundamental have been grounded in critiques of race and gender[2]—their social construction and their functions in social organization. The civil rights/Black Power/anti-racist and feminist movements emerged as large numbers of people rallied around these critiques and the social change agendas they imply. These movements have not been homogeneous; nor have they been galvanized by consensus. Rather, they have entailed large-scale internal struggles over the analyses of the systems they target: how oppression works, how entrenched it is, where responsibility for it lies, what types of change are possible and desirable, and how that change can best be brought about.

The complexities of these struggles, though, almost invariably drop out of public imagination, which reduces these critiques to their liberal versions, easily graspable within the dominant "grammar" or paradigm. This reduction results from the conscious efforts of powerful institutions, individuals, and classes; it also results, however, from the unconscious assimilative processes that any system engenders—i.e., the inexorable tendency for a system to reshape what it encounters in its own terms. For a population steeped in one grammar finds it difficult, at best, to grasp a different one it views as neutral; when the new grammar represents not neutrality, but a fundamental shift in the distribution of power, it is downright threatening, and thus all the more likely to be rejected.

Yet inroads are achieved, new grammars take hold, even if only in localized and incomplete ways. Sometimes they take hold on a large scale—though large-scale acceptance is usually contingent upon the challenge having been altered, reordered into something that more closely conforms to the original grammar. Ellen Willis writes, for instance, of the metamorphosis of feminism's initial concern with women's sexual liberation into a blander, reformist focus on a few sexual rights.[3] This metamorphosis simultaneously narrowed feminism's agenda and broadened its appeal—a dual impact that Willis's critique works to counteract. The Willises of the world keep pushing for radical change—and they continue to win adherents to their cause. For the most part, though, they go unacknowledged in accounts grounded in the status quo grammar and the interests it represents.

This book argues that this is the case with regard to the women's movement and its representation in popular culture and in academic studies. That is, the women's movement, like the anti-racist movement that preceded and accompanies it, has developed and promoted a far-reaching, radical critique of one of the cornerstones of our society—the

2

inequality of women and men. This fundamental critique has been re-cast—almost as often by constituencies within the movement as by those outside of it—as a challenge to tinker with, to modify—but not to transform in any fundamental way—the liberal ideologies and institutions that govern our society. Yet, the radical critiques have not withered away—they persist, as do efforts to promote social change that would bring social relations in line with those critiques.

This book explores some versions of these radical critiques and their manifestations in activism directed at promoting new grammars, new social paradigms through which individuals, collectivities, and institutions interpret social circumstances and devise responses to them. That is, it investigates the interpretive, discursive forms of activism that represent the most direct attempts by the women's movement to change fundamentally the way people think: feminist publishing, feminist writing, and discursive aspects of direct-action activism. Specifically, it argues that those most marginalized within and beyond the women's movement—women of color, lesbians and bisexual women, working-class women—have launched the most interesting endeavors to analyze the present "grammar" and to construct alternatives. It then looks at why these fundamental critiques "drop out" of academic accounts whose very aim is to articulate and evaluate the efforts of the movements associated with them. According to this argument, it is the pervasiveness of the grammar of liberalism, and how it imports prejudices that work to sustain it, that informs liberal feminism's[4] analyses and agendas, as well as social science's theories of power and its methodologies, in ways that render both liberal feminism and social science studies of the feminist movement profoundly myopic. This book explores the consequences for the fundamental critiques—and for those whose interests they advance—of the obfuscation liberalism imposes upon movement politics and academic investigations.

Finally, the book presents and assesses some theoretical projects—within social movement theory and within postmodern theories of the subject and identity—that offer academics, in their own language, a bridge from the liberal paradigm to more interdisciplinary, eclectic, extra-institutional approaches that might enable them better to comprehend and evaluate discursive political action and the radical paradigms—the "grammars"—that action often promotes.

With regard to human nature, liberalism subscribes to a "twofold idea of individuality and sameness": that is, it assumes that, on the one hand, we are all free to do what we please; and, on the other, "we all speak the same language, hold the same values, and know the same truths—unless, that is, we're aberrant and abnormal."[5] This paradox of individuality and sameness underlies liberalism's notion that there exists a universal standard of rationality that forms a core essence common to all "normal" people. Those who fail to act in accordance with accepted models of rational behavior do so, in this view, not because those models restrict their freedom or are, in fact, irrational in the context of their lives; they do so, rather, because they either lack reason or are consciously flouting it—in either case, to the detriment of their fellow human beings.[6]

Liberalism makes this notion of universal rationality as the essence of humanity the basis of its epistemology and politics, which valorize rational "objectivity" and its supposed embodiment in scientific inquiry and institutions of government. Essentialism enables the assumption that these "objective" standards apply equally well all around. The extension of the notion of universal rationality into a faith in argument, persuasion, and the inevitability of progress leads to the assumption that individuals in "democratic" societies who feel that they are somehow being treated unequally or unfairly need only present their case before the appropriate institutions of governance. The expectation is that these institutions will then apply their objective standards of rationality and equality under the law to determine whether mistreatment is actually taking place. If it is found that an individual has been treated unfairly or unequally, the solution is assumed to lie in a correction of the mistake which led to the unequal treatment. If it is found that the individual has been treated equally, in accordance with the rational, objective standards of liberal institutions, then any problems that individual encounters are assumed to be due to her failure to exercise her rationality—or her failure to take advantage of opportunities that are supposedly available to everyone—and are thus of her own making.

Liberalism posits what Michel Foucault calls a juridical model of power, in which power resides in a central authority and inhibits those who hold it from exploring the social and political mechanisms, including discursive production, through which "human nature" and human relations are constructed and controlled.[7]

Liberalism's focus on government at the expense of other levels of society leads feminists who subscribe to liberalism's theory of power to prioritize engagement with institutions of governance as the strategy of choice for feminist change. This is premised on the assumption that women's oppression is merely an accident or an oversight, or a rather superficial, hollow vestige of obsolete social organization, and that the machinery of liberal institutions can be harnessed to effect women's equality with men, since this goal is consistent with "equality"—a central tenet of liberalism. Though Celia Kitzinger reaches very different conclusions from those advanced by postmodern feminist theorists (see chapter 6), she

4

aptly characterizes liberalism's approach to conflict: "Ignoring the issue of power, liberalism dissolves entire areas of sociopolitical conflict into interpersonal problems which can be resolved through the learning of good communication skills." Kitzinger goes on to discuss the limitations liberalism imposes on examinations of gender relations and sexuality—areas of life thoroughly invested with power relations but presented, within liberalism, as "private" and therefore non-political:

> Liberalism . . . leaves the structure of patriarchy and the institution of heterosexuality unexamined in the belief that lesbianism is a personal choice or preference and that lesbians will achieve "equality" with heterosexual women, or women with men, through shared communication and understanding, through education and the application of reason.[8]

The limitations of liberal institutions extend as well to their responses to conflict. That is, because these institutions acknowledge a very limited scope of conflict, they also mark out a very limited range of available responses to it. One of liberal feminism's main shortcomings, then, is its reluctance to question seriously whether liberalism's available responses to conflict are sufficient to secure women's emancipation from domination. Relatedly, liberal feminism fails to question whether a definition of equality that pays only passing notice to individuals' embeddedness in social structures of inequality can ever be used to bring about actual—not just nominal—equality. (The women's movement studies also typically neglect to question the premises of liberal institutions and liberal feminist engagement with those institutions; thus, these studies run the risk—to which, I will argue, they ultimately succumb—of supporting and perpetuating discourses and institutions that themselves perpetuate the domination of women, on the basis of sex, race, class, ethnicity, and sexuality.)

Liberalism's characterization of the locus of power and domination—and thus the logical site of resistance—promises the impossible. That is, it claims that power resides in legal and governmental institutions; consequently, it views these institutions as the appropriate arena for resistance. In this view, engagement with formal governing or other policy-making institutions is the path to eventual liberation. This perception diverts attention away from the restrictive forces that emanate from sources other than these centralized, juridical institutions. Domination does not always take the form of outright prohibition; and resistance takes place in many different arenas. Forms of domination that these institutions define as "private" are seen as non-structural, not remediable via government action, and ultimately not important. Ideologies that construct power as being centralized in state institutions divert attention from other arenas and processes of domination, keeping them out of sight and thus decreasing the likelihood that they will become sites of resistance. These ideologies also divert attention away from the resistance that does take place at these levels, by failing to recognize it *as resistance*. That the studies of the women's movement prioritize the type of resistance that involves engaging with government institutions on those institutions' terms, and dismiss discursive politics and other forms of cultural resistance as something other than "politics," is evidence not of the paramount importance of formal governance and policy-making, but of the studies' rootedness in liberal notions of power, and of the limitations those notions impose.

Justice Denied: The Limits of Liberalism

Liberal institutions are premised on the principle of treating people as though they are equal, as individuals, to other individuals. As demonstrated by the civil rights and women's movements in particular, there are important, substantive gains to be made through a strategy designed to bring government practice in line with this ideology. However, these gains can be quite fragile, since they depend on the good faith and judgment of those who have power (and thus a stake in the status quo) to determine what constitutes "discrimination," "inequality," "fairness," and so on. Moreover, to the extent that liberal governmental institutions treat people as atomized individuals, they are unable to acknowledge and alleviate the large-scale social inequalities between dominant and subordinate groups—inequalities that stem, in part, from the disparate treatment of these groups by the law. In treating individuals equally, regardless of the social conditions that place them in dominant and subordinate positions, liberal institutions perpetuate social inequalities: everyone is assumed to be entitled to the same benefits, and to be burdened by the same responsibilities, even though in reality different people receive differential social, political, and economic advantages.

Sometimes, liberal governing structures do try to acknowledge hegemonic social divisions and take these into consideration in dispensing political goods and responsibilities. Liberalism's own emphasis on individuality, however, is all too easily marshaled against this attention to structural inequalities. One need only look at the success of the "New Right" in demolishing any semblance of a social safety net for poor people to understand how this works: in their recourse to liberalism's valorization of individuality, they overwhelm liberalism's focus on democracy.

The liberal political system is not a structure that feminists can easily appropriate, even on its own terms. Feminists and others who seek equality through legal institutions have found those institutions to be replete with contradictions that often work to resist intervention on behalf of marginalized groups. The four examples that follow demonstrate the tenacity of social inequalities, even in legal situations designed explicitly to ameliorate these inequalities.

Bakke

One example can be found in the pivotal 1978 Supreme Court decision on affirmative action in the case of *Regents of the University of California v. Bakke*. This case involved a challenge by a white applicant, Bakke, to the UC Davis Medical School's affirmative action program. Bakke, who was denied admission to the school, claimed he was discriminated against because the admissions committee had set aside a number of seats in the entering class for students of color. In this case, the definition of discrimination the Court utilized was that of "facial intent to discriminate." The Court's decision stated that admissions programs in which "race or ethnic background is simply one element—to be weighed fairly against other elements—in the selection process"[9] are acceptable. On the other hand, admissions processes that identify race or ethnicity as a definitive criterion[10] contain, according to the Court, a "facial intent to discriminate"—that is, they openly intend from the start to make admissions decisions based on race or ethnicity. The Court rejects such policies for institutions that have not been shown to discriminate intentionally against ethnic and racial minorities, claiming that these policies would impose "disadvantages upon persons like respondent [Bakke], who bear no responsibility for whatever harm the beneficiaries of the special admissions program are thought to have suffered."[11]

The interesting thing about this case is the Court's definition of discrimination. The Court's decision turns on an intent to discriminate, which must be demonstrated in a court of law to have been directed toward specific individuals. What this definition leaves out, of course, is the kind of pernicious discrimination that comes about not as the result of individual intent to discriminate, but as a result of socially accepted, unconsciously internalized prejudice that gets expressed in subtle but powerful and pervasive cultural biases (such as those that result in lower standardized test scores across the board for women and people of color than for white men). What the definition includes is that single form of discrimination to which white males with the privileges of affluence and heterosexuality might, in some cases, be subject. An individual's or institution's overt intent to discriminate might, on rare occasions, be directed against this privileged subject of liberalism and liberal government institutions. Ingrained, endemic, structural and cultural biases will not, by definition, be directed against this subject, and it is no accident that they are not reflected in the Court's definition.

There have been other cases in which the judicial system has recognized systemic inequalities (or at least their possibility), most notably cases that establish standards requiring employers to demonstrate that discriminatory hiring practices are necessary to adequate performance of certain jobs. These kinds of protections, however, have increasingly come under attack. The shift away from such protections indicates that while it is neither impossible nor unknown for liberal government institutions to attend to systemic inequality, such attention is by no means guaranteed. It is no accident that the Supreme Court, our society's ultimate judicial embodiment of liberal juridical power, defines discrimination in the way that it does, given liberalism's construction of the subject as equal with other subjects, combined with the current reactionary backlash against measures to remedy structural inequalities.

Women and Welfare

A second example of liberal institutions' insufficient response to hegemonic social divisions is documented by Nancy Fraser's examination of social welfare programs in terms of their differential benefits based on assumptions about programs recipients.[12] Some programs are directed toward individuals, as labor-market programs (such as unemployment). Others are directed toward households, as family-based programs (such as AFDC—Aid to Families with Dependent Children). The labor-market programs are premised on standard notions of a male, formal-sector wage laborer (as opposed to, for example, an unpaid female domestic worker). The family-based programs are premised on the assumption that a proper household is comprised of a male breadwinner and a female unpaid domestic worker. Thus the benefits allocated by family-based programs are structured so as to replace the "absent male breadwinner" in (largely) female-headed households.

The subject of the labor-market programs is the (masculinized) individual worker: those eligible for these programs make their claims as wage workers (not as parents or unpaid domestic workers), and the programs are designed to compensate for loss of the individual's breadwinning income. Women whose work is primarily unpaid domestic work, or is un-

8

recognized (such as sex work, babysitting, home typing, etc.) are ineligible for unemployment insurance and other labor-market programs. Recipients of these benefits are constructed as rights-bearers—recipients of worker's compensation, for example, are viewed as having a right to benefits distributed through programs into which they have already paid (through their employers). Generally, they are not stigmatized or seen as being "on the dole"; and they receive cash that they can spend as they see fit, without the surveillance that accompanies family-based programs.

The subjects of the family-based programs make their claims as parents, not workers, and the programs actively discourage recipients from trying to redefine their roles as workers: if a recipient takes a job, her AFDC benefits are cut by the same amount she receives from her paid job. There is a heavy component of surveillance in these programs, and unlike those who receive labor-market based benefits, AFDC recipients receive in-kind payments rather than cash, and thus have spending decisions made for them. The definition of the subjects of these programs primarily as mothers is reinforced by the programs' lack of job training and day care. Moreover, therapeutic rather than economic remedies are more often offered to recipients of family-based programs, which further pathologizes them and distinguishes them from their "deserving" counterparts in labor-market programs.

The differential construction of the subjects of these assistance programs and the differential benefits provided these subjects illustrate the tenacity of gendered stereotypes and the ease with which they are translated into public policy. They also illustrate the primacy of the male subject, who receives benefits in labor-market programs, and who is supplanted (in his absence) by social service agencies in family-based programs.

Legal Status and Treatment of Abused Children

An article in the April 1988 issue of *New Directions for Women* reported a growing sanctuary movement dedicated to sheltering children (and often their mothers) who have been placed by the courts in the custody of men who have abused them sexually.[13] The movement is spearheaded by Mothers Against Raping Children (MARC) in Gulfport, Mississippi, and the National Child Rights Alliance (NCRA) in Durham, North Carolina, which provide counseling and shelter to children and mothers who have gone underground following these court decisions.

One such case in Gulfport, Mississippi included "reams of medical evidence" and testimony from a psychiatrist that indicated repeated sexual trauma suffered by a three-year-old girl and her fifteen-month-old brother during visits with their father. The judge in the case awarded custody of both children to the father, claiming that the mother was an unfit parent. The judge contended that the mother abused the girl by taking her to "numerous and unwarranted doctors' visits and examinations."[14] The woman in the case moved her children into hiding and was ordered jailed by the judge. After forty-three days in jail, she told the court where her children were; they were then placed in their father's custody. As a condition of her release, the woman had to provide the court with a list of all the people who helped her hide her children.

In another case, the same judge awarded custody of a young girl to her abusive father on the grounds that the woman was an unfit mother because "she had no regular source of income" (she was on welfare), had two "illegitimate children," and her life "lacked stability" because she didn't marry the father of her third child.[15] The article quotes Barbara Hart of the Leadership Institute for Women as saying,

> Fathers who are sexual assailants are doing an incredible job of aggressive litigation. This type of action wears people down. . . . It tells women that if they bring charges of child sexual assault, they'll get sued for fabrication. And probably all they'll get out of it is having to pay litigation expenses and risk losing their kids.[16]

The judge's comments in the latter case make clear that the court decided the case based on traditional expectations regarding the woman's lack of deference to male authority, her class status and economic situation, her sexual behavior, and her family situation.

It is interesting and distressing to note that these women's attempts to remove their children from the custody of abusive men by going through the legal system represents the kind of strategy many liberal feminists call for: women trying to get government institutions to live up to their ideologies of equality and rationality. Not only do these feminist appropriations of the legal system fail to work to their advantage, but in some cases, these attempts also backfire, resulting in criminal charges against the women themselves. Of course, such dire outcomes are not always the case, and women have sometimes been able to secure important gains through the legal system. However, the contradictions between liberal ideology and the reality of social inequalities make liberal institutions unlikely guarantors of changes that would ameliorate social inequality—particularly, perhaps, in times of tremendous conservative backlash against those who *have* been able to secure gains from those institutions.

Hate Crimes Laws and Homophobia

A final brief example illustrates the way that social sanctions of inequality permeate a legal system supposedly organized on the basis of individual equality.

The situation facing lesbians, bisexuals, and gay men in the United States is characterized by high levels of unchecked (and, in cases such as the military, state-sanctioned) discrimination. Nationwide, approximately 185 counties and cities have enacted local ordinances that prohibit discrimination on the basis of sexual orientation.[17] However, few if any of the state and local governments that have considered or passed hate-crimes legislation have included crimes motivated by homophobia among those covered by the laws. Despite their ideology of equality among individuals, governments often codify inequality in their policies—even those policies, such as hate-crimes legislation, that are specifically designed to address systemic inequality.

Each of these examples demonstrates some of the limitations of a strategy of appealing to liberal institutions for rights, equality, and protection from discrimination and abuse. Far from being immune to hegemonic cultural biases and phobias, the institutions responsible for conferring rights and ensuring protection often reproduce those biases and phobias in public policy.

Liberal feminists who argue that true equality before the law for women and men would result in radical social transformation are probably right. However, it seems unlikely that, in reality, legal equality can be brought about *prior* to such radical transformation. Even a political system premised on the equality of individuals shows itself to be remarkably resilient in enforcing inequality in the face of challenges made by marginalized groups, remarkably able to incorporate the contradictions of an ideology of equality into a practice of discrimination and inequality. As long as prevailing social norms persist that construct, for example, women as homemakers, and as unfit mothers when they challenge male authority and abuse; affirmative action as a threat to white men; discrimination as an individual (not group) and necessarily intentional (not structural and endemic) phenomenon; and gay, lesbian, and bisexual people as undeserving of basic civil rights; as long as these constructs persist and prevail in the social imagination, it seems unlikely that the legal system will counter them to any great extent. The privileged status of white, bourgeois, heterosexual men as the subjects of liberal humanism relies on liberalism's institutionalization of these social constructs. Moreover, the notion that equality between women and men is achieved when a few women (usually white, well-educated, and well-off) move into positions of power traditionally reserved for men obscures the reality of the ongoing, systemic oppression of the vast majority of women. The seductiveness of this superficial notion of equality is, perhaps, the only way to explain a leading liberal feminist's contention that the fact that two women are the magistrate and prosecutor in the murder trial of an acknowledged wife-beater is cause for celebration (see this chapter's epigraph). If liberalism's success in focusing our attention on such token gains blinds us to such persistent systemic inequalities as the abuse of women by the men who claim to love them, it is very pernicious indeed.

What is needed to effect far-reaching social change is a variety of strategies of resistance, pursued simultaneously in different social arenas at different levels of society, but with a common focus on changing basic notions of what is acceptable. Feminist practice and postmodern and feminist theories point to several alternatives: most notably, localized, discursive resistance, and the construction of identity and subjectivity through discourse as a site for struggle and social change.

This book is concerned with articulating little-explored feminist activity aimed at transforming consciousness and examining the reasons that both liberal feminism and scholarly studies of the women's movement generally ignore that activity. As I argue in the chapters that follow, discursive activity has been central to the contemporary women's movement, more explicitly in some sectors than others. The discussion above illuminates the limitations of liberalism and of any movement for social change that relies solely or primarily on liberal strategies. The rest of this book discusses feminist discursive politics; its embodiment in feminist publishing and feminist autobiographical/theoretical texts developed and published by feminist presses; social science studies of the women's movement, and their neglect of the nature and import of discursive politics; the theoretical and methodological bases for this neglect; and theoretical and methodological strategies that facilitate a more comprehensive and nuanced understanding of discursive feminist activity.

Feminist Discursive Politics

In keeping with the women's movement's emphasis on consciousness and language, much feminist activism concentrates on changing how people think about gender, power, self-determination, and so on. Certainly any social movement, organized or otherwise, mobilizes various linguistic and non-linguistic symbolic interventions. The women's movement, however, has from the outset identified such interventions, and the territory they contest, as central to maintaining or transforming women's social, political, and economic positions. Radical feminism, for example, has consistently emphasized the ways in which women's subordination is secured through language and media images. Consciousness-raising (CR) groups were predicated in part on the conviction that women's lives can be transformed through talking with other women. Feminist publications seek to effect social change through propagating feminist discourses.

Moreover, certain sectors of the women's movement—through CR groups, speakouts, and publishing—have focused specifically on the power of women telling their stories, and placing their experiences within political contexts, in order to help other women to imagine and act on options they did not previously realize existed. But other forms of feminist discursive politics accomplish this in very different ways (and with a variety of results). The logical outcome of the sharing of experiences that took place in CR groups throughout the 1970s, for example, was often a reductive kind of identity politics that assumed a common set of experiences among women, and a common political stance following from those experiences.

Recent feminist autotheoretical writings—the subject of chapter 3—also articulate politics in terms of identity. However, because of their authorship and form, and because of the historical context in which they have emerged, the autotheoretical texts work toward a very different outcome than more reductive versions of identity politics. These texts (many of them by lesbians of color) are part of a larger challenge, advanced by women who have been marginalized both within the women's movement and outside of it, to dominant constructions of women's identities and subjectivities. The defining characteristics of these texts are that their authors engage in theoretical reflection, grounded in feminism and anti-essentialist attention to diversity and historical and cultural specificity; and that they turn that theoretical reflection to their experiences of domination and resistance as they are shaped by the particular combination of gendered, racial, sexual, economic, and cultural requirements and restrictions they face. These writings are part of a feminist strategy of discursive struggle; their authors publish their work in an effort to bring their insights to bear on other women's lives, and on the women's movement's analyses and agendas. Consequently, a reading of these texts yields a tremendous amount of information not about "gender" as a universal construct, but about the different forms that gender inducements and constraints take, given the interaction of multiple variables, including a woman's race, class status, sexuality, and ethnicity. It also yields insights into debates that have emerged within the women's movement in recent years. Writings that place issues of racism, homophobia, class oppression, and anti-Semitism, as well as gender, at the center of feminist discourses have the potential to transform those discourses, making them speak to the reality of an increasingly large and diverse group of women. Feminist presses that publish and distribute these writings on a (relatively) large scale work toward creating communities of readers. In turn, these communities have the potential to transform the women's movement and, by extension, society at large, by transforming the movement's constituency, its agenda for change, and its strategies for achieving its goals.

Chapter 3 provides extended readings of two autotheoretical texts;[18] it discusses the challenge their analyses and mixed-genre format pose to a linear construction of women's experiences,[19] and to a clear distinction between the "public/political" and "private/personal"; and it draws on literary theories about autobiography, self-representation, and identity to suggest ways for political scientists to use the autotheoretical writings without collapsing them into either the category of "fiction" or that of "objective truth," as they clearly belong in neither.

These texts embody a certain type of feminist discursive intervention that focuses specifically and directly on women's subjectivity and its constitution through discourses on gender, race, sexuality, class, ethnicity, and so on. They differ from straightforwardly autobiographical accounts and from the experience-sharing that took place in CR groups in that they not only place personal experience within political contexts, but they also conceive of those contexts as multiple and shifting. Moreover, they investigate the ways in which what gets encoded as "personal experience" is always constructed through these multiple and shifting contexts. In their formal aspects, these texts provide an opportunity for extended reflection on the complexities of subjectivity—one which is not available in forums created by CR groups and speakouts.[20]

The autotheoretical texts, then, constitute a particular aspect of feminist discursive politics: one which confronts questions of women's subjectivity in the nexus of multiple and intersecting systems of power. The texts investigate the workings of these systems at the level of daily life, with the potential of moving from the structural to the individual and back again, by examining how overarching patterns of domination construct our choices and actions, and how we might transform those patterns through transforming our language and practice.

The autotheoretical texts are significant, then, for several reasons. First, they maintain the women's movement's longstanding focus on domination and resistance at the level of daily life—a contribution to progressive politics that distinguishes the women's movement from other social movements. Second, they bring to this focus a complex understanding of a variety of forms of domination and resistance, and of arenas in which these forms of domination and resistance are enacted. Third, they seek to understand women's different situations in ways that resist reducing the subordination of women and other marginalized groups to a monolithic cause or character. In this way, the texts reflect, as well as contribute to, developments in feminist analysis that arise out of feminist activism, and thus provide readers with ways of understanding and transforming their own lives.

Feminist Presses

Feminist presses are the institutionalization of feminist production of meaning as political activism. Feminist and other progressive publishers enact, in their choices of publications as well as their efforts to effect social change through discursive struggle, the kind of non-totalizing challenge to androcentrism (with a focus on diversity among women and on decentralized forms of power) that has animated key sectors of the women's movement. Chapter 2 examines such efforts as embodied by three feminist presses, and one leftist press with a feminist list. They are Kitchen Table: Women of Color Press in Brooklyn; Firebrand Books in Ithaca, New York; Aunt Lute Books in San Francisco; and South End Press in Boston.[21] In their choice of works to publish, these presses exemplify feminist challenges to essentialism and to a conception of power as centralized and located primarily within government institutions. This is particularly the case with regard to their choice to publish autotheoretical works whose authors challenge exclusionary accounts of women's situation.

Feminist presses are crucial to the women's movement because they ensure that feminists can communicate with each other on more than a one-to-one basis and at the same time control the content of that communication. They also give feminists some control over the type and longevity of the texts they publish, as well as the livelihood of their authors. Feminist presses that make it their explicit project to publish works that challenge the ways that some feminist discourses, and some sectors of the women's movement, have marginalized women of color, lesbians and bisexual women, and Jewish and working class women are, in a sense, institutions that document the struggles of these women within the

15

women's movement and in society at large. The presses are also a central organizational arm of feminist discursive politics.

Liberalism Canonized: The Women's Movement Studies

Since the inception in the mid-1960s of the contemporary U.S. women's movement, social scientists have studied it in an effort to capture its character, aims, strategies, successes, and failures. The resulting studies of the women's movement have yielded a great deal of important information about and analysis of feminist politics. Interestingly, however, these studies all prioritize liberal feminism. They tend to give little attention to feminist discursive politics, particularly that brand that challenges homogenizing constructions of women as a category, undifferentiated in any substantial way by race, class, sexuality, or ethnicity. This is because social science studies of the women's movement focus on that sector of the movement—liberal feminism—that generally endorses governmental institutions and social movement strategies that involve engaging these institutions on their own terms.

For example, these studies can acknowledge and account for, as "feminist politics," efforts made by hierarchically-structured feminist organizations to secure legislation that prohibits domestic violence or strengthens the penalties imposed on its perpetrators. However, given their theories of power and their methodologies, they are less successful at acknowledging and accounting for, as "feminist politics," the actions of women who challenge and/or leave abusive partners—and who are able to do so because of their exposure to feminist discourses that challenge the prevailing notion that women whose husbands or lovers are abusive are themselves to blame. Nor do these studies emphasize the promulgation of those feminist discourses as "feminist politics." Feminist discursive activity is important in that it represents political activity that takes place on terms other than those set by formal institutions. Yet none of the authors of the women's movement studies seriously investigates the ways that women's initiative is obstructed by forces beyond narrowly defined legalistic ones.[22]

Social science needs to be transformed, in its approach to power and its methodology, in order that it can better account for these kinds of feminist activity. Such a transformation is crucial if social scientists are to attain their stated goal of analyzing the women's movement comprehensively. It is also necessary if they are to account more accurately and completely for the continued inability of liberal institutions to bring about "freedom" and "equality" for women, people of color, lesbian, bisexual and gay people, and ethnic and other minorities.

Feminist discursive politics has as much to do with contesting power relationships and existing social structures as does traditional electoral politics. Large numbers of women expend a great deal of feminist energy in an effort to transform, through discursive struggle, power relations at the level of daily life (already having concluded that liberalism's available responses to gendered and other conflicts are insufficient). Many have argued persuasively that feminisms that draw upon liberal principles are tainted by racism, homophobia, class bias, anti-Semitism, and ethnocentrism, precisely because they ignore these phenomena, as they imagine all women to be equal (as in the same) and ignore important differences in political priorities that stem from women's different positions within the social structure. It is particularly disheartening to note liberal feminism's continued disdain for explicitly ideological work—a disdain that is evident, often, in liberal feminist characterizations of it as "personal empowerment" or "expressive" activity, or activity directed only at maintaining alternative communities that do not directly challenge the status quo;[23] or even, more pejoratively, a useless, ineffective preoccupation, and an impediment to the "real" work of organizing for legislative change.

The fact that virtually all social science studies of the U.S. women's movement obscure the importance of discourse to power relations can be explained by their reliance on theoretical and methodological assumptions that have come under attack most recently by postmodern and postmodern-feminist theorists. The study of the women's movement, and of contemporary social movements in general, will more closely reflect the broad range of feminist activity to the degree that social scientists broaden their theoretical and methodological assumptions. With regard to the women's movement specifically, they can do this by incorporating the insights of postmodern feminist theorists and the authors of feminist "autotheoretical" works; and by examining feminist presses as embodiments of the political analyses and strategies that animate important sectors of the women's movement.

Chapter 4 examines in depth five representative social science studies of the women's movement[24] and discusses the effects of the assumptions embedded in their constructions of gender and their definitions (implicit and explicit) of power, domination, resistance, political action, and social change.[25]

Related to their neglect of discursive politics is the women's movement studies' neglect of one of the main arguments of discursive contests within the women's movement: namely, that "women" as a group cannot be reduced to the monolithic construct "woman"; nor can women's experiences and needs be distilled down to a list of common priorities. In other words, women's diversity cannot be treated superficially in the formulation of feminist analyses and agendas.

Above, I distinguished between two kinds of feminist challenges to androcentrism. The first proposes to supplant a universal male subject with a universal female one, and reproduces essentialist accounts of women's experiences. The second rejects the essentialism inherent in the project of constructing a universal female subject, and foregrounds class, racial, sexual, and ethnic diversity among women. The studies of the women's movement are by and large rooted in the first type of challenge to androcentrism, in that they counter "male" accounts of human experience and concerns with more or less monolithic "female" accounts, and reproduce universal/essentialist constructions of the meaning of gender and the category "women." And, like most social science, they employ notions of objectivity inherent in social science methodologies that define "data," "politics," and "social change" very narrowly, in terms that cannot encompass a large sector of the women's movement, the information/"data" available about that sector, its understanding of "politics" and "domination," or its efforts to bring about "collective action" and "social change."

The constructions of gender and of the category "women" that emerge in these studies begin from the supposition that women form an essentially coherent group. Women's differences from one another are assumed to be less important than what they share with each other; moreover, these differences, when taken into account, are treated as "additional" considerations to the "original" consideration of gender— they are not assumed to have any fundamental implications for the construction of gender itself in particular women's lives. Gender roles and restrictions are taken to be fundamentally similar for all women, and considerations such as class position, race and ethnic background, and sexuality are treated implicitly as extra hurdles which some women must negotiate, depending upon their specific circumstances and their proximity to or distance from the most accepted and "normalized" positions— middle-class, white, heterosexual.

Related to this monolithic construction of gender is these studies' second theoretical shortcoming: namely, a narrow and problematic view of the nature of power, domination, and resistance. One aspect of this view of power is the expectation that various forms of domination are distinct and separable from each other, so that one can discuss gender requirements apart from discussing how those requirements are molded in relation to requirements, having to do with race or sexuality, for example.

The view of power that these studies embrace is problematic in a third way insofar as it posits power as primarily centralized and governmentally exercised (Foucault's "juridical model" of power). This limits what counts in these works as "collective action," "political strategy," and "social change." The authors of these studies display a preference for those aspects of the women's movement that engage in electoral politics; nor do these studies consider the potentiality that these liberal institutions, in Nancy Fraser's words, might, "in the guise of promoting freedom, extend domination"[26] through their very insistence that "women's issues" be constructed and articulated in particular, limiting terms for them even to find an audience within these institutions.

It is not simply a matter of these authors "preferring" one type of political organizing to another, however. The problem is deeper than that: what these studies share is a collective failure to acknowledge and evaluate non-electoral political concerns and strategies (including discursive politics) on their own terms. This shortcoming has its methodological as well as theoretical side: social movement studies most often engage with movements—or aspects of movements—that identify their sole or primary opponents as formal institutions: the government or "state," political parties, formal economic institutions, and so forth. Social movements that identify as their sole or primary opponents certain ideological constructs and institutions (such as those of the family, heterosexuality, marriage, and so on) pose a problem for social movement researchers, whose received methods and assumptions simply do not "fit" such movements. This bad fit between social science methodology and important parts of the women's movement is evident in how the studies, which employ that methodology, construct "political activity," "social change," and "social movement success." Researchers of the women's movement are not entirely unaware of the methodological limitations that impede social science and thus social science analyses of the women's movement. They do, however, seem stymied by these limitations, and ultimately ignore them, first noting them and then proceeding as if they did not exist. Thus these studies tend to acknowledge, initially, a broad range of social movement activity, goals, and successes, and, in some cases, the importance of discursive struggle. For example, Ferree and Hess write,

> Already, there have been many legal and administrative changes affecting public and private life, and even if these were to be repealed tomorrow, the greater changes that have taken place within individual and social consciousness could not be so easily erased.[27]

However, these studies revert, without explanation, to traditional notions

19

of social movement success (such as electoral and policy gains, and acceptance by political elites), with the result that they reduce political activity
to only particular actions within formal institutions, and they count only
certain outcomes as successes.

The other shared weakness of these studies is methodological as well.
It concerns the imperative to generalize, often considered both a defining
characteristic and a strength of social science, but one which can lead to
analyses that obfuscate, in this case, the dissimilarities among women that
emerge from women's different situations within a social structure which
is composed of many forms of dominative power. This methodological
imperative is not in itself problematic—when one discusses politics, one
always wants and needs to move beyond discussing a particular life or a
single incident. The problem inheres in the failure to couple the goal of
generalizing with attention to specifics, differences. The result is that such
generalizations usually work to erase many of the complexities of domination and resistance that determine the texture of women's lives—particularly women who find themselves on the "wrong" sides of more than
one axis of domination and who pursue a variety of strategies of resistance beyond traditional forms of engagement with governments, political parties, unions, and the like.

Social Movement Theory

A major factor contributing to the women's movement studies' limited
focus is their grounding in social movement theory, which itself (until
very recently) has concentrated on formal movement organizations and
their reformist agendas. This has particularly been the case with "Resource Mobilization" (RM) theory, which equates social movements
with national-level, hierarchical organizations and defines success in terms
of those organizations' acceptance by political elites. Recently, some of
these assumptions have been challenged by "New Social Movement"
(NSM) theory, much of which gives greater attention to the meaning-
creating work of social movements as they seek to "frame" social issues in
public discourse in terms that support their agendas for change.

Although NSM theory's attention to discourse represents an advance
over RM theory's emphasis on movements' material resources (primarily
money and volunteers), much NSM theory tends to see that part of
movements' discursive activity that targets the construction of identity
and subjectivity as primarily psychological rather than political. This reinforces the notion of a public/private split, central to the liberal para-

digm, and misses the efforts of movements (particularly the feminist and lesbian/bisexual/gay movements) to analyze in social and political terms oppression and resistance grounded in identity.

The shortcomings in NSM theory's view of identity and subjectivity can be counteracted by a look at the more politicized view of subjectivity advanced within some postmodern/poststructuralist theories. These theories also offer an alternative to liberalism's and liberal feminism's suppression of the differences that exist among members of the same identity category. Chapter 6 discusses postmodern and feminist theories in terms of their critiques of totalizing theories of power and of essentialism, as well as the alternative theory of power, domination, and resistance they offer.

Postmodern/Feminist Theories of Power and Subjectivity

Feminists (as well as scholars involved in other political movements, such as workers' rights, anti-racist, and gay liberation movements[28]) have long disputed liberal claims to objectivity, as manifested both in institutions of government and in the natural and social sciences. Radical and liberal feminist stances against the model of the "universal" male subject of liberal society (and of various liberation movements) focus on the androcentrism of those models. These feminist arguments counter the "universal" male subject by generating what they imagine to be universal accounts of women's experiences, and universal agendas for change—or at least universal within modern Western societies.[29]

Postmodern feminist challenges to liberalism within the women's movement reject as well the essentialism underlying radical feminist accounts of women's experience and concerns. Postmodern and postmodern feminist theories offer an epistemology based on recognizing difference among people—even among those who belong to an apparently unified, coherent group. This anti-essentialism and its corollary attention to forms of domination other than gendered ones resonate with postmodern critiques of liberalism's characterization as universal those ideals that are actually culturally and historically specific. Poststructuralist/postmodern theories characterize power as dispersed throughout society and as operating through a *variety* of mechanisms (not simply the imposition of formal policies), most notably through discursive production. These critiques form the basis of a "natural alliance" between feminism and postmodernism.[30]

Poststructuralist/postmodern theories hold that various constructions of social reality define and delineate the available choices for action, and they do so always in an "interested" or "biased" way. Thus, for example, a human embryo may be called a human embryo, a fetus, or an unborn child; the removal of that embryo from a woman's uterus may be called birth control, abortion, or murder. Each of these definitions carries different social and legal connotations and consequences, different incitements and prohibitions. None of them is "natural" or self-evident; they are all social constructs, and elements of larger social discourses, which reflect and support different (often competing) political interests. The political and social strength of these discourses, and women's access to some or all of them, have direct consequences for the practical options available to women who face unwanted pregnancies. Similarly, a feminist agenda for "abortion rights" may seem irrelevant to women of color and poor women who face sterilization abuse. An agenda for "reproductive rights" that includes fighting sterilization abuse reflects not only a broader set of interests, more inclusive of the experiences and needs of poor women and women of color, but also reflects these women's struggle within the women's movement to redefine a feminist agenda that initially excluded them.

Given that people's subjectivity is not simply a matter of free will, but is constructed through language, postmodern theorists also advocate resistance at the level of discourse.[31] For example, Chris Weedon argues:

> How we live our lives as conscious thinking subjects, and how we give meaning to the material social relations under which we live and which structure our everyday lives, depends on the range and social power of existing discourses, our access to them and the political strength of the interests which they represent.[32]

Promulgating progressive discourses and augmenting their social power has been central to much contemporary feminist activism, including the development and publication of feminist autotheoretical texts. The intersection of postmodern and poststructuralist feminist theory and feminist autotheoretical texts has been investigated by a number of feminist theorists. There is a growing body of literature that could be categorized as "identity theory"—theoretical approaches to the construction of identity and its political implications—and much of this literature draws directly on the feminist autotheoretical texts. For example, Biddy Martin and Chandra Talpade Mohanty investigate questions of identity and politics in their reading of Minnie Bruce Pratt's essay, "Identity: Skin Blood Heart."[33] Katie King theorizes the construction of lesbian identities through her reading of Audre Lorde's *Zami: A New Spelling of My Name*.[34]

Bonnie Zimmerman ventured into this area of inquiry quite early on in the history of this literature with her essay on feminist first-person accounts, including some of the works I am calling feminist autotheoretical texts.[35] Norma Alarcón investigates the constructions of subjectivity by women of color in the context of Anglo-American feminism as reflected in the first-person accounts included in *This Bridge Called My Back: Writings By Radical Women of Color*.[36] Biddy Martin responds to Zimmerman's claims and theorizes the construction of lesbian identity in the autotheoretical writings of several women of color and two white Southern lesbians, making a case for the unique political implications of those texts' approach to subjectivity.[37] And other contributors to Brodzki and Schenck's anthology, *Life/Lines: Theorizing Women's Autobiography*, examine women's autobiography from the perspective of postmodern theory.

My project here draws on this literature's articulations of the intersections of insights generated by feminist autotheoretical texts and those generated by postmodern theory.[38] My aim is to bring the insights and claims of both sets of literature—postmodern/poststructural theory and the autotheoretical texts—to bear on social science studies of the women's movement.

Political/Social Science Methodology

To summarize, then, this book critiques liberal feminism's inattention to women's differences and to extra-legal aspects of oppression and resistance. It also critiques the same myopia in social science studies of the women's movement. In discussions of feminist publishing (in chapter 2) and autotheoretical feminist writing (in chapter 3), the book argues that discursive production is central to women's movement activity; furthermore, it is an especially important site in struggles to expand our understanding of differences among women, their relationship to the construction of women's subjectivity and identity, and their relationship to feminist resistance. The book goes on to analyze social science studies of the women's movement (in chapter 4), identifying in them the same shortcomings that limit liberal feminism's relevance and impact, and locating the source of those shortcomings in social movement theory (see chapter 5). Finally, the book proposes (in chapter 6) that poststructuralist and postmodern social theories have much to offer those who seek to understand the women's movement's emphasis on discourse and consciousness; and it offers (in chapter 7) some suggestions regarding the methodological changes necessary for social scientists to be able to represent the contemporary women's movement in a more complex, comprehensive way. Chapter 8 places the book's arguments in the context of my own evolving relationships to feminism and social science.

I have argued above that the static conceptions of gender employed in social science studies of the women's movement are actually constructions that best fit women who, despite being on the "down" side of the gender hierarchy, find themselves on the "up" side of hierarchies of race, class, and sexuality—in other words, women who are white, middle-class, and heterosexual. I have also argued that studies that employ such a concept of gender end up perpetuating the marginal status of women who are not white, middle-class, and/or heterosexual, by omitting or distorting their experiences of oppression and resistance; and perpetuating standards and models that normalize women who otherwise belong to dominant groups, and pathologize women who don't. If social scientists who study the women's movement, or any aspect of gender relations at all, are to avoid these pitfalls, they would do well to approach gender as a phenomenon that has multiple manifestations, and thus implies multiple feminist agendas and strategies for change. Using these autotheoretical works as "data" on gender's multiple manifestations and workings can greatly aid social scientists in such an approach.

For social science to take advantage of the information about discursive politics and the import of women's diversity embodied in the autotheoretical texts and facilitated by postmodern theories, though, it will first be necessary to revise accepted methodologies and concepts. Discursive practice is a level of analysis that continues to elude social scientists, for whom the standards defining what is acceptable as "evidence," as well as the imperative to generalize, have usually required that they adopt static constructions of domination and resistance. A methodology that recognizes the value to social science studies of the women's movement of feminist publishing and the texts they publish will be a methodology at odds with some of social science's defining characteristics and values. It will thus entail questioning the premises of these methodologies, including the divide between "public/political" and "private/personal," and between the "objective" and the "subjective"; the definitions of such concepts as "data" and "theory"; and the nature and utility of generalizations that obscure the diversity of women's experiences, political agendas, and strategies of resistance. Chapter 7 raises some questions about social science methodologies and suggests some alternatives to traditional methods and concepts. This chapter also draws on the previous chapter's discussion of the epistemological status of the autotheoretical works, and suggests some ways that social scientists can use the information presented in these works in their studies of gender, feminism, and the women's movement.

Feminist Publishing As Discursive Politics   <u>2</u>

The feminist and lesbian movement in this country is a print media movement. We literally are moving forward on the written page. . . . We are in control; we have the pen that is mightier than the sword. For some unaccountable reason, I don't pretend to know the philosophical background to this, we have lucked out—we have somehow managed to turn this rag-tag, live-in-the-trees, all-my-possessions-in-a-red-bandanna-tied-to-a-stick philosophy that permeated the feminist movement between '67 and '74 into a solid, concrete, forward-moving print media movement. We actually influence people's lives because we do infect their minds with what we put on the printed page. And that's extremely important. That's really the most important political tool I think there is, and that's what we're all doing.

—Barbara Grier, Publisher, Naiad Press

Introduction

A central thesis of this book is that lasting social change is made possible by changes in how people understand their situations and how they perceive their options for altering those situations. This book argues that progressive changes in consciousness come about through discourses that challenge oppressive constructions of social phenomena.

Language acts—including published writings—can play a crucial part in bringing about individual and collective social change. This chapter explores the efforts of feminist publishers to encourage new forms of subjectivity by creating and disseminating a particular category of language acts: mixed-genre, autotheoretical feminist writings. These texts reflect the ideas and discourses that emerge from grassroots, community-based activism and consciousness, and they influence that activism and consciousness. In their publishing work—which goes well beyond selecting a manuscript from a pile of likely submissions—feminist presses exemplify the institutionalization and the practice of a theory of power as dispersed throughout all levels of society, and an approach to activism in which discursive struggle is central. Therefore, a look at feminist presses reveals much about discursive politics, which is central to the women's movement but is thus far marginal to (or absent from) studies of the movement.

Elsewhere, I argue that the autotheoretical texts are particularly potent examples of precisely the feminist analyses and discursive interventions that have been so critical to the women's movement's evolution. My interest in these texts has dictated my focus on several presses that publish them: Firebrand Books, Aunt Lute Books, Kitchen Table: Women of Color Press, and South End Press. (South End Press is included here because of the works its Women's Studies line publishes; it is not a "feminist press" in the sense that the others are—it is run by a collective that includes men, and it publishes many works that are not necessarily feminist but are politically progressive in other ways.) In addition, Naiad Press has played an important role in networking among feminist publishers, not because it publishes autotheoretical works, but because it has been central to feminist publishing in general.[1]

These represent just a few of the myriad feminist presses operating, many of which share the political commitments of those studied here. The presses' political analyses, goals and work strategies, and their relationship to the women's movement and to feminist social change makes exploring them as feminist institutions critical to studying the women's movement.

Background

With the exception of South End Press, which was founded in 1977, the presses discussed here were all founded in the 1980s. Kitchen Table was founded in 1981, Firebrand in 1985. Aunt Lute was founded in 1982; in 1986 it merged with Spinsters Ink, and in 1990 it formed itself as a non-profit foundation, independent of Spinsters Ink. The presses vary in the numbers of books they publish each year and the number of titles they distribute. South End publishes the most—12–15 books per year; it carries 200 titles in all. Firebrand carries 84 titles, publishing six to eight books per year.[2] Aunt Lute carries 23 titles, and currently tries to publish four books per year.[3] Prior to a recent hiatus of several years, Kitchen Table had published an average of two books per year; the press had also distributed books published by other presses.

Staff Size and Income Sources

The financial viability of the presses seems secure, in that none is in imminent danger of collapsing; however, it would be a mistake to say that these are big money-making operations. South End is probably the most financially secure, with a 1–3 percent annual growth rate since 1991 and a staff of four full-time and three part-time employees. South End's income comes from sales, although it also has several spin-off projects (such as a speakers' bureau), which were started from seed money from the press and which are now paying that money back. Kitchen Table has recently moved its offices from Albany to Brooklyn; its co-founder and former publisher, Barbara Smith, has left the press and been replaced by Andrea Lockett.[4] The press has not published any new books for several years, although it has put out a couple of posters; Lockett plans to move the press back to a publishing schedule of two books per year at first, increasing later to four books per year. Kitchen Table's income since its inception has come from sales and occasional anonymous donations (channeled through progressive foundations). Beginning in January of 1994, Kitchen Table embarked on an active fundraising program developed in partnership with the Union Institute Center for Women.[5] This program has included a nationwide house party campaign that raised $130,000 in its first year, as well as substantial foundation support, secured through grant-writing assistance provided by the Union Institute Center for Women.[6] Firebrand's income comes primarily from book sales, with some income also coming from subsidiary rights (foreign rights, and movie rights on one book it published).[7]

Aunt Lute has two staff members who work full-time or close to it: Pinkvoss (the co-director),[8] and the operations manager; four others work part-time. All of the paid staff also work outside the press—a necessity, Pinkvoss says, because the hourly wage Aunt Lute is able to pay its staff is not enough to live on.[9] Aunt Lute's income comes from sales and from grants, primarily from the National Endowment for the Arts, the

California Arts Council, and the California Hotel Tax Fund, which funds the press's series of "New Voices" public readings.

Press Runs, Promotion, and Distribution

Press runs for these presses' titles are not huge—they average 2,000–5,000 books per run for Kitchen Table, Aunt Lute, and Firebrand, and 4,000–10,000 for South End's feminist books. The "break even" point for books varies from book to book. Each press has one or more mailing lists to which it mails catalogs and promotional flyers. Again, South End's mailing operations are the biggest. Its own list has 20,000 individual book buyers and organizations, and about 4000 faculty members.[10] In addition, South End rents numerous mailing lists (on average four for each of the 12 books it publishes each year), with a combined total of about 130,000 names. The press mails its catalogs to about 10 different lists per season, and mails promotional fliers to about 48 lists. Aunt Lute has six different lists that "target different community interests" (e.g., a Chicana list, a Latina list, etc.). The press mails its catalog to its lists annually, and does additional, targeted mailings appropriate to the books it publishes in a given season. Kitchen Table's mailing list has 14,000 individuals, organizations, and institutions; the press has been mailing to its list irregularly, but planned to move to annual mailings in 1996 and semiannual mailings in the future. Firebrand has seven mailing lists: individuals; bookstores; organizations, women's centers, periodicals, and agents; movie/production companies; libraries; women's bed and breakfasts; and Native American organizations and tribal offices. Firebrand mails its catalog to all but the Native American list twice a year, and does more targeted mailing to the Native American list, sending out fliers for each new title with specifically Native American interest.

Competition; the Presses In Context

In 1991, none of the presses seemed to feel any competition from academic or mainstream presses because the materials being published are so different. Each publisher said that their niche in the publishing world was specific enough that competition simply did not exist, not even from other feminist/alternative presses. On the one hand, this augured well for the presses' being able to continue their work without having to face stiff competition; on the other, it indicated that if any one of these presses went out of business, the resulting gap in feminist publishing would be strongly felt.

Aunt Lute, Kitchen Table, Firebrand, South End, and other small presses that publish autotheoretical and other explicitly political, feminist writings are on the cutting edge of feminist publishing. This continues to be true even as some mainstream publishers have discovered a market for such texts. As both Nancy Bereano of Firebrand Books and Joan Pinkvoss of Aunt Lute Books point out, mainstream publishers wait to take up these kinds of texts until academic presses have done so; and academic presses wait until smaller presses have published them for a while, and it becomes clear that a market for them exists. This state of affairs can actually benefit small presses financially, according to Bereano. This is because the large houses don't bother to publish a wide range of feminist writings, but rather focus on particular subjects—Bereano gives the example of black women's fiction—so that the feminist presses are still the only publishers of most of these writings. This situation also reinforces the position of small feminist presses at the political cutting edge of feminist publishing:

> It's the nature of small presses to be on the cutting edge because economically that's the only way they're going to survive. As soon as the large houses are competing with you, you're going to lose. So in some rather bizarre way, the fact that they're racist and homophobic and sexist, and all of those other things, and very big business, and more big business than they were fifteen years ago, is in the favor of stabilizing and making more secure small press publishing, including women's publishing.[11]

Such was the situation in 1991. More recently, however, the rise of large bookstore chains has changed the marketing of feminist books in such a way that small presses sometimes find themselves in direct competition with large publishers. That is, the growth of chains such as Barnes & Noble and Borders, coupled with their interest in capturing the market for feminist and lesbian books, has led large publishers to become interested in publishing books that can go on the shelves of the Women's Studies and Lesbian and Gay sections of these bookstores. Bereano says that, as a result, she now finds herself in direct competition with some of the large publishing houses:

> For several years, small publishers really benefitted [from the growth of chain bookstores] because we were selling to a new venue that wouldn't have looked at [these books] before.

But then the large trade publishers began raiding small press authors[12] and publishing feminist and lesbian books. Now, Bereano says,

> I'm competing head-to-head on the shelf with the big houses, something I've never chosen to do—it's ridiculous, I'll lose, but now I am competing against them.[13]

Bereano, Pinkvoss, and San Juan all believe that large chain bookstores' and large publishers' interest in feminist and lesbian and women of color writing will prove ephemeral. They also note that chain bookstores and large publishers are driven by profits, not politics, and thus do not take on the labor-intensive work that each of these presses does in helping new authors complete viable manuscripts. But the publishers also concur that large bookstores' and publishers' interest in feminist and lesbian books has not changed the fact that small presses are still the mouthpieces of certain constituencies, political analyses, and agendas to which the large houses have no access, and which they show no inclination to tap into. For example, San Juan, then a member of South End Press's publishing collective, argued in the early 1990s that alternative presses are important in getting women into print. With feminist and alternative presses,

> [w]omen can get their work published where people are sympathetic to them . . . they're not going to find a voice in corporate America until corporate America decides they're saleable. So we need to exist to maintain that critical edge for the industry.[14]

San Juan maintains that this is still the case in the mid-1990s. Carol Seajay, creator and editor of *Feminist Bookstore News*, notes that feminist publishing helps "keep mainstream publishers [who publish feminist work] honest," by providing the impetus for the mainstream houses to publish work that is less "watered-down" politically than it would likely be if feminist presses weren't publishing more radical writings.[15]

Pinkvoss echoes this observation. Despite the fact that large publishers are expanding into areas that once were the sole province of feminist presses, she says, this is more the case with lesbian and gay books than with the multicultural, feminist books Aunt Lute puts out.[16] Aunt Lute maintains its particular niche:

> We do so few books each year [that] . . . we pretty much choose our books to be leading edge stuff. . . . Eventually, the major presses catch up with us, but it takes them a while because the theory has to come

out of our own community, and that's always been what Aunt Lute has been strongest in, its community niche. . . . So we're trying to do very different things, that change what the face of things looks like. When it comes out of communities that are vital, then it's always ahead of anything that can come out of New York [publishing houses], so [competition] is not a problem for us.[17]

Pinkvoss adds that "Mostly, we do community people, like Melanie Kaye/Kantrowitz . . . and Chicana authors, that New York [publishers] wouldn't know what to do with."

Because small feminist and progressive presses occupy this position, they are crucial to the production of innovative feminist ideas and texts and are therefore institutions that play a key role in the women's movement. Moreover, many of these presses go to great lengths to publish texts whose politics reflect recent challenges to the women's movement's conceptions of who women are as a group, and what women's experiences of oppression are.

Publishing As Feminist Activism

These presses are driven by political motives, not simply financial motives; and though they define their political missions in a variety of ways, these shared motives distinguish them from mainstream, commercial presses. Their political commitments are reflected in practices that can be grouped together in four (overlapping) categories: (1) what the presses publish and how they go about procuring the works they publish; (2) work that presses do beyond that strictly related to publishing (including methods of promotion and community education); (3) the way the presses handle the business and financial aspects of publishing; and (4) how the presses interact with each other. Each of these practices is necessarily informed by how each of these publishers conceives of her work in political terms. It is significant that each publisher considers her work to be a form a feminist activism. All of the publishers maintain that publishing the works they do contributes to social change, though their ideas about the nature of that contribution differ.

Nancy Bereano of Firebrand, for example, emphasizes the need for lesbians to control sufficient means of (textual) production so that they can communicate with each other on more than a one-to-one basis.[18] She sees facilitating this communication as part of the broader mission of her press, which is to publish work by lesbians and feminists to help increase consciousness, open up worlds to people because of what's being written about, and to be part of a cultural arm in helping to make a revolution. I don't think that books alone can do that, I have no illusions about that, but I don't think it's possible without a cultural arm . . .[19]

Barbara Smith, formerly the publisher at Kitchen Table: Women of Color Press, also believes that publishing facilitates dialogue on a large scale:

That's the thing that's great about books . . . you never know who you might reach. People who you can't ever meet and have dialogue with, you can reach through words, through something that's published.

In addition, she emphasizes that the works Kitchen Table publishes provide support for activists and others working for social change:

I'm not under the illusion that a book gets written and then people begin to mobilize, but the thing is it's a synergistic process, and once a movement is in motion, then books are a way of people having dialogue with each other . . . that can inspire [them] to keep on struggling. Most of the books we've done are catalysts, particularly for younger people who may be open to doing things in new ways.[20]

Smith says that she generally believes that publishing reflects, rather than guides, the direction a movement takes, though she also believes that certain "very theoretical or analytic" texts (she give the example of Marxist theoretical works) can be more strategic in identifying what kinds of conditions and efforts can move people to act. She emphasizes that Kitchen Table's role in publishing has been to provide support for people of color and to break down the isolation they may feel; she also suggests that the works Kitchen Table publishes provide white feminists with "a window onto the experiences of women of color," which can be their motivation for taking an explicitly anti-racist stance. Her comments suggest that the supportive and reflective functions of feminist and progressive publishing are not so easily distinguishable from its political and galvanizing functions. That is, though she maintains that the impact of publishing is not that it mobilizes people, her example of white feminists being moved, by reading the work of women of color, to resist racism is an example of exactly that process.

Karin San Juan, formerly of South End Press, places a greater emphasis than does Smith on publishing's ability to influence, as well as to reflect, political activity. South End's mission, she says, is to publish books that fuel social change, whether that means that people who are political already read them and find information that's helpful in their work, or to some extent we're able to preach to the unconverted . . .[21]

South End makes its decisions about what to publish with the needs of political movements in mind:

> At South End, we say, "How do we want to shape the movement?" And sometimes that's a little bit grandiose, and sometimes it's something we can do. . . . The weird thing about publishing is that it can legitimate a movement to a certain degree. That's one of the functions of [*Women, AIDS and Activism*, a South End book edited by the Women and AIDS Handbook Group of ACT UP/New York]. . . . It makes it visible and encapsulates the whole movement. That is shaping the movement, it's giving it some definition.[22]

Cynthia Peters of South End concurs with this view:

> I believe that our feminist publishing does both reflect activism in the community and give shape to it. In the current political and economic crisis, I believe our greatest contribution is that we try to understand problems using a race, gender and class lens.[23]

Joan Pinkvoss echoes San Juan's observation that putting something into print makes it seem more legitimate and serious: this was the case with Aunt Lute's book, *Why Can't Sharon Kowalski Come Home?*, about a lesbian who became severely disabled as the result of a car accident and her partner's struggle to get custody of her from her homophobic parents. The book's account of the struggle galvanized support and aid throughout the women's movement for Kowalski's partner, Karen Thompson.

Even when the subject matter is not as specific as that in *Why Can't Sharon Kowalski Come Home?*, Pinkvoss considers the books she publishes, and the other work she does as a publisher, to be a form of political activism, one that unites women politically and socially: "Having women's bookstores and women publishers is what's given real cohesion to this movement."[24] Moreover, a good deal of the work that Aunt Lute Foundation does involves grassroots efforts to assist urban, working-class women in writing and revising manuscripts; to teach young women of color about publishing through an internship program, and thereby "change the face of publishing"[25]; and to network with activist, academic, and community organizations for the purpose of promoting Aunt Lute books to readers who might not otherwise have access to the ideas they articulate. Firebrand and Kitchen Table also do some of this sort of work.

Both Bereano and Pinkvoss link their choices of which works to publish with larger political and social developments and their own relationship to them. Although resources are still mainly concentrated in white hands, Bereano says, people of color are emerging as the real leaders: "Being in the world as a white, middle-class, Jewish woman, I have to be responsible to what that means, and part of how I do that is through the publishing."[26] Pinkvoss shares this sense of responsibility. Regarding her decision to publish Gloria Anzaldúa's autotheoretical work, *Border-lands: La Frontera: The New Mestiza*, Pinkvoss states:

> One of the lessons I learned from being around the women's move-ment . . . for the early years was that we kind of failed the first time around in that it stayed a white, middle-class women's movement and it never became anything other than that as far as I was con-cerned. And the reason for that is that we had never made a space for other ethnic groups to be part of the movement, or that we had defined the movement because we hadn't let any other voices define it. Of course there were other women out there speaking, I mean Barbara Smith has been speaking her heart out for years, and other women of color who have worked both inside and outside the movement to try and make it clear where we've failed. Audre Lorde certainly has spent a lot of time and energy trying to make that space. . . . If you look at the feminist publishing world, it's all run and owned for the most part by white, middle-class women because that's who's going to have access. There's some variation in that . . . but that's been a long time coming, and still most of the control is in the hands of white, middle-class women. So obviously we have an obligation, if we have that control, to make [works such as An-zaldúa's] available to women. So that's the philosophical end of it. In my own heart, I've always been interested in and excited by other voices.[27]

In contrast to the other publishers, Smith of Kitchen Table says that she has only recently come to consider her work to be a form of activism. In a 1989 article, Smith writes:

> Recently, I have begun to acknowledge that Kitchen Table does indeed play an important role in making political change. When we began I was hesitant to confuse our cultural and ideological work with grass roots organizing and activism. Having done a great deal of the latter, I believed that it was inaccurate to view the cultural work of the press as

identical to the grueling work of directly taking on the power structure around such issues as economics, housing, education, jobs, racial violence, violence against women, and reproductive rights.

After seven years I have started to see things differently, perhaps because I have had time to experience the difference it makes for women of color to control a significant means of communication, a way to shape ideology into a foundation for practical social and political change. . . . Kitchen Table: Women of Color Press is a revolutionary tool because it is one means of empowering society's most dispossessed people, who also have the greatest potential for making change.[28]

Moreover, insofar as Smith considers Kitchen Table's work to be a form of activism, it is in part because the press performs many functions not normally associated with publishing, such as distributing works that are published by other presses but that are relevant to Kitchen Table's political commitments.[29] The press has expanded its non-publishing political activities even further since Smith's departure.

Smith stresses that political activism culminates in written work and not the other way around, and she describes her own process as being active in political movements and then turning the consciousness she gains from that activism to her writing and her editorial and publishing work. She has this in common with other feminist publishers who have been and are now involved in grassroots activist efforts, in addition to their publishing work.

Lockett, Smith's successor at Kitchen Table, articulates the nexus of publishing and activism this way:

I think as this political situation becomes more and more conservative and regressive, there is really a mandate for feminist publishers to become more politically active. Barbara has always been, and that was the foundation on which Kitchen Table was founded, and for us, we see the changing political situation, and we have to respond. Publishing books is one way of responding to it. Getting involved in the community is another way. Helping to empower people in the community is another way. . . . I think it's going to be more and more important to help support and mentor more and more women and more and more people of color in the publishing world, because we're losing other places right now where our voices can be heard. It's becoming fashionable to silence people.[30]

Each of the feminist publishers sees her work as political, then, and though each of them holds a slightly different view of what that means, for all of them it is related to how they see feminist publishing affecting

women's consciousness and subjectivity, and affecting the women's movement and other movements for social change.

Political Commitments of Presses as
the Foundation of Their Work

Although feminist publishers generally agree that their work to disseminate new discourses and ideas is a form of political activism, each of them
draws different boundaries around what she considers to be "political."
This is where some significant conflicts among the presses have emerged,
especially as these differing conceptions of what is political have informed
the ways that the presses network with each other. These conflicts are discussed later in this chapter.

Perhaps the most striking way that feminist presses' political commitments affect their practices is that political considerations have at
least as much influence over what the presses publish as do economic
considerations—and politics is often the primary criterion in publishing
decisions. As Pinkvoss puts it,

> I can't imagine any one of us who doesn't [consider her work in pub-
> lishing to be a form of activism]. I don't know that there would be any
> other reason to do this for as little money as we do it for. It's our way
> of contributing.[31]

Other publishers echoed her sentiments.

The fact that each of these presses is motivated at least as much by
politics as by financial considerations informs the way that the presses network with each other. It also informs their structure, the way they do
business, the way they promote and distribute their books, their relationships to the communities they seek to empower, and the ways that they
procure manuscripts and see them through to publication.

Content and Procurement of Manuscripts

The most obvious reflection of the feminist publishers' political commitments is what they choose to publish; indeed, many of their business and
other decisions follow from their commitments to publish certain kinds
of material.

Chapter 6 examines postmodern and poststructuralist theories of identity and the subject. In very different language, but in terms that closely parallel postmodern critiques of the notion of a universal subject, feminist publishers speak of their commitment to publishing the works of women of color, lesbians, and others who challenge hegemonic constructions of "women" and "gender"—constructions that dominate the women's movement studies discussed in chapter 4. These works are the autotheoretical texts described in chapter 1 and discussed at length in chapter 3; they also include books of theoretical essays and anthologies that mix genres.

These presses are committed to publishing work that addresses how people's relationships to configurations of racial, gendered, sexual, and other inducements and prohibitions construct their identities, mold their experiences, and delineate possibilities for their resistance to domination. The texts confront this task by foregrounding the perspectives of women of color, lesbians, working-class women, Jewish women, and others whose insights into the multiple forces—including, but also exceeding, gendered ones—that operate in their lives challenge the implied "neutrality" of the voices, identities, and subjectivities that have been central to most feminist discourse. For example, many of the contributors to the groundbreaking, mixed-genre anthology *This Bridge Called My Back: Writings by Radical Women of Color* directly addressed the damage to women of color and to the women's movement done by feminist discourse, images, analyses, and agendas that assume a universal, white subject. The writers thereby expose the racist consequences of assumptions of whiteness, the relationships between race and subjectivity, the entanglements of race and gender, and the costs of such racism to women's solidarity. In this way, they also undermine the notion that racism structures the identities and subjectivities only of women of color, that homophobia structures the identities and subjectivities only of lesbians, and so on.

The politics reflected in these publication choices, then, involve a rejection of essentialized notions of identity and the rigid approaches to subjectivity they imply. This is a politics which seeks to denaturalize apparently ontological categories and which refuses to reduce any identity to an essential condition. These texts take identity as one of their central foci, but in a way that moves beyond some of the limitations of identity politics (as described in chapter 6) while retaining its other, more productive aspects. Thus the content of these texts (which these publishers go to great lengths to procure and disseminate) is broadly subversive, both of racist, homophobic, and other oppressive tendencies within feminist discourse; and of essentialist notions of identity and the limitations those notions impose upon the possibilities for theorizing and enacting individual and collective resistance to a variety of dominations.

All of these publishers are actively involved in the *creation* of these texts—not simply in getting them to a reading public. Publishing decisions are politically strategic; the publishers seek out, work closely with, mentor, and develop women who can write and edit books that advance certain visions, grounded in de-centering notions of who women are and in views of power and politics that are much broader than those reflected in the women's movement studies. The mixed-genre autotheoretical works and the anthologies organized around identities that are the products of these efforts are unique to feminist publishing. Bereano asserts:

> With history, with hindsight, the absolutely overarching contribution that the women's presses will have made to literary history in the United States will have been the encouragement of multi-genre work. Most people still don't do that, and nobody had even thought of doing that before. Even with anthologies, you'd have an anthology of poetry or essays, but not mixing things together around a subject area or ethnicity. All of that came out of the women's presses, and I think the women of color by and large and some white lesbians are the ones who pushed that, because in fact their lives cannot be compartmentalized.[32]

Pinkvoss argues that publishing mixed-genre work reflects a commitment to writing by women who are activists, or who for other reasons don't have the time to sustain a book-length writing project. The mixed-genre format of the book-length autotheoretical texts also lends itself to the reality of the lives of women who can't be full-time writers. Says Pinkvoss,

> A lot of women don't have the time to sit and write long works—they'll write a poem right now, an essay next year. It's very hard to get long pieces of work from someone who has another life. . . . You just have to let women move at their own speed . . . most don't have the time or money apart from their [paid] work.[33]

The content and structure of these texts, in addition to reflecting their authors' concerns, also reflects the political agendas and efforts of their publishers. Each of the feminist publishers uses methods to obtain manuscripts that go far beyond waiting for them to arrive in the mail. (In fact, Kitchen Table has never had a manuscript they received through the mail result in a book. Aunt Lute's record is similar: Pinkvoss states, "[We're] often a big part of making the book happen—of the 30 books I've published in my lifetime, only three of them have come through a manuscript pile."[34]) Rather, each publisher has encouraged authors to write a book, or has taken an idea for an anthology and looked for editors to match with it, subsequently working with them very closely, showing them how to edit a book. Barbara Smith spoke of doing this with a book forthcoming from Kitchen Table, *Third Wave*: she identified the need for an anthology of the sort *Third Wave* will be (a kind of "next step" feminist collection featuring writing by women of color), and then asked several women she knows to edit the book. Since these women had never edited an anthology before, Smith worked closely with them to teach them the ins and outs of the task. In the end, these efforts will result in both a new anthology and several more women of color who know a great deal about editing.

Nancy Bereano of Firebrand also works closely with new authors, helping them to produce work that satisfies political as well as commercial concerns. She describes her efforts to be conscious of, and take into account, the ways that culture and ethnic identity can enter into the writing and editing processes. For example, a Native American author unaccustomed to direct, "confrontational" collaborative style may need time to digest Bereano's editorial suggestions before being able to say which of them she accepts and which she rejects. Bereano tries to make space and time for this process.[35] Or an author may wish to write a feminist mystery that breaks with established conventions and constructs a less linear, more circular story line, because that is consistent with her cultural background. Bereano will support that project whereas another publisher might insist, for commercial reasons, that the writer conform to the standard formula.[36] Working closely with authors, for Bereano, means paying careful attention to class, ethnic, and other differences that inform their interactions, adjusting her own style, and ensuring that she and her authors are able to communicate through these differences to achieve a clear understanding and agreement on editorial decisions. It can also mean investing a lot of time in the editorial process, as when she travels to where an author lives so that they can edit face-to-face.

Bereano has also instituted an internship program at Firebrand that enables young women to learn about publishing, and to "work in a lesbian institution and see what that's like."[37] Kitchen Table has an internship program as well, which brings students from New York-area colleges and universities to the press to gain knowledge about publishing, as well as to participate in discussions based on readings from Kitchen Table books. Moreover, the press has conducted writing workshops with battered women, and produced a locally-distributed book of their works, as a means to empower them and underscore for them the power they have as writers.[38]

Other publishers also bring their commitments to diversity to bear on their editorial work. Aunt Lute works directly with women of color who are new writers in a number of capacities. In the case of Gloria Anzaldúa's *Borderlands*, for example, Pinkvoss had heard Anzaldúa reading her poetry, and told her that she ought to get her work out but that Aunt Lute couldn't afford to publish a book that was just poetry. Pinkvoss encouraged Anzaldúa to write some essays as well, which she did—*Borderlands* was result. Pinkvoss states, "Part of what we do is try to give people the confidence that this is what they should be doing."

Aunt Lute works to instill confidence in new writers through its "New Voices" public readings series, funded through California's hotel tax fund. Aunt Lute arranges public readings that feature well-known writers—such as Joy Harjo or Sandra Cisneros—along with new and unpublished writers. The "big names" attract an audience, which then also gets to hear from the newer writers; the event includes a dialogue, held after the reading, between the audience and the new writers. Pinkvoss believes that when new writers have an audience and receive feedback, they take their writing more seriously and spend more time on it. "New Voices" is also a series of publications—a print forum for these same new writers, who don't have complete manuscripts that are acceptable or appropriate for publication, but have one or two publishable pieces. The first in the series was edited, moreover, by a fairly new writer who, according to Pinkvoss, found the editing experience helpful and instructive for her own writing.

Another way that Aunt Lute plans to develop new writers and bring their perspectives to the movement is to pair them with established writers who will work with them one-on-one to develop and edit their manuscripts. To this end, Aunt Lute has paired Cherríe Moraga with a new writer, Reid Gomez, whose first book Moraga will edit.

Aunt Lute has identified other ways to involve feminist activists from diverse backgrounds in the press's operations. A manuscript committee of nine activists reviews manuscripts and participates in publishing decisions. An advisory committee of faculty from various campuses will meet with Aunt Lute staff at major academic conferences (such as the National Women's Studies Association and the Modern Language Association conferences) to plan campus visits by Aunt Lute authors.

South End also works closely with authors to produce books it sees as being politically necessary. For example, South End published *Prime Time Activism*,[39] a how-to manual for activists. The author is a grassroots organizer, not a writer, "and so it took a huge editorial effort to get [the book] out because we had to show her how to write a book."[40] These and other instances in which publishers engage in heavy editorial work with their authors and editors reflects the presses' commitment to publishing work that fills particular political needs.

Promotion and Distribution of Books—Political Aspects

The feminist publishers' political commitments are also evident in their methods of promoting and distributing their books. Each press uses traditional methods of promotion—catalogs sent to individuals, libraries, bookstores, and college professors; review copies sent to bookstores and literary publications; book-signing parties and readings. However, some of their promotion and distribution work goes beyond these methods, and involves community-based networking and education.

Some of the presses use mailing lists in innovative ways to promote certain of their books to target audiences. South End, for example, promoted its book *CIA Off Campus* through a mailing list provided by the National Committee Against Repressive Legislation, which also provided funding for the mailing. Kitchen Table mails to its own mailing list, but has also mailed to those of anti-racist political organizations such as the Southern Poverty Law Center and the Center for Democratic Renewal. These promotional efforts are also the results of political coalitional efforts between presses and political organizations.

When it became clear to Nancy Bereano of Firebrand Books that her press was publishing a fair amount of work by Native American women, she tried to find a mailing list for Native American institutions, such as libraries, Native American studies programs, tribal schools, reservation and Bureau of Indian Affairs schools. She found that none existed, so she created one. She contacted a Native American friend in Minneapolis who was doing work on AIDS and had her send Firebrand her AIDS tribal mailing list. Bereano also used a book about sightseeing in Native American areas that contained a lot of information about Native American organizations. From the information gathered from these sources, Firebrand created a mailing list, which continues to grow and which, according to Bereano, may be the most complete mailing list of its kind. Bereano reports that the response has been good; the Choctaw tribal office in Oklahoma, for example, ordered books to go in all of its libraries. Bereano, who subscribes to several national Native American newspapers to "keep up in a marginal, white kind of way," has found that the process of working to ensure that the material Firebrand publishes is available to potentially interested readers has taught her a lot:

It's really an education. Clearly people are just really hungry for books by their own and are willing to overlook some of the "problematic" issues like some of these women are lesbians, because like a lot of women of color, these women are writing about their lesbianism, but in the context of writing about the other things that they are also inseparable from. So any open-minded reader from that ethnicity will not feel excluded because they're not being excluded. It's very gratifying. It's financially gratifying, but it's much more than that, because it's like, okay, that's *exactly* what I wanted to have happen. And then they get these books, and in the back of the books, it says "Other titles from Firebrand Books include" and it says *Dykes to Watch Out For*, and I have no idea what they think. They don't send me letters saying "We're throwing these books off our shelves because they have these words in them." And I think, isn't this interesting, isn't this really interesting.[41]

Aunt Lute also engages in special promotional efforts designed to bring relevant material to particular audiences. One example involves *Tight Spaces*, a book by three African-American women telling their stories to each other about growing up in Detroit.[42] When *Tight Spaces* came out, Pinkvoss phoned bookstores in Detroit, the Bay Area, and around the East Coast to encourage them to carry the book. She also called public libraries in these areas to find out where the nearest library outlet in surrounding black communities was, so she could call them and ask them to add the book to their holdings. Aunt Lute did the same sort of promotional work in Puerto Rican communities for Carmen de Monteflores's book, *Singing Softly/Cantando Bajito*.[43]

Authors are also involved in promotional efforts that go far beyond mailing lists. Again, in the case of Aunt Lute's *Tight Spaces*, the authors did readings and speaking engagements for NAACP chapters and church groups. One of the authors carried copies of the book with her, and approached other African-American women with the question, "Have you read my book?"

Kitchen Table has in the past sought to provide authors with the opportunity to promote their books by sending review copies to relevant radio talk shows, a strategy that has sometimes resulted in authors being invited to appear on the shows. Media appearances have worked particularly well for Kitchen Table, Smith reported in 1991. She attributed this success to the fact that the press's function is so specific that it receives media attention not just related to the books it publishes but also related to the press itself, and to Smith's own reputation as an author and activist.[44] Smith also used to travel widely to conferences to promote Kitchen Table books, as well as the other books the press distributes.

Kitchen Table has also distributed books that they did not publish themselves. In the past, they have put a good deal of effort into distributing other presses' books, regularly purchasing books at a discount from other presses and including them in Kitchen Table's catalog. They have done this, Smith says, because, as a women of color press, they believe in supporting the writings of women of color wherever they have been published; and because they feel that these are writings to which Kitchen Table's target audience needs access. Kitchen Table still does some of this work, distributing books published not only by other feminist presses, but also by other Third World presses, such as Africa World Press and Arte Publico Press.

Smith, who says that she finds it "interesting that none of the white women's presses do this," says Kitchen Table participated in these distribution networks because of the press's commitment to "the liberation struggles of all people who are oppressed, not just women, and not just lesbians."

While Smith's formulation may overdraw the differences between Kitchen Table's politics and those of other presses, it is nonetheless true that differences in the degree to which some presses emphasize gender over other concerns has become a point of friction between the presses. This friction is particularly apparent in such practical actions as networking, as discussed below.

Structure, Business, and Finances

Each of these publishers describes strategies they employ to maintain their press's financial viability and still be able to publish political writings that they believe are important and necessary. These strategies reflect the publishers' political commitments and the ways those commitments combine with concerns about economic viability.

Firebrand, Aunt Lute, and South End all arrange their publishing schedules so as to balance titles that won't sell particularly well with other titles that will sell well and will subsidize the others. This is how Firebrand, for example, is able to publish poetry, as well as autotheoretical texts and other political works: "The best-selling books are not necessarily the books that are the serious books. . . . Alison Bechdel [a lesbian cartoonist] sells more than Audre Lorde, who sells more than the Moraleses."[45] Pinkvoss describes Aunt Lute's strategy of balancing lists this way: "You pick a book that's going to sell really well and put it against a book that's politically important."[46] Aunt Lute's decision to publish in an English translation the first lesbian book from a mainstream press in Mexico[47] is part of this strategy: it's a good book, Pinkvoss says, "but it just doesn't purport the same things in life that I care about . . . [but] part of our readership will be really excited about this book." Aunt Lute is publishing it partly "because it's historical and partly because it will help sell Edna Escamill's books,"[48] (i.e., by subsidizing them)—books which more closely reflect the press's mission and politics.

Kitchen Table has not followed this practice of balancing its publishing schedule. Smith said in a 1991 interview that this was because the press wasn't doing as many books at a time as other presses, and therefore it didn't need to be quite so strategic as the other feminist presses. She said she also chose manuscripts that she was sure would sell well, and would "still be selling in ten years." (As Kitchen Table emerges from a hiatus from publishing new works, and comes more under the control of its new publisher, the ways it makes its publishing and financial decisions will become clearer.) In addition, however, Kitchen Table's financial strategies are shaped by its publishers' efforts to run the press "on a shoestring" (even down to planning meticulously in order to avoid using Federal Express); and by the fact that the press was not the primary source of income for any of its staff members until 1990. The argument could be made that Kitchen Table's small list and its recent hiatus from publishing do little to recommend its operating strategies. Again, Kitchen Table's financial operations, and their impact on the press's viability and political effectivenss, will become clearer as it resumes publishing.

Aunt Lute and Kitchen Table are both non-profit foundations. Their non-profit status enables them to secure grants to fund their publishing work as well as their grassroots efforts that extend eyond publishing. Both presses see their decisions to go non-profit as a strategy that makes it possible for them to publish political books.

In 1986, Spinsters Ink and Aunt Lute Press merged operations as Spinsters/Aunt Lute. After about four years, however, it became clear that there was not a sufficiently lucrative market for the books Pinkvoss wanted to publish. After consulting with financial advisors, Pinkvoss and Sherry Thomas of Spinsters decided to form a nonprofit foundation—Aunt Lute Foundation—to publish the kinds of "multicultural" fiction and essays that interest Pinkvoss. Pinkvoss says her first commitment is to publishing political works, and she makes her financial decisions with that commitment in mind. Regarding changes she sees in feminist publishing, and how those changes might affect what Aunt Lute does, Pinkvoss says she is worried by trends toward "escapist literature" such as romances and detective novels, and away from serious, thoughtful, issue-oriented books. "I don't have a moral judgment about that, but it scares me to think that really the political climate in the United States is making people shut down, rather than get on the horse and fight. But if it got to the point where the books we're publishing here didn't have an audience, we would just shut down."[49] Pinkvoss says she would not go into publishing romances, as some presses have done, but she notes that her choice to go to grants instead is not unproblematic, and that in the end Aunt Lute may be shut down for not publishing work that is acceptable to funders.

Smith at Kitchen Table has even stronger reservations about the directions some feminist publishing is taking. In addition to the decline of feminist periodicals, Smith sees an increasing commercialism among feminist presses—what she refers to as white women's presses—manifested in decisions to publish romances, mysteries, cartoon books, astrology books, erotica, potboilers, how-to books, books about "unexamined spirituality," and "books that are for entertainment, that may have been written by the right person demographically, but in truth are at least seven-eighths fluff." Publishing these sorts of books, Smith says, gives the wrong message about the political situation facing women and oppressed people in general:

> It's fine for people to be entertained. The reason Kitchen Table will not be publishing those sorts of books is that our resources are quite limited and our target audiences have incredibly serious problems. I trust that our target audiences, which are all people of color, not just women of color, will find places to be entertained elsewhere, and that they look to Kitchen Table for something else, which is political inspiration and support and even strategies for making actual political change. I think we would look quite foolish if we published some of those kinds of books that I mentioned, because it would be sending a message to the world at large that maybe things are not quite as serious as they thought they were.[50]

Smith sees publishing decisions as directly political, and her notion of what is politically appropriate to publish is quite specific; she is critical of the strategies adopted by some of the other feminist publishers. Whereas those publishers talk about balancing their lists and other decisions in political terms, Smith asserts that these decisions reflect primarily financial motives: "Many of the [white women's] presses are not as motivated by serving the movement as they are by making a buck. . . . The publication of women of color by most of the women's presses is done for reasons that are not particularly laudatory. It's clear that books by women of color sell and are popular."[51]

45

While it is true that Kitchen Table's anthologies—*This Bridge Called My Back*[52] and *Home Girls: A Black Feminist Anthology*[53]—sell quite well, there are many other books on the market by women of color that don't sell as well, probably at least in part because they are not such obvious candidates for introductory Women's Studies courses. Bereano and Pinkvoss are two white feminist publishers whose presses put out expressly political nonfiction and fiction by women of color (and by white women doing anti-racist work). They have devised different strategies that enable them to publish these works in spite of their limited commercial appeal—Pinkvoss by going nonprofit, and Bereano in balancing her lists so as to subsidize the serious political works by women of color and others with better-selling, less politically potent material.

Although exact numbers are not available in every case, publishers at Aunt Lute and Firebrand indicate that few of their books by women of color enjoy as wide an audience as some of South End's books by bell hooks[54] or Kitchen Table's *This Bridge Called My Back: Writings by Radical Women of Color* (with 100,000 copies in print) and *Home Girls: A Black Feminist Anthology* (with 30,000 copies in print). Gloria Anzaldúa's *Borderlands*, at the high end of Aunt Lute's list in terms of sales, has sold 35,000 copies[55]; most of the presses' books by women of color have sold far fewer. Morales and Morales's *Getting Home Alive* (Firebrand) has 11–12,000 copies in print. Pratt's *Rebellion*—an autotheoretical work authored by a white woman doing anti-racist and other progressive work (Firebrand)—has 6000 copies in print. And Moraga's *Loving in the War Years* (South End) has 11,505 copies in print.

But the differences between the smaller non-profits (Kitchen Table and Aunt Lute) and the larger one (South End) may have to do with more than simply their size. Whereas Kitchen Table and Aunt Lute do not currently or have not in the past paid their staff liveable wages, South End not only pays sufficient salaries that collective members need not hold down other jobs; it also provides benefits, including sabbaticals. While financial well-being is obviously a requisite for providing liveable wages and benefits—and for South End is partly a function of its appeal to "the left" more broadly—at issue is also a strategic choice to ensure the press's longevity and effectiveness by creating working conditions that are less likely to lead to burn-out and attrition.

Moreover, just as "non-profit" need not necessarily equate with "financially precarious," neither does it necessarily equate with "politically effective." Nor is the alternative necessarily limited to commercial voracity and political treason. Firebrand's commercial status has not kept it from publishing radical books. Nor has it yielded enormous salaries, or even more than a couple of paid positions at the press. Rather, it has produced a mix of heavy-hitting political abooks and lighter forms of entertainment, as well as salaries and benefits that help to keep burnout at bay.

It is impossible to reconcile these different positions on the political and financial aspects of publishing works by women of color; it does, however, seem clear that each small press that chooses to publish political works, including those by women of color, must make a compromise in its structure and finances. These strategies, as Smith points out, have different political implications. However, despite Smith's implication that one choice is politically progressive and another is simply commercially motivated, it does seem that, whatever strategy is pursued, a small press that decides to publish expressly political (often theoretical) nonfiction by women of color or by white lesbians must make financial compromises, and must therefore have an overriding political concern. Though their strategies differ, this seems equally true of Kitchen Table and the other small feminist presses.

The situation facing South End, on the other hand, is somewhat different, not least because although it is nonprofit, it is a large press—a million-dollar operation; but also because it has published books by bell hooks, arguably a "star" among African-American women theorists, whose books sell well and enjoy widespread course adoption. The popularity of hooks's texts and of other lines South End publishes (which include a number of popular texts by top-selling authors, such as Noam Chomsky) lend South End additional financial flexibility not available to the smaller feminist presses. This financial flexibility translates into political flexibility: South End is able to publish books it knows won't sell well but finds politically important (such as a book on the U.S. involvement in the Gulf War), secure in the knowledge that other, better-selling works will subsidize the less popular ones.[56]

Since specific figures on salaries are not available, a precise comparative analysis on this issue is not possible. A more viable and fruitful approach may be simply to explore and assess the variety of strategies presses employ in terms of their consequences for producing politically important work, getting that work into as many hands as possible, and doing so over a long period of time. Thus, for example, one can weigh the more purely political concentration of Aunt Lute's and Kitchen Table's resources against Firebrand's stability and longevity. And one can consider both in relation to South End's different economies of scale and broader constituency.

Networking among the Presses: Harmony and Discord

The feminist presses, and South End's Women's Studies line, then, all employ somewhat different strategies, financial and otherwise, for procuring feminist works, getting them into print, and distributing them to a wide range of audiences. In this sense, the presses could be said to be working in ways that complement each others' efforts. Yet, not all of the publishers hold this view. Barbara Smith, in particular, has been critical of some of the strategies employed by the white-owned and white-run women's presses, as discussed above. Where both the harmony and the discord among the presses are most starkly apparent, however, is in the realm of networking. This can be attributed, in part, to the identity-politics approach underlying the networking efforts of the feminist and lesbian/gay presses, and differences in what various publishers consider to be the more immediately engaging aspects of their identities. The feminist and lesbian/gay presses experience a degree of harmony to the extent that they feel a sense of shared purpose or common experience, and they build on that sense in their networking efforts. On the other hand, conflict emerges to the extent that identity-based constructed commonalities conflict with the institutional arrangements expressed in networking and exhibiting at the American Booksellers Association annual convention. That is, they emerge to the extent that a "women-owned" press network or a "feminist and lesbian/gay" aisle operate according to criteria that exclude some publishers who share the political commitments, but not the identities, suggested by these groupings.

Networking among feminist publishers has taken many forms and worked toward many goals. Among them are skill- and information-sharing, as well as other forms of mutual aid: working together to enhance the representation of all feminist presses' publications, for example, by exerting pressure on *Library Review* to review more books published by feminist presses, or by taking out joint ads in *Publishers Weekly*; or working together to retain sales representatives who are knowledgeable about feminist publishing and will work to get more of these presses' books into bookstores and out to wholesalers. According to Pinkvoss of Aunt Lute, the feminist publishers' networking efforts and solidarity make it less likely that they will be overlooked by the publishing and book selling industry. These efforts depend upon instances in which publishers pursue the interests of the group as a whole:

For example, I might have more time than another publisher to go to *Library Journal* and ask them why they're not doing more reviews of our books. It's been a team effort to really make it clear what women's presses are trying to do. . . . How can we be feminists and not do that? How can we be feminists and cut each others' throats? Yes, we have to be good businesswomen, and it's amazing how many good business-women are in this trade, but you have to figure out what your line is. I think we've done pretty well.[57]

Barbara Grier of Naiad press echoes these assertions about the impor-tance of cooperation among feminist presses and the diversity in inter-ests and approaches that enables that cooperation. Grier, a pioneer in feminist publishing who helped to found Naiad Press in 1973 articu-lates the reason for this ethic of cooperation among feminist publish-ers:

It's why we all survive. . . . There are enough people out there who are [opposed to] seeing the feminist press take over the world that we need each other, we need to be a strong, structured base. And we need not to be competitive [with each other]. Ninety percent of the battle is that we don't go to war over each other's authors. . . . It's become fairly ob-vious that if we all go about doing what we all want to do, and we all have a slightly different flavor, that we not only do not have any reason or need to compete, but that we add tremendous strength to each other by being cooperative and helpful. Not for a moment am I naive enough to believe that everyone out there from time to time has not said, "Well, if we shoot Barbara Grier there will be a bigger pie to divide up," but as a matter of fact, most of them do not want to publish what I publish.[58]

An example Grier points to of the type of cooperative effort that takes place is when various feminist publishers will work in concert to create a collective advertisement and pressure the business managers at *Bookseller* or *Publishers Weekly* to sell ad space to the group at half price. Grier her-self has been in a position to help numerous other feminist presses, as well as feminist bookstores, offering the accumulated expertise of more than 20 years in the publishing business. In addition, she has provided financial assistance to several presses and bookstores[59]—a practice that is probably unheard of in mainstream commercial publishing. Grier maintains that providing such help is

self-serving. Yes, what I'm doing is good, and yes, I have helped a lot of people, but I do this because I'm bright enough to see that if we all

help each other we will all get stronger as a result of it. It isn't just no-
bility, it's common sense.[60]

Bereano points to other instances of cooperation among the feminist
publishers, including taking another publisher's books to a conference if
she is unable to attend, or working together with other publishers who
do attend. She cites a conference in Montreal at which she and Pinkvoss
"helped each other out to the extent that we learned the raps about each
other's books and were in and out of each other's cash boxes."[61] A fair
amount of cooperative networking takes place informally, over the
phone, throughout the year as well. And in 1996, about ten feminist
presses participated in networking retreats held at the Hedgebrook writers' colony, in Pinkvoss's words, "to see where we are and kind of take
stock, and to do it with the people we've been in business with for years,
and know and love."[62] The point here is that the operations of the feminist presses reflect *political* considerations—as much or more than financial
ones. In other words, their publishing work is the political work of disseminating new ideas, transformational discourses with profoundly subversive potential.

This work is not without its pitfalls and paradoxes, however, and
those become most pronounced when politics is treated as if it were syn-
onymous with identity, as if someone's political stances will be determined by her identities. This has been most clearly the case in the
networking efforts among the presses.

Much of the skill sharing and other networking the presses engage in
takes place at an annual meeting of the feminist presses, held immediately
prior to the American Booksellers' Association (ABA) convention (which
meets each June); and under the rubric of the feminist and lesbian/gay
exhibit aisle at the convention itself. The meeting of feminist presses usually takes place the Thursday before the convention, and is open to any
woman-owned, women-run press that describes itself as feminist. The exhibit aisle itself is also open to gay male-owned presses.

It is in relation to the definition of "feminist" and its coupling with
the "woman-owned" criterion for inclusion in these networking efforts
that discord has arisen among publishers. The requirement that presses
participating in the networking meeting and the exhibit aisle be women-
or gay male-owned has effectively excluded presses whose political commitments may be compatible with the presses involved in the network or
aisle, but whose structure and/or ownership disqualifies them from participation. South End Press is one example: the press is collectively structured, and although its charter stipulates that the majority of collective
members be women and people of color, there are male collective mem-

bers as well. And, though it publishes feminist works, its publishing mission also includes a wide range of political works that aren't explicitly feminist.

Bereano, who initiated the women publishers' meetings, decided at the outset to restrict participation to women-owned, women-run presses. This policy has endured:

> The only other press that ever challenged [this decision] was South End, by saying: "we do women's books, we have lesbians on the staff," and I think the position was, "Look. Women control very little economically in this country. . . . It is very important for women who have the means of production to be able to talk and share information. It is not that we do not think that you [the women at South End and other progressive presses] are good guys, but you do not control what happens at your press. For better or worse, we control what happens at our press. If you want to organize a meeting of progressive publishers and ask us to participate, we'll consider it, but this is really the bottom line." I feel very, very strongly about that, and I pushed real hard. Nobody fought against that, I don't think, and for me it's not a separatist position, it is a very clear [issue]. Sasha Alyson [of Alyson Publications] has different goals, and different needs over the long haul, than women-controlled presses. He deals with a bank differently, he has access to capital differently, it's just different. It's true, and that's a function of the economic system and all of the isms and stuff. . . . I think that the women who do women's publishing come out of a grassroots political world that starts as a feminist and lesbian world. . . . So there are enough pressures that exist that I think it's important that we know that we're the ones who get to make the choices and that we're bound by the larger historical reality, but we don't have to ask anybody's permission or negotiate with anybody else. It's us. . . . But if there's a women's representative from South End, she's got to deal with guys in making decisions about feminist kinds of stuff. . . . People can get the information they need in other ways. It's much harder for women to figure out how to do things that allow us to be out there in the world.[63]

Of course, it is also true that people of color control very little in the way of capital and other resources, which would seem to suggest that the feminist presses could find an obvious alliance with, if not South End Press, presses owned and run by people of color. Such an alliance would have to be based on a politics of coalition along political and economic lines, rather than a politics of identity, given the reality that most (though not all) of the feminist publishers are white and lesbian, and most (though not all) of the publishers of color are heterosexual. At least for some of the white feminist publishers, their choices of allies seem to be based more on identity and assumptions about common experiences and common politics than on shared politics and shared economic constraints across lines of gender, sexuality, and/or race.

This policy of forging alliances along identity categories of gender and sexuality was overtly reinforced in 1988. According to Barbara Smith at Kitchen Table, Third World and left presses had been coming into the exhibiting consortium begun by the feminist and lesbian/gay publishers. Following the 1988 ABA convention, Sasha Alyson, the gay male publisher at Alyson Publications who initiated efforts to establish the exhibit aisle, sent letters around to those who participated in the aisle that year stating that the consortium was only for feminist and lesbian and gay presses. Although Kitchen Table was feminist and lesbian-run, it chose to cease participating in the aisle because the criteria for inclusion implicitly excluded people of color who work in alternative publishing, but not in that part of alternative publishing comprised of women- or gay-owned presses, or presses that are exclusively feminist.

Smith says that this question of criteria for inclusion also came up at the feminist press networking session prior to the 1990 convention. There, the discussion revolved around whether women who worked at presses that were not women-owned should be allowed to participate in the networking sessions, and the consensus was that they should not be. This decision effectively excluded women of color, including Karin San Juan from South End, as well as other women of color who work at Third World presses. Smith's sense of the discussion was that it was guided by competitiveness and a fear that a more inclusive policy would lead to struggles over information and authors. The decision, Smith says, "had distinct racial consequences—it excluded women of color who work at presses."[64]

In response to the exclusive criteria for membership in the women-owned networking sessions and the feminist and lesbian/gay exhibit aisle, Karin San Juan began working to establish a political aisle for the ABA convention. She began these efforts by organizing (together with a woman from Monthly Review Press) a reception for independent publishers. The reception, San Juan says, was groundbreaking in that it pulled together feminist publishers along with other independent publishers who publish political works but are not necessarily considered feminist because they don't publish feminist works exclusively:

> This was important because in the past there have been big rifts between women-owned, women-run [presses] versus publishers like Third World Press or Kitchen Table. Kitchen Table has stepped out of the circle of feminist publishing because they feel that their concerns as

women of color are not fully met by a label that says "we are women's presses." So there's a big political debate among us about who's feminist and who's not. I do see my work as a feminist intervention into the world as much as Cleis or Aunt Lute or Firebrand. But our actions as publishers haven't always been coordinated, and I'm trying to coordinate them.[65]

San Juan went on to create a distinct political aisle "not because we're politically separate, but because we are not included in that [feminist, women- or gay male-owned] definition. . . . To me, women-owned, women-run does not describe feminism. But it's a functional definition. . . . we need to just pull together another grouping, and have some dialogue and find out where we share goals."[66]

The political aisle was established in 1993, and between five and eight presses participate in it each year.[67] San Juan had hoped that those participating in this new network would exhibit their books together at the ABA, but would also share ideas about marketing; communicate with each other about common problems (such as how to convince distributors to carry all of their titles, and not just the biggest-selling ones—a problem common in alternative publishing); and discuss with each other the politics of how they structure their work and run their workplaces. But little of this has come to pass, and, just as Pinkvoss and Bereano note the limited usefulness of the women-owned networking group to long-established presses, San Juan voices doubt about the ability of the (as yet undeveloped) networking potential of the political aisle to overcome material disincentives not to attend the very expensive convention:[68]

I think there's a lot of feeling sometimes like, "Who cares about these conventions?" And I think South End is getting to that, so that, even as much as the political aisle made it an exciting place for us to be, if it's not really helping sales, or if it's not really helping the network on some other level, you have to sort of reevaluate. The networking, if it were happening, would be a really good reason to go.[69]

Differing approaches to concerns about racism influence the discord among the presses, but the way the feminist presses have constituted themselves as a group of women-owned, women-run presses (for the networking group) and as feminist and lesbian/gay presses (for the exhibit aisle) suggests that concerns about homophobia and sexism, in addition to those about racism, are central to this conflict. Smith, who participated in the political aisle its first year,[70] had long been dissatisfied with the way the other feminist presses have constituted themselves.

I would say that I have much more contact with Third World presses, that is, people of color presses, than I do with the white women's presses at this point. It's because of the fact that I see the white women's presses as being limited politically, and also racist. . . . I have found it much easier to deal with Third World presses that are usually not women-run, but they seem to be more sympathetic to what Kitchen Table is doing. I would rather deal with the homophobia, and say, sexism that I've experienced dealing with other people of color presses, [which] doesn't even hold a candle to the racism I've experienced with the white women's presses.[71]

Bereano, for one, concedes that "issues of racism exist in the white feminist publishing group that exist on a larger level" in society. She suggests that some of the dissent among the publishers stems from a decision the group made several years ago not to make time on the agenda for "pure political discussions" on issues such as racism, something that Smith had suggested, but which Bereano feels is out of place at a meeting she sees as being about business and marketing, rather than politics.

If I were going to have a political discussion, it would not be with this group. The common denominator that draws us together is not one of political like-mindedness except in the broadest sense of the term . . . people [in the group] are all over the map.[72]

Clearly, some of the dissension flows from differing ideas about the function of the meeting, the problems that are most urgent for the presses, and whether "political like-mindedness" is an appropriate criterion for engaging in political discussion. But it also appears that dissimiliar approaches to concerns about sexism and homophobia are central to the conflict as well. Bereano notes, for example, that "it's a pleasure to work on the [feminist/lesbian and gay] aisle—there's much less homophobia there." She articulates the situation thus:

I think that there is an unspoken assumption that gays and lesbians have something in common that straight people, regardless of their other politics, do not have. Sort of being in the same boat, that they're going to come for us in a different way from how they're going to come for other people. . . . It makes perfect sense that [South End and other leftist presses are] where the overtures are coming from, but I think yeah, I probably would rather struggle [with gay men].[73]

Bereano's and Smith's comments exemplify different priorities and approaches in dealing with these concerns. Just as Smith says she would rather deal with the sexism and homophobia of the people of color presses she has chosen to ally with than with the racism of the feminist presses, the "feminist" and "women-owned" criteria for inclusion in the women's publishing network, and the alliance between these presses and gay male-owned presses, is at least in part a response to homophobia and sexism within and beyond the publishing industry. That is, the feminist and lesbian/gay exhibit aisle is designed to provide lesbian and gay publishers with a buffer against homophobia and sexism. Both Grier and Bereano mentioned that the presses in the networking group and on the aisle are almost all lesbian-run: there are few heterosexual women or gay men involved. As for the networking meeting, rejecting the participation of women who work at non-women-owned presses in the feminist press network was intended to maintain the network as a resource specifically for women in a male-dominated profession.

However, the other side of this choice—as Smith and San Juan point out—is that women of color who might define their priorities differently from white feminists, or who might simply be in the position of working for a press that is not women- or gay-owned, find themselves in a difficult bind. There is no similar buffer against racism for women of color who wish to network with other women/lesbians and gay men. Each assemblage of presses (the feminist and lesbian/gay groupings, the informal networks among presses run by people of color, and the more recently formed political aisle) is constituted in ways that address certain forms of oppression and not others; and while there is overlap in the types of exclusion each consortium addresses, none of these groups engages all the different parts of everyone's identity nor addresses all of their political concerns. Racism persists in the feminist and lesbian/gay press networks; homophobia persists among the leftist presses; sexism no doubt emerges in each from time to time; and so forth.

These choices about alliances, however, are also influenced by publishers' perceptions of the book selling market. Bereano maintains that the objective of the ABA convention is to disseminate ideas by selling books, and that the more effectively that can be done, the better. The feminist/lesbian and gay aisle, she says,

> is a good idea from a marketing point of view, which is what the ABA is. That's not a political aisle for me, those are not the presses that I necessarily love the most in the world, I might be much more comfortable with South End than I would with one of the [gay] boys' presses.[74]

But, she notes, it costs a great deal to attend the ABA convention, and presses need to make the event as lucrative as possible so that it contributes to their well-being, rather than detracting from it. For Bereano, this means that feminist, lesbian, and gay presses should group themselves together to deal with booksellers in a way that is consistent with the booksellers' expectations about what kinds of books are available from these presses. Though the publishers of feminist, lesbian, and gay books may themselves share the political ideals of leftist and people of color presses, she says, it makes good business sense for them to group together as publishers of gay and feminist books so that booksellers can find them, and so that they can assist each other by directing booksellers to the appropriate press. Bereano also sees some potential for mutual assistance taking place between participants in the feminist/lesbian and gay aisle and those on the political aisle, but her primary alliance (both politically and economically) is with other women-owned and gay presses.[75]

The tensions between ideology and practice that come into play in networking are even more apparent in the pre-conference meetings (whose marketing implications arguably bear a less direct relationship to fulfilling booksellers' expectations) of white feminist publishers who have mostly chosen to create alliances along the lines of gender and sexuality, rather than across lines of race. This would seem to reflect a strategy (characteristic of identity politics, and certainly not without both its pitfalls and its uses) of separating and buffering oneself from potential adversaries, rather than a politics of coalition which requires engagement. Among this strategy's strengths is the fact that these publishers find themselves less hindered by homophobia and sexism than they would likely be in some other constellation of presses. However, the contrived distinction between politics and business, and the unwillingness or inability to entertain serious discussions of racism and other political issues, seems to hold the potential for compromising the presses' political missions.

This inability to grapple with the political implications of these choices is reflected in several publishers' understandings of the dynamics between the presses. For example, Barbara Grier of Naiad states, "I don't think [there have been publishers who were unhappy with the network], but I do not know that. I have a way of refusing to see difficulty, on the grounds that if you ride right over the top of it, it'll disappear."[76] This is, of course, precisely the kind of approach that is likely to exacerbate conflicts that involve any type of exclusionary practice. Nancy Bereano, who is well aware of the conflicts surrounding the criteria for inclusion in the network and on the aisle, sees their effect of excluding women of color in the publishing industry as "very unfortunate" but implicitly unavoidable:

> I don't know what to do about that, what to think about that, beyond that it's unfortunate. None of us, South End or Firebrand, has the time

or energy . . . to do the kinds of thrashing that needs to be done. It's a very strange thing when you're doing something that your economic survival depends on, as well as your politics being invested in it. It's very hard sometimes, as opposed to if you take on a project . . . it's very hard when a business is the thing that has to be juggled.

Bereano sees the political aisle as a means for people with political common ground to undertake joint efforts without having to resolve all the differences between them:

the women's publishers have been doing this for years . . . we have been there and we have been steady. . . . I don't think that there's a built-in disagreement, an ideological thing that says we will never do anything jointly [but] I think it's much better for people not to do the melding too quickly. I think there's too much at stake. I think if the political aisle is doing its own set of activities, there will be much more possibility for saying, "Okay, this is what we need [to do together]," rather than inviting people in to what's been done with certain assumptions.[77]

What emerges from these interviews, then, is a mixture of publishers' insights into the shortcomings of the strategies in use, on the one hand, and their unwillingness to look closely at the implications of those shortcomings both for networking among publishers and for feminist publishing in general, on the other. If feminist publishers are unwilling to engage each other in discussions about how their practices might reinforce racism, sexism, or homophobia, they may miss a rare and crucial opportunity to extend such examinations into the realm of what they publish and its potential impact on the women's movement. On the other hand, the publishers' decisions not to confront these issues directly with each other may reflect a strategy of maintaining their focus and concentrating their resources on their publishing work.

Based on these interviews, there seem to be contradictions between the white feminist publishers' commitments to anti-racist work and their lack of awareness of—or willingness to do much about—the de facto racial exclusivity of their networking efforts. There also seem to be contradictions between the women of color publishers' commitments to work against sexism and homophobia (and indeed to acknowledge their own identities as women and as lesbians) and their neglect in addressing the role that those concerns play in the white lesbian publishers' reluctance to alter their networking and exhibiting structures. On both sides, these contradictions can be attributed, at least in part, to the tension between a politics based on identity categories (women, lesbians and gay men, people of color) and one based on shared political commitments and the coalitions they necessitate. Networking and exhibiting constellations based on a politics of coalition would likely look rather different from the networks that exist. On the one hand, they would be more inclusive of different but overlapping political agendas. On the other hand, as Bereano points out, the presses are not simply political projects but are in fact businesses. Moreover, their success as businesses has direct consequences for their political effectiveness: the more books they sell, the more widespread the influence of those books' messages will be. The networks do address some aspects of the economic realities facing these publihsers; and, because expanding existing networks to include new participants raises questions about the viability of such an undertaking, there seems to be no clear path toward resolving the conflicts between publishers. It does seem clear, though, that if the publishers suppress these conflicts, if they "ride right over the top" of them, they will lose a significant opportunity to expand both politically and economically.

It may be that there is no solution to these conflicts at this point. Indeed, several publishers indicate that, while these conflicts have not been explicitly resolved between the early and mid-1990s, recently they seem to be less pressing. The conflicts, after all, reflect a tension that exists at a larger level: between identity politics and coalition politics.

Finally, while conflicts around race and presentation may not have been resolved over the years, some publishers feel that, currently, intergenerational conflicts are the most pressing. Both Bereano and Pinkvoss—who come from the older, first generation of feminist publishers—argue that young women who are just coming into publishing, whether as staff members at existing presses or owners and publishers of new presses, often seem unaware of the pioneering work that the more established presses have done, which has paved the way for newer presses and younger women just entering the industry. Moreover, Pinkvoss notes that younger women seem more reluctant to work the long hours at low pay that their predecessors took for granted, as well as more optimistic about what coordinated effort among the presses could yield.

> I see a different tone between the women who have been doing this for years and the new women. The new women will want to form a group and name it and do all these things, and us old people who are jaded say, "yeah, when are you going to have time to do all that?" . . . I think the major conflict now is intergenerational. I think that what's happened now is everyone realizes they have their own political image that they're going to do, finances have forced us to not be as unified on the floor [of the ABA convention], and [we're] even questioning whether

ABA is worthwhile. A lot of us go to ABA just to go to that meeting rather than [to exhibit] . . . the people who've been around for a while really aren't getting as much out of it—they see themselves more as teachers. We've talked about things like buying paper together, doing all these things together that would help us financially, and it's never happened.[78]

Bereano echoes Pinkvoss, saying that the pre-ABA networking meeting has changed a lot as the needs of newer and older presses become more distinct.

Each of the publishers I interviewed seemed to articulate political commitments based both on the notion that certain groups of people who share the same identity and experience of oppression need to band together; and on the notion that people belonging to different (and sometimes conflicting) oppressed groups need to band together in order to seek political change more effectively. These approaches sometimes come into conflict, yet because they both have merit—and, perhaps more important, because they are both discourses on political reality and social change that carry a great deal of influence—there seems at this point to be no easy reconciliation of them, in theory or in practice.

Conclusion

As Barbara Grier's observatin indicates (in the epigraph that opens this chapter), feminist presses are important to the women's movement as purveyors of writings that encourage shifts in consciousness and action. But even beyond this function, the presses actually generate ideas and forums for those ideas' public expression through their efforts to develop and encourage certain kinds of writing and writers, to extend the tools and resources required for writing to people who ordinarily lack access to them, and to get books to audiences who would especially benefit from reading them. As such, the presses are, as Bereano asserts, the "cultural arm" of the women's movement; and as Smith says, the books they publish facilitate dialogue between people who would never otherwise engage with each other. The presses and their books are thus catalysts for change.

The impact of these efforts, and the extent and nature of the presses' influence on the women's movement, needs to be explored as part of the general social science inquiry into the movement as a whole. The presses are interesting and revealing as examples of institutions whose political commitments to feminism and other struggles for liberation inform their work at almost every level, from the editing processes to the structure of their operations, from financial arrangements to promotion and distribution efforts, from editor-author relations to inter-press relations. The presses have institutionalized a multi-dimensional approach to power, based on a view of power as being dispersed rather than centralized, that has characterized important sectors of the movement, and that social movement theorists have found particularly difficult to study.

The conflicts between publishers are perhaps especially revealing. On the one hand, they illuminate certain limitations in the degree to which presses have been able to incorporate some of feminism's insights into their interactions with each other. These limitations are evident not in the simple fact that conflict exists—after all, it would be impossible for the presses completely to resolve, in their interactions with each other, conflicts that persist at a larger, societal level. Rather, the limitations are evident in the degree to which the conflict is suppressed. On the other hand, the fact that there is any recognition and dialogue at all also underscores the political commitments that underlie the work of the feminist publishers. Moreover, the pull between identity politics and coalition politics approaches should be viewed as a real dilemma, and not in every case as the failure of feminist publishers to make their actions "catch up" with their politics. The presses, in their political commitments and in their impact on the women's movement and on feminist/progressive social change, deserve the attention of scholars and others who seek to understand the women's movement or social change in general.

The Autotheoretical Texts 3

My words are not deeds, but they can lead me toward another reality.

—Minnie Bruce Pratt

C hapter 2 discusses feminist publishing as the institutionalization of discursive political activism. It investigates some presses' efforts to counter discourses that homogenize "women," and that reify the concerns and strategies of relatively privileged women, with other discourses that center on the experiences and perspectives of women traditionally marginalized on the grounds of race, class, ethnic or religious background, sexuality, physical ability, and so forth. These counter-discourses also examine the political implications of the construction of identities, and how this construction also structures possibilities for resistance to (or acquiescence in) domination.

This chapter examines some of those counter-discourses directly, as they are exemplified in a certain genre of writing—which I am calling "autotheoretical"—that has emerged from the women's movement. My focus specifically on this embodiment of a discursive type of political action, which decenters the hegemonic subject of feminism, is not meant to argue for the centrality to the women's movement of the particular texts examined herein.[1] Rather, I argue for the importance to the women's movement of the kinds of politics these texts advocate and exemplify. Similar arguments could be made, of course, with regard to a variety of discursive forms of political action, a range of challenges to the assumptions about class, color, and sexuality that operate in and on feminism. I have chosen to focus on the autotheoretical texts first, because the intentionality and conscious effort involved on the part of feminist publishers in bringing them into being testifies to these texts' role as representative of a specific and highly-developed political strategy; and second, because they are books rather than slogans, informal speech acts, or direct action campaigns, and so on, and as such they offer sustained and well-developed discussions of the politics of discourse and of identity and subjectivity in relation to gender, class, race, sexuality, and other major social divisions.[2]

Why Read Autotheoretical Texts?

One reason for those interested in understanding contemporary feminism and the women's movement to read autotheoretical feminist texts is that they constitute a form of "documentation" of the emergence within the movement of new discourses around women's differences—discourses that have transformed feminist political agendas.[3] The debates that gave rise to these discourses emerged nationally in the early 1980s (though they had local incarnations earlier). These debates challenged the discursive construction of differences among women that prevailed at the time, and that held that these differences were superseded by women's common experiences and concerns. This challenge came from several quarters.

The publication of *This Bridge Called My Back: Writings by Radical Women of Color*[4] in 1981 gave voice to the frustration and anger of many feminists of color whose own lives belied the assertion that women shared a special bond, more important than bonds between people of shared racial, ethnic, or class identity. Moreover, the essays challenged simple notions of *any* category, with many of the pieces addressing the specificity of particular forms and manifestations of oppression. Thus, this anthology of writings by women who share the fact of racial oppression in the contemporary United States was intended not to crystallize a fixed meaning of such oppression, but to articulate some of the myriad manifestations of racism, the ways racism combines with other forms of oppression, and some of the strategies for resistance available to women of color (and suggested for white women). Also important was the way the anthology addressed not only racism, heterosexism, and classism in the women's movement, but also sexism and homophobia within communities of color. This attention to communities of color underscored the authors' membership in and need for those communities, and the fact that many women of color felt themselves to be marginal to the women's community, which professed to be home for all women.

The following year, 1982, saw the publication of *Nice Jewish Girls: A Lesbian Anthology*.[5] Like *This Bridge*, *Nice Jewish Girls* addressed (at least) two communities, reflecting the multiplicity of its contributors' identities and allegiances. And as *This Bridge* did vis-à-vis racial and ethnic identities, the essays in *Nice Jewish Girls* illustrated the complexity and diversity of both Jewish and lesbian identities. Both *Nice Jewish Girls* and *This Bridge Called My Back* attempted to render the category "women" much more complicated than many feminists generally assumed it to be. In addition, *Nice Jewish Girls* challenged the notion that prevailed at the time that there was nothing redeemable for women in historically patriarchal religions or the cultures based on them. And, like *This Bridge*, the writings in *Nice Jewish Girls* belonged to a variety of genres, and brought critical reflection to bear on individual lives by locating and analyzing them within larger, complex political contexts.

In 1983, the anthology *Powers of Desire: the Politics of Sexuality*[6] was published, followed in 1984 by *Pleasure and Danger: Exploring Female Sexuality*.[7] These collections contested another aspect of the ostensibly universal set of female characteristics and experiences: sexuality. Much feminist discourse around sexuality in the 1970s had centered around the argument that women's sexuality is essentially different from men's—purer, gentler, less imbued with power and lust, more connected to love. Furthermore, discourses on lesbian sexuality often cast it as the ultimate expression of femaleness and liberation, the most politically and morally evolved form of sexual expression. This construction of lesbian sexuality left lesbians in a paradoxical position of moral superiority, on the one hand, and unfulfillable responsibility (for creating models for liberation) on the other.[8] Moreover, the late 1970s and early 1980s saw the increasing polarization of the women's movement around the issue of women's, and particularly lesbians', sexual practices. In the early stages of these "sex debates," lesbians who acknowledged the presence of lust and power plays in their sexual repertoires became the targets of vicious criticism, contempt, and rejection from other women—lesbian, bisexual, and heterosexual alike—who had a stake in viewing lesbian sexuality as transcending lust and power (which they associated with patriarchy). It was from this historical and political context that these two anthologies emerged and contested these constructions of female and lesbian sexuality, identifying the anti-sex, reactionary nature of a vision of women's sexuality that dichotomizes liberation and lust.

Though most of the pieces in *Powers of Desire* and *Pleasure and Danger* belong to theoretical/scholarly genres, rather than the hybrid of the-

ory and autobiography that the essays in *This Bridge* and *Nice Jewish Girls*
represent, all of these books and others—and the presses that publish
them—have spawned a new genre of feminist writing: autobiographical
works that are also explicitly theoretical in nature. These books and
presses work to challenge and transform the assumptions around which
many sectors of the women's movement initially mobilized. The period
since 1980 has seen a "sea change," a growing emphasis in parts of the
women's movement on acknowledging and promoting diversity,
whether it be in grassroots political campaigns, cultural events, or college
curricula. It is examples from this genre that I explore here, because
these works reflect this sea change in the women's movement in a way
that social science research on the movement and popular depictions of
the movement do not.

The need to document the history of these debates within the contemporary women's movement, then, constitutes a good reason to examine
these and other texts.[9] Another reason to read these texts—and one way in
which the texts might be unique, and not easily substituted by movement
news periodicals—has to do with the sorts of phenomena the autotheoretical texts reveal that are generally obscured within the genres of news reporting and social science scholarship. The ability to communicate certain
realities can sometimes depend on the genre in which one writes, an argument that is increasingly being made by scholars and writers from several
disciplines. Regarding the emergence within legal scholarship of mixed-
genre writing that draws on personal experience, Jon Wiener notes that

> A body of work is appearing that is radically different from the typical
> law-review fare, not only in content but also in form. "The traditional
> way of doing legal scholarship doesn't do justice to our experience,"
> says Harvard Law School professor Derrick Bell. . . .
>
> The work challenges the way knowledge is constructed by the legal
> profession and addresses the relationship between knowledge and
> power. Articles by the new legal scholars of color draw explicitly on
> personal experience, include storytelling and family history, and mix
> dreams and fantasies with the more familiar apparatus of scholarly cita-
> tions and analysis of cases and court decisions.
>
> In the process, the authors—like many feminist scholars—reveal
> much more about their own lives than one finds in conventional legal
> writing.[10]

Law professor Richard Delgado agrees with Derrick Bell that this writing enables insights into experiences that are generally excluded from traditional scholarship:

"The debate is about voice," Delgado concludes, "about making everybody speak one language. Certain cries of pain lose a lot in the translation. The whole idea of the dominant legal discourse is to limit the range of what you can express, the range of argument you can make."[11]

Patricia J. Williams's writing is one of the most powerful examples of this kind of text.[12]

The need to rely on genres other than traditional/academic ones in order to communicate certain realities is a prominent theme in some of the feminist autotheoretical texts. In one such book, co-authored with her daughter, Rosario Morales explores the restrictiveness of certain accepted forms of writing as she encountered it in her frustrated graduate studies in anthropology:

> Let me tell you about the dolphin. The fish dolphin, as my biologist husband is quick to correct, not the mammal dolphin. When this fish is killed, pulled out of its life-giving water and asphyxiated in the life-denying air, it changes colors as it slowly chokes to death. . . . They say as it dies it turns beautiful colors, iridescent blue to electric green to dark purple to purple red. All over its body these colors pulse while we watch. Anthropologists watch murdered peoples die and look at the colors of their customs, the movements of the rigor mortis. And the emotional ones write vivid descriptions, the methodical ones take meticulous notes, the scientific ones make careful measurements. All the while the dolphin dies, the people writhe as their mothers die or their children or their friends, and we write and publish and get promoted, give or receive prizes and grants, and we never mention pain or sorrow or anger or death.
>
> I tried. It's like describing the contents of an unflushed toilet at a garden party. That's what it all was: one long prolonged tea party serving dying dolphin.[13]

It can be argued that political science methods require that the researcher work primarily in general terms, rather than moving from the general to the specific and back to the general, and that the researcher maintain a distance from the subjects of study—in this case, women—in the name of "objectivity." If and when a researcher's methodology does impose these constraints, then in the process what gets defined as outside the realm of good scholarship is an approach that investigates the quality of people's lives, as they experience and articulate it, and much is lost.

Certainly, it is necessary to avoid simply reproducing people's expressions of their experiences and taking them at face value, as if they are irreducible to some prevailing patterns from which one can make general claims. In chapter 6 I argue against the notion that people's experience represents "truth" and that people are able to represent their experience transparently and "objectively." On the other hand, it seems contrary to the very project of political science—a project which I take to be the identification and investigation of power relationships[14]—to exclude methodologies that involve considering people's perceptions of their lives. Eve Kosofsky Sedgwick has written of the cost of such exclusion in studies of sexuality. Her point applies equally well, I believe, to other subject areas, including those under consideration here.

> The impact of such a list [of people's different experiences of their sexuality] may seem to depend radically on a trust in the self-perception, self-knowledge, or self-report of individuals, in an area that is if anything notoriously resistant to the claims of common sense and introspection. . . . Yet I am even more impressed by the leap of presumptuousness necessary to dismiss such a list of differences than by the leap of faith necessary to entertain it. To alienate conclusively, *definitionally*, from anyone on any theoretical ground the authority to describe and name their own sexual desire is a terribly consequential seizure. . . .
>
> The safer procedure would seem to be to give as much credence as one finds it conceivable to give to self-reports . . . weighing one's credence, when it is necessary to weight it at all, in favor of the less normative and therefore riskier, costlier self-reports.[15]

When people we purport to study are denied the articulation of their experience, what is lost may be "certain cries of pain," as Delgado asserts regarding law scholarship, or "pain or sorrow or anger or death," as Morales asserts regarding anthropology. It may also be the story of large-scale social divisions and forms of power *as they operate at the level of individual, daily life* (that link between the "macro" and "micro" levels) and the forms of resistance that are mounted to those exercises of power—both of which the autotheoretical texts do much to articulate. Sedgwick's point that such an exclusion comes at a high cost is apt.

So, in addition to charting the evolution of debates within the women's movement regarding the status of differences among women, the autotheoretical texts can be useful to those who are interested in understanding the women's movement not only at an organizational level, but also in terms of the intersection of hegemonic forms of power with individual lives, and individual (as well as organizational) responses to that power. Again, reading the autotheoretical texts is not the only means to examine feminist politics on a variety of levels. It is, however, one particularly good method for doing so, given the function of the texts both as documents of movement debates and efforts to transform feminist discourse (and women's subjectivity); and as products of feminist institutions—presses—whose politics and workings participate in and reflect a discursive approach to creating feminist social change.

Strategies for Reading the Autotheoretical Texts

The concern may be raised that if, as I argue, identity and experience are constructed, then looking to autotheoretical texts for material useful to critical analysis of the women's movement will necessarily involve a shift away from the clear domain of "objectivity" toward the murky region of "subjective experience," and thus will foul any attempt to arrive at some truth about women and feminism. This objection, however, reflects the rather narrowly drawn boundaries that social science has used to mark out what it looks for, and how it looks for it. As I argue in chapter 6 and elsewhere, the concept of "objectivity" implies that certain people or institutions are in a position to judge what truth is. With regard to politics, liberal institutions have set themselves up as arbiters of justice in such a way as to obscure the partial nature of the realities to which those institutions can address themselves. Social science, for its part, has accepted many of the same liberal premises that underlie liberal institutions, with the effect that social scientists often seem to be attempting to reduce differences down to some single (or primary) essential truth. Postmodern theory, and the lessons of the women's movement, suggest a different approach—one which acknowledges and studies the multiplicity and diversity of social reality, as well as the importance of subjectivity and its construction through language. This approach draws on people's own understanding of their experiences.

The goal of social science to collect and analyze information in order to arrive at generalizable claims is an excellent one, and is crucial to any useful understanding of social and political reality. Such efforts will be severely hindered, however, if the methods they employ do not enable an analysis of how large-scale social forces affect people's lives and actions, and vice versa. This kind of analysis and these generalizable claims are mutually enhancing, not mutually exclusive.

It should be noted that some feminist theorists have expressed objections similar to those I anticipate from within social science. Bonnie Zimmerman, for example, has criticized what she sees as a tendency in feminist first-person accounts to view articulating and celebrating identities as an end in itself, rather than undertaking such a project for more explicitly political ends.[16] Zimmerman's critique, though, insufficiently distinguishes the political implications of autobiographical "coming-out stories" from those of autotheoretical work of a more sustained and critical nature. Biddy Martin has made this point specifically with regard to autotheoretical texts by women of color, arguing that ". . . the autobiographical writings of women of color, indeed, the conception of that category itself, also have the potential to challenge conventional assumptions of identity and its relation to politics and writing."[17] Martin goes on to argue that

> There is no attempt to specify the relations between gender, sexuality, race and ethnicity in the abstract; Moraga and other contributors [to *This Bridge Called My Back*] instead address the question of relationships and priorities by examining how they intersect at specific historical sites.[18]

Social scientists who read the autotheoretical texts will gain access to information; but they will also gain insights into methodology, as these texts suggest a method of moving back and forth between the lived life and the social structure, and assessing the impact of each on the other.

Certainly some social scientists rely on first-person accounts, such as interviews, as part of their data, and these data can be very useful. The autotheoretical texts are much more deliberate, complex, and nuanced than interviews, though. Moreover, what I am suggesting is a strategy of reading that looks beneath the surface of the texts to identify their theoretical underpinnings and to locate them within the women's movement. This strategy also considers the text as a whole, and the political origins and implications of its formal features. In using these texts to support and expand on my challenge to some of the assumptions in social science research on the women's movement, I employ a set of interpretive strategies and assumptions that resist humanist and realist frameworks, and instead insist upon a contextual and strategic interpretation of the works.

In her book *Sexual/Textual Politics*,[19] Toril Moi draws on Derrida, Kristeva, and Freud to critique what she identifies as humanism and realism in literary criticism. She defines humanism as an interpretive framework that assumes that there exists a unified self that an author can/must portray and that that self is ultimately rational. Humanism also assumes that there is something universal to all rational selves; and that language is a transparent tool through which a speaker/writer can convey, intact and undisturbed, any thoughts or feelings in such a way that others are able to experience them just as the speaker/writer has done—that is, the writer can transmit, and the reader can receive, a transparent, coherent account. Moi defines realism as an interpretive framework that assumes that a text can be a total, "true" representation of reality, and that reality exists outside of and prior to discourse.

Humanist and realist assumptions have worked together in some feminist literary criticism to create the expectation that there exists some category of "women's experience" that is identifiable (rather than constructed through language); and that this experience is universal to all women. That is, realist criticism assumes that all women somehow share some common experience that is essential to "womanness" and transcends social/historical/political contexts. Moi's critiques of humanism and realism are compelling precisely because they correspond to (and perhaps derive from?) ongoing debates within the women's movement involving challenges to totalizing constructions of women's realities and identities.[20]

The power of the autotheoretical texts lies, in part, in their insistence on situatedness and embodiedness.[21] The writings' autobiographical nature clarifies the origins of their insights, and thus underscores the contingency of their claims (indeed, of claims about social reality in general). It also works as an invitation to the reader to examine her own multiple positions—in relation to the author/narrator (the relationship is not always one of identification) and, by extension, to other readers and authors; and in relation to various aspects of the social structure. These texts combine autobiography with theoretical reflection and with the authors' insistence on situating themselves within histories of oppression and resistance. The effect is that the texts undermine the traditional autobiographical impulse to depict a life as unique and individual. Instead, they present the lives they chronicle as deeply enmeshed in other lives, and in history, in power relations that operate on multiple levels simultaneously. Moreover, in their shifting back and forth between the narrators/authors as individuals and the larger social forces in which they are caught—and which they seek to transform—the texts *perform* the politics for which they argue. Pratt's essays, for example, circle back on themselves: she starts with some mundane event—walking down the street, or going to visit a monastery, or recalling looking through a high school yearbook, or describing the closets in her childhood bedroom—and then moves to a more general level of analysis. For example, she assesses her interaction with an African-American man on the street in the context of white men's historical practice of justifying violence toward black men on the grounds of protecting white womanhood. In another example, she analyzes the frescoes in a monastery, and the maps in the back of the Bible her parents gave her as a child, in the context of the long history of Christian anti-Semitism and the contemporary conflict between Israelis and Palestinians. In shifting back and forth between herself, her background, the groups to which she belongs (women, whites, lesbians, and so on), and the relations of domination and resistance in which these groups have been caught up, in the past and present, Pratt performs the very politics of location she advocates.

What I mean by a politics of location is twofold. Such a politics holds, first, that the forms of domination to which one is subjected, or to which one subjects others, as well as corollary forms of resistance, are in some way the products of one's position within the social structure. Second, it insists that one's perspective is also, to some degree, shaped by one's position within the social structure; and that this position should therefore be examined and articulated in relation to the claims one makes, since one's perspective, and its contingence upon one's position(s), informs those claims. The authors of the autotheoretical texts strive to articulate perspectives that have been suppressed because they spring from those located on the margins of hegemonic cultural positions; simultaneously, they work to locate themselves and their perspectives within the nexus of cross-cutting discourses and mechanisms of power.

Though a politics of location—related to yet distinct from identity politics, as discussed in chapter 6—is central to these texts, it is combined with a different impulse, also central: the belief that subjectivity can shift, that people's understanding and the actions that follow from their understanding are not completely determined by their identity. Articulating marginalized perspectives is strategic: the point is to enable others to bring those perspectives to bear on their own lives. Indeed, these authors demonstrate in their writing the power of the discourses they have encountered to alter their own subjectivity, for better and for worse, as well as their desire to use discourse to affect positively the subjectivities of their readers. Thus Pratt writes, in "My Mother's Question,"

> And in the work that is my poetry, and my writing, I am beginning to understand that I can effect material change. A woman writes to me that she has read over and over something I have written, to keep herself from going crazy, and killing herself, to help herself go on with a new way of living. When this happens, I know that I can speak and write in ways that can make something possible that has not existed before. My words are not deeds, but they can lead me toward another reality.[22]

Likewise, Cherríe Moraga's need to articulate a Chicana feminist theory grows out of her conviction that such a theory, by positing as mutually beneficial those identities usually constructed as mutually antagonistic, would facilitate stronger bonds between Chicanas, strengthen Chicano resistance to Anglo cultural hegemony, and broaden the appeal and impact of the women's movement.

Simply stated, the authors of the autotheoretical texts suggest an approach to identifying and analyzing oppression, mounting resistance, and thus creating social change, that does not replace more traditional, liberal approaches to social change, but that complements them and goes a long way toward addressing their shortcomings. Their works also offer an alternative to power, domination, and resistance. This is true particularly in the way that the texts work consistently to articulate a method of analysis that places individuals within larger social contexts, and that analyzes those contexts in terms of their differential impact on people who inhabit different positions within them.

Minnie Bruce Pratt's *Rebellion: Essays 1980–1991*

Chapter 4 explores the ways that liberal feminism and its representation in social science scholarship on the women's movement construct women as a more or less monolithic group, often by identifying "women's issues" or "feminist concerns" in such a way as to suggest that certain manifestations of sexist domination have an equal impact on all women, and are unmediated by other forms of domination (such as racism, class oppression, or homophobia). For example, some scholars and activists call for feminists to focus on "universal goals related to all women."[23] The irony, of course, is that such calls for a strategy that incorporates the needs of all women, rather than seeking the liberation of a more "limited" group, comes in the context of constructions of feminist concerns that advance, as universal, an agenda that is in many ways more relevant to relatively privileged women than to relatively marginal ones. Pratt and the other authors of autotheoretical texts—in their method that focuses on individual lives and links them to broader social forces—advance strategies and agendas that ultimately can appeal to a broader spectrum of women than do the (unwittingly) exclusive "universal" agendas of much liberal feminism.

For Pratt, resistance begins with identity—though, as the quote above indicates, and as critics Biddy Martin and Chandra Talpade Mohanty argue,[24] this is not an unreconstructed "conflation of experience,

71

identity, and political perspective."[25] Pratt's essays tell the story again and again, in bits and pieces, of how she came to political consciousness, and political work, through coming out as a lesbian and consequently losing her children. Writing of coming into consciousness and working for social justice, Pratt says:

> . . . I began when I jumped from my edge and outside myself, into radical change, for love—simply love—for myself and for other women. I acted on that love by becoming a lesbian, falling in love with and becoming sexual with a particular woman; and this love led me directly, but by a complicated way, to work against racism and anti-Semitism. . . . It was my joy at loving another woman, the risks I took by doing so, the changes this brought me to, and the losses, that broke through the bubble of my skin and class privilege around me. . . . I speak here of how I came to my own fight, through the oppression I suffered as a lesbian and a woman; and how I came to an understanding of my connection to the struggles of other women and people different from myself.[26]

And in an essay on her work as a lesbian writer, Pratt cites as one of the main motivating forces behind her writing the fact of having been "driven to the edge of madness by my losses and punishment as a lesbian."[27] Pratt's work begins with the aspects of her identity that have to do with her oppression, but always moves out from there to more humbling terrain. This move outward reflects her stated commitment to an identity politics that acknowledges the multiple subject positions each of us inhabits and attempts not to resolve the tensions between those positions but rather to mobilize the identities they spawn, whether as "oppressor" or "oppressed," in the service of change for the better.

> This is a politics of identity, but I understand *identity* to include *all* of our identities, our multiple selves, the one who has been hurt, the one who has worked hurt on another, the one who has despised, the one who has gloried in another and in her self.[28]

Her insistence on looking at "*all* of our identities" leads Pratt continually and rigorously to evaluate and reevaluate her own assumptions and actions. For example, Pratt's excavation and reassessment of her past work with NOW—a reassessment she undertakes in light of debates that emerged within the women's movement with regard to difference, and in light of her later inquiry into the history and demographics of the North Carolina town in which she was organizing—lead her to articulate a different approach to the same kind of organizing:

We wanted to change the world; we thought we knew how it needed changing. . . . We were doing "outreach," that disastrous method of organizing; *we* had gone forward to a new place, women together, and now were throwing back safety lines to other women, to pull them in as if they were drowning, to save them. . . . I needed desperately to have a place that was mine with other women, where I felt hopeful. But because of my need, I did not push myself to look at what might separate me from other women. . . . When we worked to establish a battered women's shelter . . . I didn't wonder if it would be experienced as a "white woman's home" or if a Thai woman with perhaps her own language needs, a Jewish woman with perhaps her own food needs, a Black woman with perhaps a need not to experience white ignorance of her life, if any of these women or others might feel so dubious of their "safety" that they would choose not to come.[29]

This passage from "Identity: Skin Blood Heart" illustrates both the political commitments and the archeological method that exemplifies most of the essays in *Rebellion*. Politically, Pratt's project is almost always to break through the harmonious gloss that certain events or traditions, or groupings of people, take on, and to investigate the underlying dynamics. In the above example, this means operating with a non-essentializing concept of who women are, and a non-totalizing approach to identifying women's issues. Methodologically, she consistently begins with her own position and perspective, and then examines it for the ways it is shaped by her position within various social hierarchies, in order to move outward and imagine other positions, other perspectives. Such imagining involves the excavation of suppressed histories—of social movements and other efforts on behalf of social justice, of towns and regions, of oppressed peoples. The epistemology that undergirds this project is one that views ignorance not as the absence of knowledge, but as something structured into our lives in ways that are neither accidental nor random. Knowledge is shaped, in Pratt's words, by "my constricted eye, an eye that has only let in what I have been taught to see."[30] What that eye sees is influenced by Pratt's physical location, but also by her positioning in relation to ideology and dominative practices. Her project of expanding her constricted eye, then, is a project of investigating other realities so as to imagine other locations, both geographical and social; but also of interrogating the ideologies that accompany her own position, to see how she might be perpetuating certain exclusionary practices.

For Pratt, learning "a way of looking at the world that is more accurate, complex, multi-layered, multi-dimensional, more truthful"[31] is necessary not simply because she lacks a complete picture, but "because

I've learned that what is presented to me as an accurate view of the world is frequently a lie . . . [and] what I think I *know* is an accurate view of the world is frequently a lie."[32] She is motivated to seek a more "accurate view" by her keen awareness of the ways that "inaccurate views" separate her from other women. She is also motivated by her knowledge that such views are inculcated and perpetuated as part of the ideological functioning of systems of oppression. The experience of recalling Arlington National Cemetery as rows and rows of crosses, only to be presented, by a Jewish woman, with photographs of the cemetery's headstones with crosses or stars of David engraved over the names, presents Pratt with an insight into what Biddy Martin (in an essay on the kinds of autobiographical writings I examine here) refers to as "the ideological quality of memory itself."[33] Investigating how ignorance, knowledge, and memory are structured by ideology is part of Pratt's method for beginning to grasp the dimensions of what she does not know and why she does not know it.

In Pratt's writing, domination takes many forms and comes from many sources—including, potentially, the well-intentioned efforts of white feminists to assist battered women or to get the ERA passed.[34] Again and again, Pratt's rhetorical strategy is to shift back and forth between her self as oppressed and her self as oppressor; and between her complicity in the domination of others and her resistance to that domination, and to that complicity. She writes about reading a newspaper article about how several thousand Gypsies, fleeing poverty in Rumania to prosperous areas of Germany, had been placed in a fenced-in camp. The mayor of Berlin was quoted as saying, "We are just not a multiracial and multicultural society. We are a really pure, good German society." Pratt discusses how she noticed that while the story briefly mentioned the murder of Gypsies in concentration camps during the Holocaust, it made no mention of the treatment of Jews during the Holocaust. And she writes:

> In this story I recognized the place within me that has obliterated lives, particularly Jewish lives, by assuming their nonexistence, the place that is then used to *justify* nonexistence. But in my recognition I also saw the place I have made, within me, with my work, to acquire new information, experience, ability to act, through a journey to the imprisoning and imprisoned images, and, finally, to a place where I have puzzled over, admitted, welcomed Jewish lives, the place where new images overlay the old . . .[35]

Pratt also writes, in the same essay, of times when she has intervened when someone made anti-Semitic comments; lectures she has given and essays she has published on anti-Semitism; groups she has worked with to confront anti-Semitism; and so on. Here again, she exemplifies for her readers the shifts in perspective and in action that can come from a close examination of one's position within hierarchies of domination.

Pratt's work implicitly invites her readers to engage in the kind of political self-reflection that she performs, and to take up a position of resistance, whatever their identity may be, and whatever their relationship to a given form of oppression may be. She does not assume that positions of resistance are the province solely of the oppressed; on the other hand, neither does she relinquish the notion that identity, and related experience, are contingent to a degree upon subject position.

This point becomes clear in an essay entitled "Watching the Door," the text of a speech she gave when she received the Lamont Poetry Selection Prize for a collection of poems about losing her sons because she is a lesbian. "Watching the Door" was first published in *Gay Community News*, a (now defunct) newspaper published in Boston and distributed nationally. The appearance of the piece in this forum adds another dimension to Pratt's characteristic invitation to her readers to follow her example in examining their position in the world and potentially altering their actions.

That this invitation comes in an essay entitled "Watching the Door" is also significant, as it refers to a political reality particular to queers. Pratt implies the need for an identity-based understanding of this political reality at the same time that she invokes a non-identity-based "coalition politics" approach in locating herself within the history and trajectory of a variety of struggles (civil rights, women's liberation, gay and lesbian rights). "Watching the door" was a built-in part of a night out at a queer bar in 1975, the year Pratt came out, in Fayetteville, North Carolina, with its anti-sodomy statute outlawing homosexuality. The bar's patrons always turned to see who was coming in the door whenever it opened, to see if it was the sheriff or the military police from Fort Bragg, "come on another raid to check I.D.'s, to arrest queers."[36] Pratt writes of a night when three (apparent) heterosexuals,

> a woman and two men, all three dressed elegantly in black and white, slumming for the evening, came to lean smiling and laughing against the cigarette machine while we danced. The three of them looked at us with avid eyes, heterosexuals watching us seek love in the midst of great danger, watching our laughter, our defiance, our erotic intensity, our fear. They never once turned to look when the door opened.[37]

The political reality of sexual persecution does not exist for some people in the same way that it does for others, and Pratt's description of this event makes clear the legitimacy of making general claims on the basis of identity. However, her work resists the temptation to stop there, and instead pushes through to deconstruct apparently coherent identity categories without doing away with them altogether. Pratt's tireless interrogation of how hierarchies of domination operate within groups of people often assumed to be "in the same boat" enables a politics of coalition based not necessarily on shared identity but on shared interest. But her unwillingness to do away with identity, her skill at sliding back and forth between individual lives and power structures, ensures that the politics she articulates is anchored in the reality—and *specificity*—of people's daily lives. This "anchor" is common to the works in this genre in general, and has the advantage of being accessible and appealing in ways that more abstract manifestos may not be.

Thus Pratt anchors resistance in—but does not subordinate it to—identity. Her identity politics is not of the individualistic sort criticized by feminists who fear the loss of activism to endless introspection. Nor is it, generally speaking, an identity politics that relies on essentialized notions of identity. Her momentary tendencies in that direction, in fact, have a disruptive effect on her prose and her argument. The most pronounced such moment occurs in "The Friends of My Secret Self," an essay in which Pratt contemplates a number of women who were friends, acquaintances, or neighbors when she was a child and are lesbians as adults. Pratt tries to unearth "the lesbian in us,"[38] to discover why she and these other girls were hidden from each other in childhood, unrecognizable as lesbians. This reading from adulthood backwards into childhood to establish continuity is a classic characteristic of lesbian coming out stories. Pratt's effort to explore the ways young girls are socialized into heterosexuality, pushed away from lesbianism, is important; yet, her unquestioning assumption of lesbianism as seamless continuity, differentiated only by degree of suppression, leads to such clichéd, essentializing (and, relative to the rest of her work, contradictory) statements as "my lover Joan tells me that my years of heterosexual training are wearing off, and that no woman who is not a lesbian walks, talks, or dresses like I do."[39] It also leads Pratt to devalue "femme" lesbians, including herself, insofar as she talks about femme qualities only in the context of how they enable femme lesbians to pass as heterosexual, to get heterosexual privilege, or how her possession of femme qualities, combined with her class privilege, has made her experience of lesbianism easier than those of her working-class, butch counterparts. This would seem to be an ideal moment for Pratt to pursue her usual strategy of articulating the complexities of a situation—for example, to talk about her own femmeness as something which simultaneously enables her to pass but also enables others to deny her lesbianism. Her willingness to embrace the terminology of "butch/femme"—anathema to the brand of Lesbian-Feminism that valorized a particular variety of androgyny—coupled with her failure to complicate Lesbian-Feminism's valuation of butch and femme qualities provides an interesting and productive tension, one which can reveal some of the competing sexual discourses circulating in the women's movement and lesbian communities in the wake of the feminist sex debates.

Pratt's momentary impulse toward some essentialized notion of lesbianism is also interesting for what it reveals about the continued appeal of easy, self-evident identity categories. Pratt's project in this essay is, largely, to examine differences between herself and other adult lesbians and their childhood selves. The jarring impact of the piece's essentializing impulses simply underscores the importance of the rest of the project, and the continuing competition between these different ways of understanding identity.

Generally speaking, then, Pratt's aim could be said to fall under the rubric of "social constructionism," to locate the individual life in relation to the larger social reality. She also locates it historically.

In "Watching the Door," Pratt writes of the only other time she ever received an award for poetry: one hundred dollars for "a little poem called 'The Shell' ":

> At that time in Alabama, and in the South, a revolution was under way; all around me, Black people and some white people were giving their lives, being blown up, shotgunned, set upon with dogs, for asking for the simplest needs of human life. But I was oblivious to all this: I was a scholar and a poet. A sorority sister told me I should take the prize money for my poem and buy something that would be a good investment. So I used my hundred dollars to buy a string of pearls, which lies now, unworn for many years, in my bureau drawer.[40]

In the paragraph that follows, Pratt returns to the acknowledgments she offers earlier in her speech, when she states "I would not have begun to live as a lesbian nor have survived to write these poems without the women's liberation and the gay and lesbian liberation movements," and refers to "the people who made the political and cultural realities that helped me survive."[41] Pratt charts her shift in perspective, in subjectivity and action, in the next paragraph:[42]

> But when I began to live as a lesbian, what I needed to know to survive despisal, and to do my work, was the knowledge of those who had

come before me, who I had not acknowledged, those in the Black civil
rights movement, in the women's liberation movement, in our gay and
lesbian past. So it gives me much satisfaction to be able to say that, this
time, I am returning my award money to those communities, who have
given me my life.[43]

Again, Pratt exemplifies the kind of shift in understanding—and thus
in action—enabled by activism and by critical intellectual engagement
with one's surroundings and circumstances. Over and over, her work
demonstrates the variety of ways of being within the *only apparently* homogeneous and static position of white, middle-class woman in the
United States in the latter part of the twentieth century. And her work
emphasizes that that variety of ways of being exists not because she has
willed it, or because she alone has invented new ways to be, but because,
as she writes in "Money and the Shape of Things,"

> The only reason that I can now choose to piece together my financially
> precarious but deeply satisfying way of making a living is because many
> women, those in the women's liberation movement, the civil rights
> movement, the gay and lesbian liberation movement, have made places
> within the economic system where I can do my work and be paid for
> it. I can work because folks established women's studies programs . . . ;
> students put together cultural programs about women's and lesbian is-
> sues; women began feminist and lesbian publishing houses, magazines,
> newspapers; women started women's bookstores and travelling libraries
> that operated out of the trunk of someone's car; women in small com-
> munities formed production companies to bring visiting artists to
> town.[44]

Moreover, Pratt's shifts in perspective, and her effort to locate the
sources of those shifts in discourses and material realities created by social
movements, moves her from an individual solution to threats to her security—a string of pearls as a "good investment" on which she can rely
later—to a collective solution: returning benefits that accrue to her to the
communities that have "given me my life." What has sustained her are communities and movements that have, in one form or another, fought inequalities. Thus, in Pratt's logic, the appropriate form of resistance for her as
an individual is that which bolsters those communities and movements. She
makes this point even more clearly in "My Mother's Question":

> I attempt to keep my income low . . . : to resist paying any, or to pay
> hardly any, federal taxes; to resist feeding my money into a system that

supports militaristic capitalism rather than the old women who live on social security and very little food in my apartment building. I do some organizing in my building, have worked with other tenants to prevent rent increases, have assisted the older women in applying for exemptions from rent pressures—all partial, erratic efforts. When I face the women I see my own old age, living not merely on the margin, but sunk, going under, my old age unless I grab at security, make more money, contribute constantly to a retirement fund. I struggle to resist this fear, the fear of losing my little bit of security unless I pour my work *into* the system.

Instead I try to push myself to overturn these fears, to stress the need for change in the structure of privilege in this country.[45]

Pratt's strategy, and her articulation of it, reflect a question that has divided the contemporary women's movement from its inception (and which an exclusive focus on public policy skirts but does not resolve). That is, the question of whether "the system" can be expanded and transformed to include those whom it currently excludes, or whether it is inherently—or at least unresolvably—exclusionary, such that seeking gains within it bolsters it, including some of its oppressive aspects. Pratt not only takes a position on this question different from that implied by liberal feminism and social science scholarship on the women's movement; she also illustrates an agenda that reflects her convictions, an array of "personal" acts that have political motives and consequences.

It is important to note that Pratt does not eschew altogether engagement with governmental institutions. "I Plead Guilty to Being a Lesbian" documents her action group's participation in civil disobedience at the Supreme Court as part of the 1987 National March on Washington for Lesbian and Gay Rights and in response to the Court's decision in the *Bowers v. Hardwick* case, which upheld the constitutionality of sodomy laws, even when applied primarily or exclusively to homosexual behavior. It is also important to note, though, that what strikes Pratt about the March and other events associated with it is that, with so many queers in D.C. for the occasion, she feels safe for once, and must notice "how constantly I had guarded against a destroying look, a hateful sneer . . . until that weekend, I did not understand the tense inner barrier that had guarded me for years from how I might be recognized as a dyke out in the world; the barrier that kept one aspect of my self always apart, expecting hate, not joy."[46] Moreover, in discussing the *Bowers v. Hardwick* case and Justice Blackmun's dissenting opinion, in which he defended the inclusion of adult, consensual, homosexual sex in the Constitution's concept of the right to privacy, Pratt notes:

> But his opinion disclosed no understanding that our lives as lesbians and
> gay men are more than one kind of sex act performed behind a closed
> door; no statement that *our kind of loving, made public, could be a liberating
> possibility for others.* Justice Blackmun didn't mention that the majority
> might have some lesson to learn about themselves if they could bear to
> look at the joy of me and Joan, walking down the street after dinner,
> Saturday night, holding hands; if they could bear to consider why our
> sexual pleasure has been condemned by them as sexual crime.[47] [em-
> phasis added]

Pratt does not ignore government institutions and the power they
wield over individual lives; she gets arrested for protesting the abuse of
that power. But she also works to articulate other exercises, other
abuses of power—ones that don't carry the sanction of law but that
have equally powerful effects. It remains unclear how Pratt conceives
of the relationship between these two types of domination, or how she
reconciles her strategy of not pouring her work "*into* the system" with
her demands within the system (in this example, her demand for the
Court's accountability to non-heterosexuals). Just as the women's
movement studies do not address, much less resolve, the apparent contradictions between strategies of engagement and strategies of detach-
ment, neither does Pratt confront directly the questions raised by this
tension within her own work. However, in exhibiting this tension
(rather than burying it entirely), Pratt's work alludes to debates over
strategy that have preoccupied the women's movement, despite their
absence from social science accounts. This tension thus illuminates a
site for further inquiry, reflecting as it does at least two different discourses on power and change that circulate within the women's movement.

It is clear, however, that what is at the core of Pratt's view of domination and her vision of resistance is the power to define what is possible
and desirable—and its relationship to identity, discourse, and daily life.
This is evident throughout all her essays; it is also evident in the ordering
of the essays in her book.

The title essay of Pratt's collection, and the first to appear in the
book, is all about the political necessity and potential of speech. Pratt's
subject in this essay is her own experience with silence and complicity,
which she intersperses with excerpts from Mary Boykin Chesnut's Civil
War-era *A Diary From Dixie*, so as to examine the history in the South of
silence, as well as of what gets cast as "rebellion," and to investigate what
is at stake in each. The excerpts from Chesnut's diary generally have to do
with silence, with manners and remaining within the bounds of proper

behavior in the face of the unfolding Civil War; they have to do with women's silence in particular, the efforts women expended to remain within those bounds.

By moving between Chesnut's silences and her own, Pratt works to distinguish between the strength required to endure an oppressive situation and actual rebellion against it. Again, Pratt explores the "ideological quality of memory" (Martin's term) as well as the connection between discourse and change, as in this passage:

> I have often asked my mother about events in her past, and had her say that she really didn't remember how she felt about them, that this or that was "just something that had to be done." I used to think that the silence which still surrounds the emotional lives of her and her sisters was deliberate, a deliberate withholding from me of their secrets and knowledge as women. But now I think that this loss of memory is a result of the silence, of the never talking, never thinking about what may lie under the surface, the awful truths. It is a result of years and years spent trying to do what was right in silence and isolation, as my mother did, within a system which she thought could not be changed. . . .
>
> It was not a possibility that *talking about something would release a passion for change and thus bring about change.*[48] [emphasis added]

Pratt's whole project is about remembering and speaking out to bring about change. Remembering, for her, includes interrogating her own memories and also locating present events and power relations in historical contexts, unearthing the origins of the present in the past as a way to greater understanding of current problems and how to effect change. It also involves unearthing the history of resistance so as to build on past lessons and strengths: as when she writes, "I remember Mary Boykin Chesnut, her strengths and her weaknesses, in order to live like her, in order to live differently from her."[49] And speaking out, for Pratt, is the way to change:

> I found out exactly how manners, doing what is "reasonable," can be used to cage us and keep us from shouting for changes, as I argued with my husband who told me to leave the house until I could behave in a "civil manner," and then hit me when I would not keep quiet. For a while I valued this incident for the insight it gave me into how men control women's words and actions by violence. Lately it has taken on for me an added significance, as an example of how when we speak, say certain things, certain words, we rebel; we put ourselves outside manners and civilization; we step over a boundary into the forbidden.[50]

81

She goes on to describe another way of crossing the boundaries—wearing a "Stop the Klan" button around Fayetteville, North Carolina after an anti-Klan march, and the verbal abuse she encountered from white men when she wore the button, when she "crossed their line between white and Black; I had, to them, repudiated whiteness and joined with the others."[51] For Pratt, that abuse signals the degree to which she is pushing at boundaries set up to control people's actions and their relationships to each other. Those boundaries become, for her, sites of resistance, places where dominative power is exerted and must be countered.

> I am trying to teach myself to cross these boundaries, many of which I have lived within my whole life and have never seen. I practice seeing the limits, and then crossing them, if I am brave enough at the moment. . . . I begin to understand that a white woman of the South can live and write, but not of the dead heroes. She can live and write a new kind of honor, the daily, conscious actions of women in true rebellion.[52]

Pratt's focus on history is fundamental to her project of denaturalizing the boundaries that her mother and aunts took for granted, of calling into question the assumption that certain things "just had to be done." And the combination of this historical archeology and her relentless insertion of herself into history, into her excavations and examinations of forms of domination and resistance, acts as an invitation to her reader to do the same, to practice seeing limits and going beyond them.

Having laid out in "Rebellion" her view of how domination gets perpetuated—through silence and complicity—and the centrality of speaking out to resistance, Pratt moves to issues of identity in her next essay, "Identity: Skin Blood Heart." The themes Pratt addresses in this essay have been discussed above; the placement of the essay at the beginning of the book, just after her explication of her theory of power (not in so many words) in "Rebellion," underscores Pratt's contention that politics is a matter of identity, but identity understood politically. That the next essay, "I Plead Guilty to Being a Lesbian," weaves together insights about daily dominations and daily resistances, on the one hand, and a protest against the nation's highest court, on the other, adds another layer to Pratt's argument, to her political vision. In the rest of the essays, Pratt moves back and forth between her lesbianism as the original and continuing source of her political motivation, and the other sites of the struggles in which she engages.

For Pratt, then, resistance is multilayered because domination is multilayered. It begins not with some apparently self-evident "universal women's issue," but with a process of locating herself in history, and in power relations, so as to ensure that the form her resistance takes does not reinforce someone's oppression in ways not immediately apparent to her. It is this recognition of the contingency of interests, coupled with a desire truly to effect *fundamental* change, that leads her to this strategy that attends to both local and general/historical considerations.

Most important, though, is Pratt's commitment to working for change through discourse, whether that be writing and publishing essays, teaching women's studies courses, or wearing a "Stop the Klan" button in an area of intense Klan activity and challenging those who want to make a joke of such activity. That commitment is evident throughout all of her work, both in the materiality of the essays themselves and in Pratt's method of theorizing her own life, uncovering new possibilities for resisting both the roles of oppressor and oppressed, and inviting her readers to do the same.

Cherrié Moraga's *Loving in the War Years: lo que nunca pasó por sus labios*

Like Pratt, Moraga is concerned with locating her life within larger historical, political, and cultural contexts. Both Pratt and Moraga strive to explore the relationships between the "personal" and the "political," and indeed both their books have the effect of collapsing any rigid opposition between the two. Both texts also work to reveal the constructedness of identity, particularly the ways that race, gender, and sexuality are constructed through each other, rather than being imbued with some inherent, essential, and fixed meaning.

These two texts share a number of features with each other and with other texts in this genre. One such feature is the authors'/narrators' concern to articulate the events of their lives in political terms, and their need to deconstruct the identities they acquired as a result of their particular backgrounds and their positions within the social structure, and to reconstruct for themselves identities which enable them to resist various forces of oppression. The texts also commonly challenge facile dichotomies between oppressor and oppressed, and complicate simplistic notions of women as a category, and of how oppression and resistance can and do function. Even more important, these authors reveal the dimensions and material consequences of psychic forms of oppression, and make these processes public, through writing, in an effort to aid their readers in undertaking similar reflections and achieving similar shifts in subjectivity.

In the culminating essay in *Loving in the War Years*, entitled "A Long Line of Vendidas," Cherríe Moraga writes:

> *The right to passion* expressed in our own cultural tongue and move-ments is what this essay seems, finally, to be about. I would not be try-ing to develop some kind of Chicana feminist theory if I did not have strong convictions, urgent hunches, and deep racial memory that the Chicana could *not* betray a sister, a daughter, a compañera in the service of the man and his historical institutions if somewhere in the chain of historical events and generations, she were allowed to love herself as both female and mestiza. . . . The extent to which our sexuality and identity as Chicanas have been distorted both within our culture and by the dominant culture is the measure of how great a source of our po-tential power it holds. We have not been allowed to express ourselves in specifically female and Latina ways or even to explore what those ways are. As long as that is held in check, so much of the rest of our poten-tial power is as well.[53]

The right to passion, and how access to that right is constructed and me-diated through race, culture, gender, and history is the subject of Mor-aga's book. Through essays, poems, dream narratives, and journal entries, Moraga charts her exploration of her identity as a Chicana feminist les-bian, and locates it in relation to broad social forces. The catalyst behind Moraga's writing in the first part of the book is her desire to construct an account of the origins of her lesbianism, as well as the conditions for its possibility within her particular family and within her culture (and in the context of having been alienated from that culture). Later in the book she discusses how gender and sexuality are constructed through race and cul-ture, and vice versa, in the context of the legacy of Spanish conquest in Mexico as well as Anglo imperialism in Chicano culture. Throughout, her project is to investigate and reconceptualize the relationship between her lesbianism and feminism, her light skin, class, and education, and her Chicano culture and identity so as to make a place for herself in both the Chicano community and the women's movement. Thus, her work un-derscores the constructedness and interrelatedness of gender, sexuality, race, ethnicity, and class.

For Moraga, the site of Chicana oppression is identity—specifically, gender, sexual, and ethnic identity. That is, these are the grounds on which Chicanas' "right to passion" is withheld. Having thus located the *site* of Chicana oppression, Moraga sets out to explore the *sources* of that oppression by examining the construction of Chicana subjectivity, both her own within her particular family, and in general within the Chicano cultural legacy of Spanish and Anglo imperialism. She also addresses the women's movement's construction of lesbianism and feminism, and the ways that its Anglo cultural assumptions are at odds with its claims to universality.

Within her own family, Moraga came to associate passion with her mother, and thus with brownness and Chicana identity. From the beginning of her account, then, sexuality is complicated and mediated by race and ethnicity—Moraga's mother is Chicana, her father Anglo. The combination of Chicano culture's inculcation in its daughters of reverence for the mother, the sexism and heterosexism of that culture and the dominant culture, her Anglo father's passionlessness, and her own light skin and lesbianism place Moraga in a conflicted position vis-a-vis race, culture, and sexuality. In an essay addressed to her sister, Moraga writes, "Maybe you'll understand this. My mother was not the queer one, but my father . . . *it is this queer I run from.* This white man in me."[54] She writes of a conversation she has with her mother about her father's passionlessness, in which her mother enlists her as sexual confidante, revealing secrets of Moraga's father's sexual incompetence—secrets from which, her mother insists, her sister must be protected. Moraga is also placed in the role of the son, charged with the task of taking her mother's sexual concerns to her father, whom Moraga's mother suspects may be queer, "'different like you. . . .' "[55]

Throughout, Moraga writes of her desire for her mother's love. This desire's sexual dimension is fueled by the paradoxical position in which her mother places her, as well as by the contrast between Moraga's Anglo father's lack of passion and her Chicana mother's very present, yet unrequited, desire. Gender, race, and sexuality become inextricably intertwined: "To be a woman fully necessitated my claiming the race of my mother. My brother's sex was white. Mine, brown."[56] Moraga's sex is brown not simply because she identifies with, and desires, her brown mother's passion, but also because her politics have defined her alliances. Again, she contrasts this to her brother:

> . . . after I began to make political the fact of my being a Chicana, I remember my brother saying to me, "*I've* never felt 'culturally deprived'." . . . And yes, I can see now that that's true. *Male in a man's world. Light-skinned in a white world. Why change?*
>
> The pull to identify with the oppressor was never as great in me as it was in my brother. For unlike him, I could never have *become* the white man, only the white man's *woman.*[57]

This passage, like some of those in Pratt's work, underscores both the constructedness of identity and affiliation and the necessity of a political understanding of how some fairly immutable facts—such as one's categorization as a woman—have profound effects on one's experience and daily reality. That is, to say that identities are constructed is not to say that they are necessarily mutable; moreover, their mutability or immutability may depend on a particular context. On the other hand, identities can be quite fluid in both their content and their importance, depending on context and the discourses available for constructing those identities. In Moraga's text, the categories of "race" and "ethnicity" are highly mutable. This mutability is related to Moraga's light skin (and later, her education); it is the product of the fact that the dominant discourses available define "being Chicana" in a way that excludes from Chicana identity someone with her skin color and education.

For example: Moraga recounts her mother's emphasis on getting a good education, and the fact that only she and her light-skinned brother and sister "were *the* success stories of the family. Within our sex, we have received the most education and work in recognized professions."[58] But Moraga faced differential treatment not only outside of her community, but within it as well—and in each case, the treatment was both enabling and restricting, and involved both pleasure and loss. Passing in the white world by denying her Chicana heritage not only facilitated Moraga's movement in that world: it also gave her a stake in rejecting her community, her past, and her identity. Moreover, it cultivated in her a hatred for her own brownness, as well as a hatred for her whiteness. Moraga writes of how she experiences her skin color paradoxically. On the one hand, she followed "like a white sheep" the path laid out for one with her skin color—assimilation into the Anglo world. On the other hand, because this was the path that was assumed within the Chicano community (as well as in the dominant culture) to be appropriate for light-skinned Chicanas, Moraga felt pushed away from Chicano community in many ways, from her grandmother's lack of interest in her— "Mi abuela raised the darkest cousins herself, she never wanting us the way she molded and managed them"[59]—to her dark-skinned girl friends' rejection of her. The cost of this rejection—not only by her adolescent girl friends/potential lovers, but by Chicano community in general—is what Moraga tries to come to terms with in this book, simultaneously with coming to terms with the varied meanings of her feminism and lesbianism.

In these passages, then, Moraga designates neither race, culture, gender, nor sexuality as fundamentally determinant or imbued with essential meaning, but rather makes clear how they are constructed *through* each other. Thus, for her, claiming "the right to passion expressed in our own cultural tongue and movements" necessitates deconstructing and reconstructing the relationships between race, culture, gender, and sexuality, in order to articulate the possibility of different relationships between them than the generally accepted ones. That is, if discourses on racial and cultural affiliation and loyalty are constructed in sexist and heterosexist terms, or in terms of dark skin color, then in order for Moraga to make a place for herself and others like her within Chicano community, she needs to—and does—argue for the importance, to Chicano resistance to Anglo imperialism, of allowing Chicanas the full range of their power. Likewise, in order for her to make a place for herself and others like her within the women's movement, she needs to—and does—argue that that movement weakens itself to the degree that it remains complacent about the marginalization of women of color and lesbians.

Another of the book's essays, "A Long Line of Vendidas," illustrates at length this process of deconstructing and reconstructing the relationships between gender, sexuality, race, class, culture, and resistance. In this essay, Moraga refers to the Mexican tradition of "putting the male first," and explores the tradition's reflections through the Mexican myth of Malinche and its persistence among contemporary Chicano activists. In this way, she brings feminism to bear on her analysis of Chicano culture and its treatment of women and sexuality. She also challenges totalizing feminist accounts of sexism that assume that it has the same origins and manifestations across cultures, and white feminists' assumptions that the women's movement constitutes for women of color a haven, free from oppression. Thus Moraga locates herself at the intersection of the cultures that form her heritage. Hand in hand with "putting the male first" goes a devaluation and suppression of the importance of mother-daughter bonds among Chicanas. Moraga explores these phenomena through looking at Anglo imperialism and the Mexican legend of Malinche, a legend whose effects are pervasive:

> Chicanas' negative perceptions of ourselves as sexual persons and our consequential betrayal of each other finds its roots in a four-hundred year long Mexican history and mythology. It is further entrenched by a system of anglo imperialism which long ago put Mexicanos and Chicanos in a defensive posture against the dominant culture.[60]

The Mexican history and mythology to which Moraga refers is the legend of Malinche, an Aztec woman who became the translator, advisor, and mistress of Cortez, whose Spanish conquest of Mexico all but wiped out its indigenous peoples. Feminists and others have discovered evidence that Malinche became Cortez's abettor because he arrived at the moment that Aztec myth predicted the return of Quetzalcoatl, the feathered serpent god, to save his people, and Malinche believed Cortez to be Quetzalcoatl. Nonetheless, the legacy of Malinche is the Chicano and Mexican suspicion that women will betray their race through sex. The "inherent unreliability of women, our natural propensity for treachery"[61] is further reinforced by the part of the mythology that holds that Malinche was betrayed by her mother, who supposedly sold her into slavery so that Malinche's half-brother would be heir to the father's estate.

Moraga connects this legend to the current status of Chicanas within Chicano culture:

> Ask, for example, any Chicana mother about her children and she is quick to tell you she loves them all the same, but she doesn't. *The boys are different.* Sometimes I sense that she feels this way because she wants to believe that . . . through her son she can get a small taste of male privilege, since without race or class privilege that's all there is to be had. The daughters can never offer the mother such hope. . . . As a result, the daughter must constantly earn the mother's love, prove her fidelity to her. The son—he gets her love for free.[62]

Moraga discusses the privileging of the males in her own family (for example, the requirement that she and her sister wait on her brother and his friends) and its corollary—the endless competition between the women in her family. Her introduction to the book, "Amar en Los Años de Guerra," begins with a dream narrative in which Moraga and a lover are being held in a prison camp in wartime. Facing certain death, Moraga contemplates escape, but, realizing that only one of them—if that—could make it without being spotted, she immediately understands that they must stay together, even at the risk of their lives. From this dream narrative, Moraga moves to a series of scenes of women's loyalty to women in Chicana culture: women at a Mexican basilica defying the inexorable motion of the moving sidewalk that carries them past a portrait of the Virgin of Guadaloupe in order to stay and worship the Virgin; the endless competition between her mother and aunts for the favor of her grandmother; and another dream narrative, in which Moraga is pulled, torn between her grandmother's deathbed and her own bed, where a woman waits for her. Moraga writes of the suffering Chicanas go through in their loyalty to their mothers/La Virgen:

It's the daughters who remain loyal to the mother. She is the only woman we stand by. It is not always reciprocated. To be free means on some level to cut that painful loyalty when it begins to punish us. Stop the chain of events. La procesion de mujeres, sufriendo [The procession of women, suffering] . . . . Free the daughter to love her own daughter. It is the daughters who are my audience.[63]

Elsewhere in the essay, Moraga writes: *"I write this book because we are losing ourselves to the gavacho. I mourn my brother in this."*[64] She also writes of her own estrangement from Chicano culture:

I grew white. Fought to free myself from my culture's claim on me. It seemed I had to step outside my familia to see what we as a people were doing suffering. This is my politics. This is my writing. For as much as the two have eventually brought me back to my familia, there is no fooling myself that it is my education, my "consciousness" that separated me from them. That forced me to leave home. This is what has made me the outsider so many Chicanos—very near to me in circumstance—fear.[65]

In dedicating her book to the daughters and stating that she writes it out of fear that Chicanos are losing themselves to Anglo culture, Moraga underscores the tension between the things she tries to reconcile throughout the book: retaining Chicano culture, yet freeing women, "the daughters." The pull between the cultural certainty her grandmother represents ("su memoria a de noventa y seis años [her memory of ninety-six years] going back to a time where 'nuestra cultura' [our culture] was not the subject of debate")[66] and Moraga's lesbianism, her feminism, and the "right to passion"[67] (represented by the woman in her bed) as laid out in this introduction reflects the theme that is the foundation of the collection. Moraga explores the contours of her desire for women and the contours of Chicano culture, teasing out what seems mutually exclusive about the two and reconstructing their meanings so as to reconcile them. She reconciles her lesbian self with the culture from which she has become estranged yet which she desperately needs, not least because it is the women from this culture she desires. Moraga's dedication—indeed, her whole book—also performs the politics she advocates: affirmation of the bonds between Chicanas, and a steadfast refusal to separate culture, class, and sexuality, *especially* when her affiliations along those lines are defined as mutually exclusive within hegemonic discourses.

Given pervasive sexism and homophobia, in dominant Anglo culture and in Chicano culture, and given the Chicano legend of women betraying their race through sex, Moraga finds herself in a terrible bind as a feminist and a lesbian. This bind is worsened by leftist Chicano discourses that construct resistance to Anglo imperialism in terms that reinforce sexism and heterosexism. Within these constructions, a woman's pursuit of any kind of independent sexuality brands her as a traitor, since women's sexuality is constructed as the grounds on which they betray men and the Chicano race. Pursuing lesbian sexuality—sexuality which does not center around men—leaves Moraga even more vulnerable to charges of "*vendida*" ("traitor"). And this pull between culture and sexuality, between her Chicana identity and her lesbianism, is complicated even further by the fact that Malinche is seen not only as a traitor, but also as passive, violated, "*La Chingada*" ("the fucked/raped one")—the effect being that Malinche, model of Chicana sexuality, is represented as "having been violated . . . not, however, an innocent victim, but the guilty party—ultimately responsible for her own sexual victimization."[68] Her male counterpart, the active sexual subject, *el chingón*, is the one who commits such violence, who violates *la chingada*. As a woman but also the queer in the family, her mother's sexual confidante but also identified with her, Moraga found herself in paradoxical relation to the available roles: "For what, indeed, must my body look like if I were both the *chingada* and the *chingón*?"[69] Again, Moraga seeks to articulate the complexity of the situation, identifying the paradoxical role available to her as the product of both culture and religion: "The resemblance between Malinche and the Eve image is all too obvious."[70]

Moraga locates her sexuality at the intersection of multiple, often competing discourses: the repression of female sexuality by Catholicism and Chicano culture; the latter's construction of it as the site of Chicanas' betrayal, as well as their violation; the homophobia and racism within the women's movement and the dominant culture; the homophobia in Chicano culture. Like Pratt, Moraga models for her readers a method for analyzing individual lives within their historical and political contexts. She begins from her own position and identity, and examines them in relation to larger forces of oppression and privilege so as to understand the options constructed by these forces. From articulating and understanding these cross-cutting forces, these discourses about Chicana/lesbian sexuality, feminism, and resistance to Anglo imperialism, Moraga can move on to construct a different discourse about Chicana lesbian sexuality and political practice that locates her within both Chicano culture and the women's movement. Though she names "the daughters" as her audience, her audience is also the (white) women's movement and the Chicano left, both of which she castigates for the contradictions between their pur-

portedly inclusive/progressive intentions and agendas and their exclu-
sionary/reactionary practices.

Moraga's affiliations—and frustrations—with the Chicano and
women's movements are evident in the attention she gives to both
throughout her book. It is particularly evident in the theme and structure
of her discussion of her Chicana identity and her lesbianism in "A Long
Line of Vendidas." After exploring the impact of the myth of Malinche
on Chicana women's lives and (hetero)sexuality, she shifts to a discussion
of how the fact of her being Chicana and lesbian has made her an outcast
both among heterosexual Chicanas/Chicanos and among Anglo lesbians
and feminists. Just as the former have constructed a Chicana sexuality
premised on sexism and heterosexism, the latter have constructed a les-
bian/feminist sexuality premised on abandoning (non-Anglo) cultural
backgrounds and, indeed, abandoning history altogether.

> . . . I became increasingly aware of the fact that *my* sexuality had not
> only made me an outcast from my culture, but if I seriously listened to
> it, with all its specific cultural nuances, it would further make me an out-
> cast from the women's movement. . . . What the white women's move-
> ment tried to convince me of is that lesbian sexuality was *naturally*
> different than heterosexual sexuality. That the desire to penetrate and be
> penetrated, to fill and be filled, would vanish. That retaining such desires
> was "reactionary," not "politically correct," "male-identified." And
> somehow reaching sexual ecstasy with a woman lover would never in-
> volve any kind of power struggle. . . .
>
> The fact of the matter was that all these power struggles of "having"
> and "being had" were being played out in my own bedroom. And in
> my psyche, they held a particular Mexican twist.[71]

Quoting an article she published in 1982 in *off our backs*, a national feminist news journal, she continues:

> What I need to explore will not be found in the feminist lesbian bed-
> room, but more likely in the mostly heterosexual bedrooms of South
> Texas, L.A., or even Sonora, Mexico. Further, I have come to realize
> that the boundaries white feminists confine themselves to in describ-
> ing sexuality are based in white-rooted interpretations of dominance,
> submission, power-exchange, etc.[72]

Moraga goes on to critique the anti-materialism and ahistoricism of Radical Feminist discourses of sexuality, resistance, and identity politics, moving from there to a discussion of black feminist identity politics (as

elaborated in the Combahee River Collective's "A Black Feminist Statement")[73] and finally to a discussion of the need for, and character of, a Third World women's movement. Moraga repeatedly argues here for the importance of counterhegemonic discourses in creating new possibilities for subjectivity, and, out of those, new directions for social movements and social change. The Combahee River Collective statement, she writes,

> had considerable impact in creating an analysis of U.S. Third World women's oppression. . . . The appearance of these sisters' words *in print,* as lesbians of color, suddenly made it viable for me to put myself in the center of a movement. I no longer had to postpone or deny any part of my identity to make revolution easier for somebody else to swallow.[74]

The availability of a discourse on oppression and resistance at the center of which Moraga could locate herself was crucial to her becoming politically active, resisting forces of oppression. Alienated from white feminism's ahistoricism and construction of a "universal" (white) female experience of sexist domination, Moraga, who had been pushed by her family and community to acculturate to Anglo society, was alienated from the Chicano movement as well. Her discussion of this alienation reveals a totalizing construction of "the Chicana" within the Chicano movement that paralleled the women's movement's construction of "the woman":

> During the late 60s and early 70s, I was not an active part of la causa [the cause]. I never managed to get myself to walk in the marches in East Los Angeles (I merely watched from the sidelines); I never went to one meeting of MECHA on campus. No soy tonta. [I'm not stupid.] I would have been murdered in El Movimiento—light-skinned, unable to speak Spanish well enough to hang; miserably attracted to women and fighting it; and constantly questioning all authority, including men's. I felt I did not belong there. Maybe I had really come to believe that "Chicanos" were "different," not "like us," as my mother would say. But I fully knew that there was a part of me that was a part of that movement, but it seemed that part would have to go unexpressed until the time I could be a Chicano and the woman I had to be, too.[75]

Split into different "selves" by discourses and movements that had no room for a light-skinned, Chicana lesbian, Moraga lacked a channel for what could be her political energy.

> I had heard too many times that my concern about specifically sexual issues was divisive to the "larger struggle" or wasn't really the "primary

contradiction" and therefore, not essential for revolution. That to be concerned about the sexuality of women of color was an insult to women in the Third World literally starving to death. But the only hunger I have ever known was the hunger for sex and the hunger for freedom and somehow, in my mind and heart, they were related and certainly not mutually exclusive. If I could not use the source of my hunger as the source of my activism, how then was I to be politically effective?[76]

Here, like Pratt, Moraga argues that coming to terms with one's identities is a necessary precursor to engaging in resistance. But she also makes clear that she is not advocating simply a "multiplication of identities" and thus of movements, where the circles get drawn with increasing specificity and narrowness. In "La Güera," ("The Light-Skinned One"), a piece she also published earlier in *This Bridge Called My Back: Writings by Radical Women of Color*, Moraga writes:

Do we merely struggle with the "ism" that's sitting on top of our heads?

The answer is: yes, I think first we do; and we must do so thoroughly and deeply. But to fail to move out from there will only isolate us in our oppression. . . .[77]

In this piece, she also refers to Emma Goldman's statement about the need to enter into the lives of others, and she writes of this by way of arguing for a politics that is neither abstract/anti-materialist in its definition of a universal subject and a standard set of political concerns purported to be relevant to all; nor so mired in specificity that it fails to make connections between parallel forms of oppression, and fails to connect resistance struggles as well. She takes up similar themes in the poem "Winter of Oppression, 1982," in which she connects her struggles to those of Jewish people. She does so in the context of resisting the impulse, inculcated in her through her religious upbringing, to decide "whose death/has been marked/upon the collective forehead/of this continent, this/shattering globe/the most indelibly." She ends the poem by reminding herself, "Whoever I am/I must believe/I am not/and never will be/the only/one/who suffers."[78]

In bringing together these themes of identity, commonality, and difference, in working from the specificity of identity outward to larger connections, Moraga illustrates and enacts the fundamental principle underlying coalition politics in the late twentieth century: the linking of shared struggles that takes place simultaneously with maintaining differences and acknowledging the specificity of different realities and needs.

The structure of Moraga's discussion of the shortcomings of both feminist and Chicano politics underscores the message of its content: that is, Moraga elaborates her critique of Chicano cultural discourses on women's sexuality and on resistance to imperialism, but then follows immediately with her critique of counterpart discourses in the women's movement. This can be read as a response not only to the ethnocentric assumptions underlying much of U.S. feminism in general, but also to more overtly racist discourses generated by feminists who had begun to look at differences based on race and ethnicity. These feminists started from an Anglo-centric perspective that assumed non-Anglo women to be subject to worse forms of sexism within their cultures than operated in white cultures; and that offered up the (Anglo) women's community and movement as the answer to such problems—a kind of feminist assimilation. Moraga works against this feminist "solution" in the way she structures her book: her "emotional/political chronology" sketches her Anglicization as a child, adolescent, and young adult by virtue of her light skin and the education available to her as one moving from poverty into the middle class; her rejection of that move into whiteness and respectability; and her embrace of the very culture and identity that the dominant feminist discourses of the time might have described as oppressive.

Moraga's mix of poetry and prose is yet another means by which she strives to retain different aspects of her self, refusing to subordinate one to another even when doing so would lend the appearance of a unified self, devoid of unresolved contradictions:

> The combining of poetry and essays in this book is the compromise I make in the effort to be understood. In Spanish, "compromiso" is also used to mean obligation or commitment. And I guess, in fact, I write as I do because I *am committed* to communicating with both sides of myself.
>
> I am the daughter of a Chicana and anglo. I think most days I am an embarrassment to both groups. I sometimes hate the white in me so viciously that I long to forget the commitment my skin has imposed on my life. To speak in two tongues. I must. But I will not double-talk and I refuse to let *anybody's* movement determine for me what is safe and fair to say.[79]

It is in her mix of Spanish and English, though, that Moraga's project of reconstructing her subjectivity is most startling and intrepid, and this is because Spanish is a language she has had to learn as an adult, having grown up one of the many children of immigrants whose parents seek to ensure their children's success by pushing them to assimilate, linguistically and otherwise, into mainstream U.S. culture. In learning and using Spanish, Moraga refuses to remain within accepted notions of "authenticity" as it relates to identity. That is, she does not accept the white-washed subjectivity instilled by her complicated background; nor does she accept the essentialism inherent in the notion that identity (as reflected through language) is fixed. At the same time, she insists (with Pratt) that one cannot shed an old identity and adopt an entirely new one. The political implications of the possibilities for *shifts* in identity and subjectivity that both Moraga and Pratt argue for have powerful liberatory potential.

> In returning to the love of my race, I must return to the fact that not only has the mother been taken from me, but her tongue, her mother-tongue. I want the language . . .
>
> Quiero decir [I want to say] that I know on the surface of things, this is not to make any sense. I spoke English at home . . . but what I must admit is that I have felt in my writing that the English was not cutting it. Entiendes? [Understand?] That there is something else, deep and behind my heart and I want to hold it hot and bold in the hands of my writing and it will not come out sounding like English. Te prometo. No es ingles. [I promise you. It is not English.] And I have to wonder, is it so that I have felt "too much," "too emotional," "too sensitive" because I was trying to translate my feelings into English cadences?[80]

In this passage and others in which Moraga mixes English and Spanish, the reader is confronted with the performance of one of her main themes: that her background and identities are mixed, and she is committed to all the different parts of them. The Spanish-speaking, Chicana reader who may see Moraga as the outsider to be feared[81] because of her light skin and acquired Anglo ways is confronted with her move back into Chicano culture and identity, including at the level of language. And the non-Spanish-speaking, Anglo feminist is confronted in an undeniable way with what Moraga continually points out in her arguments: that is, the limitations to such a reader's own perspective, her own potentially totalizing construction of women, and the limits in her own identification with Moraga as woman, feminist, and lesbian.

In the back of the book, Moraga includes a three-page glossary of English translations of some—but nowhere near all—of the passages that appear in Spanish in the text. The glossary, in what it includes as well as what it excludes, again places the non-Spanish-speaking reader momentarily in a marginal relationship to the text—one which parallels, in some ways, the marginal relationship that many whose first language is Spanish have to dominant U.S. culture. This untranslated heteroglossia[82] may move some readers to consider the position of a non-English speaker's relationship to an English-speaking dominant culture; it also invites readers to consider the conditions under which such a mixing of languages is possible, and what that mix usually connotes. Moraga explores this theme explicitly in her poem, "It's the Poverty," in which she writes of her anxiety about acquiring the language and education that has been used against her people (and has also been used by her people to separate her from them):

> *I lack imagination* you say.

> No. I lack language.
> The language to clarify
> my resistance to the literate.

> Words are a war to me.
> They threaten my family.

> To gain the word to describe the loss,
> I risk losing everything.
> I may create a monster,
> the word's length and body
> swelling up colorful and thrilling
> looming over my *mother,* characterized.
> Her voice in the distance
> *unintelligible   illiterate.*

> These are the monster's words. . . .[83]

Moraga's theme here (and elsewhere in her book) is her ambivalent position vis-a-vis writing and education. Her "resistance to the literate" is also her resistance to the use of words to marginalize and negate the lives of people of color, her community and family—a use that has been central to Anglo imperialism against Chicanos. The rhetoric of this imperialism is tangible and immediate for Moraga—her own mother and her family are threatened in this "war" of words as "unintelligible" and "illiterate"—words often used to characterize those who mix Spanish and English in a culture in which the "English-only Movement" and ethnocentrism in general define English as the language of the intelligent, and other languages as symbols of cultural and intellectual inferiority. The risk for Moraga is that she may find that participating in this war of words by gaining the language to describe its effects on her, her family, and her community, will ultimately mean that her own words become part of this imperialist rhetoric, that they will be used to uphold and perpetuate the very practices she wishes to subvert. By learning the language that has been mobilized against her people, she risks betraying them herself. She subverts this possibility to some extent—and calls attention to it as well—by her strategic heteroglossia.

Conclusion

The autotheoretical texts, exemplified by the two considered here, are important in a number of ways for those interested in the women's movement. The texts are examples of recently emerging feminist efforts to create social change through transforming discourse and thus subjectivity. Taken together, they form a documentation of debates within the women's movement that have concentrated on the construction of women as a category; of differences in women's identities and subjectivities based on race, sexuality, class, ethnicity, religion, and so forth; and of feminist concerns and strategies. These debates have involved the articulation of fractured—rather than coherent—identities and the political implications of the multiple alliances suggested by those fractured identities. They have also, significantly, involved the efforts (some successful, some not) of women who have been marginalized within the women's movement and outside of it to bring their experiences of domination and resistance to bear on feminist analyses and agendas.

While the autotheoretical texts suggest a theory of power similar to that which underlies feminist appropriations of postmodern theory, these texts go beyond strictly theoretical works in that they provide a "thick descriptive" account of domination and resistance at the level of identity and daily life. They proceed from the same conceptions of power that postmodern theory does, but they move beyond the latter's realm of abstraction into the materiality of lived experience. They do this, moreover, in the context of theoretical reflection and as part of the project of linking individual lives to hegemonic and counterhegemonic social forces. The autotheoretical texts share postmodern theory's focus on discourse as central to constructing subjectivity and agency: indeed, one of their chief concerns is to chart the shifts in subjectivity and agency made

97

possible by the availability and political strength of resistant discourses. In this way, the texts show how discourses produced collectively can affect individual lives, as well as transform the politics of a movement (or at least some sectors of it). Moreover, they show that even within a given set of social relations and a particular political system, there are multiple possibilities for how subjectivity gets constructed, what forms of action are available, and how resistance can be mounted to both juridical and dispersed forms of power. They also provide some direction for those interested in effecting change at the level of discourse as well as at the level of legislation and explicitly stated social policy. That is, these texts explore how shifts in consciousness—and thus action—can be achieved. At the same time, they work toward achieving such shifts by insisting on the situatedness within the social structure of authors and readers, and modeling for readers, through discursive acts, a method for investigating their own situatedness and taking up positions of resistance to hegemonic forms of domination.

These texts also represent the possibility of incorporating into social science studies of the women's movement the voices of some of the women on whose behalf the movement purportedly operates. Herein lies the potential for social science to study not only organizations, but also the impact of dominant social forces on actual, individual lives. This latter objective is important: the study of power is incomplete without an analysis of its impact, on multiple levels, on the people who are subject to it.

Social Science Studies of the Women's Movement: Problems in Theory and Method

Scholarship on the women's movement in sociology and political science has attempted to capture its character, aims, and impact. Because of some common features these studies share, however, they tend to reflect a relatively traditional, interest-group perspective on feminist action. This is particularly true of those studies that focus exclusively on feminist legislative activity. Some recent studies have enjoyed greater success in examining other types of feminist activity as well, and some of these later works even seek to evaluate non-policy activity on its own terms. Nevertheless, legislative activity remains the dominant concern of scholarship on the women's movement even in these works. Moreover, feminist discursive activity, aimed at transforming cultural paradigms, remains inadequately specified even in those texts in which it is identified and examined.

This omission (in some cases) or shortchanging (in others) of feminist discursive politics has consequences not only for how scholars describe and analyze sexist domination and feminist resistance to it, but also for how they assess feminist success. Moreover, a policy emphasis renders some data (legislative changes, election results, lobbying records) legitimate, and others (discursive and symbolic activities, including speech acts, writing, publishing, dissemination of visual images, etc.) illegitimate for the study of a movement. Consequently, the participants and ideas associated with the former are highlighted, while those associated with the latter are elided.

The fundamental approaches that produce the studies' uniform perspective on domination and resistance can be summarized in the following ways.

1. These studies tend to construct women in essentialist and homogenizing terms (often through the narrow range of concerns the studies identify as feminist).

To varying degrees, the studies of the women's movement tend either to treat women as if they are all basically the same, sharing a common set of gendered experiences and feminist goals; or to divide women into apparently coherent subcategories, between which (but not within which) minor differences exist. This static treatment of women results from the assumption that gender is the primary fact of life for all women—i.e., that gender is essential to women's subjectivity whereas other factors, such as race, sexuality, or class, are not.

2. These studies emphasize liberal feminism, with important consequences for their treatment of race, sexuality, religion, class, and ethnicity.

To varying degrees, these studies accept the premise, which operates in social science methodology generally, that social phenomena are best explained when variables are disaggregated and treated separately or additively, rather than interactively. In studies of the women's movement, this premise implies that gender can be—and is best studied when—separated out from class, race, ethnicity, and sexuality; and that the way to achieve this separation is to focus on women whose relation to social divisions other than gender appears neutral. It is a fallacy, however, to assume that a position of power vis-à-vis a social division, such as race, is a neutral position. Those subject positions that appear "neutral" do so because they are hegemonic, powerful, and thus "unmarked." Thus, in a tacit effort to isolate the dynamics of sexist domination from other dominations, and "feminist" concerns from "other" concerns, the studies tend to look to experiences and concerns that, for example, *appear* not to be racialized, but only because of the hegemonic, "unmarked" status of white perspectives. One of the practical consequences of this approach is that feminist organizing within socialist, anti-racist, anti-homophobic, and other progressive organizations is omitted from consideration; likewise, feminist organizations that are explicitly grounded in anti-racist, anti-homophobic or working-class interests are omitted, likely because they are viewed as "unrepresentative."

Moreover, the concerns these studies emphasize—principally, legal/administrative and economic barriers to women's formal equality with men—and the implicit analyses from which they derive invoke an ideal-typical white, middle-class, heterosexual woman at their center. This is not to say that the concerns these studies focus on are equally important to all white, middle-class, heterosexual women, nor that attention to these concerns would be sufficient to achieve the end of domination of this group of women. Nor is it to say that women who fall outside these privileged categories have not gained in important ways from legislative change. Rather, the point is that the definition of politics most widely accepted among social scientists researching the women's movement leads them to fix their gaze most steadily on liberal feminism. And while liberal feminists pursue a variety of reforms that are relevant to a broad constituency, part of how liberal feminism gets constructed (through media, academic studies, and so on) is through a focus on educated, professional, white heterosexual women (and the concerns most relevant to them). This is because these women are the most visible and vocal feminists who engage in this type of activism, and because they are the ones who the media and academia are most comfortable representing. Consequently, social scientists' focus on liberal feminism constitutes a focus on relatively powerful, less marginalized women whose activism generally takes place in the arena of electoral politics.

Thus, the studies implicitly ratify entrenched hierarchies of race, class, and sexuality, both in the concerns they identify as central to feminism and in the types of activism—and the arenas in which that activism takes place—that they identify as legitimately "political."

3. These studies offer narrow representation of the strategies of resistance feminists have developed and employed.

To the degree that the women's movement studies treat liberal feminism as primary, they do so with regard not only to its concerns but to its tactics as well—indeed, the two are inextricable. Thus, the studies reflect a liberal feminist paradigm in their emphasis on legislative and administrative barriers to women's equality with men. They reflect this paradigm as well in their emphasis and on liberal feminism's favored tactics, including lobbying legislators, aiding the election campaigns of local, state, and national candidates who are sympathetic to feminist concerns, establishing and administering political action committees (PACs), mobilizing women's movement constituents to pressure their government representatives to pass legislation favorable to women, encouraging women to run for office, and providing political campaign education to women candidates,[1] and so forth.

Conversely, some of the studies say little or nothing about feminist challenges—even those emanating from liberal feminist organizations such as NOW—that take place at an ideological level, or that reflect a more fundamental agenda for social transformation. Other studies acknowledge ideological and discursive activity, but subordinate it nonetheless to policy initiatives, either because they see the latter as constituting the more important feminist activity, or because they simply don't treat discursive or symbolic activity in specific terms, exploring the goals, tactics, and impact of these efforts.[2]

One consequence of this emphasis on liberal strategies is that the studies perpetuate a view of domination that locates it at a more superficial level than do analyses that concentrate on discourse, public consciousness, and entrenched social paradigms. Misleading in a way, liberal approaches can suggest that sexism and other forms of domination are more tractable than they really are.

The texts discussed here are the most comprehensive of the women's movement studies, in that they seek to treat the movement as a whole, rather than *explicitly* restricting their focus to public policy.[3] The distance between their stated goal of treating the women's movement comprehensively and their actual representations of the movement provides the starting point for my critique—which focuses most closely on those studies whose representations are the most complex. That is, though I examine five central texts here, I dwell considerably less on those whose shortcomings are most obvious and focus more on those works whose omissions and prejudices are the least apparent, relatively submerged, or subtle.

Consequently, some of the criticisms articulated below may seem picayune, and the shortcomings they address trivial, particularly to those who have attempted, either in academic writing or in activist work, the truly impossible task of "representing everyone." Yet my critique is not meant to be an indictment of particular works or their authors; rather it is meant to call attention to the insidiousness of privileged perspectives, even in the work of those who seek to overcome the hegemony of those perspectives; and to illustrate the relationship between an attachment to liberal paradigms and established methodologies, on the one hand, and a recalcitrance of prejudice, on the other.

The Women's Movement Studies

Myra Marx Ferree and Beth B. Hess, *Controversy and Coalition: The New Feminist Movement* (1985)[4] and Ferree and Hess, *Controversy and Coalition: The New Feminist Movement Across Three Decades of Change* (1994) (revised edition)[5]

Ferree and Hess trace the contemporary women's movement from its roots in the history of U.S. feminist organizing and ideology and in postwar demographic changes through its emergence as a full-fledged social movement in the 1960s and 70s, and its development through the early 1980s (in the first edition) and through the early 1990s (in the second).

They approach the various strands of feminism animated by the movement's diverse ideologies, goals, and strategies through the typologies of career, liberal, socialist, and radical feminisms, and of small groups and national organizations/the women's policy network. In discussing the movement's variety, they focus specifically on the challenges that this diversity of goals, participants, and structures presents to the movement as a whole.

While the first edition of *Controversy and Coalition* offered the fullest account of the varieties of feminist issues and resistance of any of the studies that had been published at that time, it nonetheless displayed the same shortcomings of the studies that preceded it. These are particularly apparent in its treatment of collectivist organizations, radical feminism, and women's differences.

The second edition of Ferree and Hess's study reflects the authors' deepening awareness of the diversity of women's experiences and needs, and of the importance of what they call "cultural change." Of all the studies of the women's movement, this edition provides the most well-rounded, complex view of feminism's varied dimensions.

Barbara Ryan, *Feminism and the Women's Movement: Dynamics of Change in Social Movement Ideology and Activism*, 1992[6]

From the perspective of this study, the chief contribution Ryan makes to the literature on the women's movement is her inclusion of the category "discursive politics." By including this concept, Ryan acknowledges forms of domination and of feminist resistance to that domination beyond those typically recognized.

Ryan's other main contributions are, first, that she focuses on intramovement dynamics to explain the course various sectors of the women's movement have taken, and thereby complements analyses that concentrate on external factors; and second, that, although her loyalties clearly lie with more traditional forms of political action and goals, she does investigate small group and radical feminism at some length and even, for the most part, on its own terms.

Ryan's discussion of intramovement conflict centers on three splits: that between radical feminists and NOW; that between lesbians and heterosexual women; and that between women of color and white women.

Jo Freeman, *The Politics of Women's Liberation* (1975)[7]

When Freeman's book came out in 1975, it was the first social science text to examine the women's movement as a political movement. Freeman states her purpose as the examination of the relationship of feminism to the policy process, but in fact she addresses the broader women's movement. She examines and evaluates the origins, goals, strategies, and efficacy of the "older" and "younger" branches of feminism, the two strands of the feminist movement that she identifies (only the former of which, in her taxonomy, is concerned primarily with policy change). As the first study of its kind about the women's movement, Freeman's work provided a foundation for political science analysis of the women's movement upon which subsequent studies built. The book thus warrants attention here, despite the fact that the political context in which it was published differs in important ways from the political context from which the later works emerged.

Ethel Klein, *Gender Politics* (1984)[8]

The central argument of Klein's study of the emergence of mass feminist consciousness and movement in the 1960s and 1970s is that the quintessential dilemma facing women as a group is the task of balancing the competing demands of marriage, motherhood, and career. Klein argues that women developed feminist consciousness in the 1970s largely because of their recent entry into the labor force: "Women's contribution to the economy has changed dramatically over the course of the century. They now work outside the home."[9] Moreover, she argues, women are able to do so not because of changes in social expectations of women, and the consequences of these changes for women's subjectivity, but rather the other way around. That is, according to Klein, women's roles changed first, and consciousness followed.

Joyce Gelb, "Social Movement 'Success' "[10] (1987) and *Feminism and Politics* (1989)[11]

Gelb's article and book comprise a comparative study of the women's movements in the United States and Great Britain.[12] Like Freeman and Ferree and Hess, she breaks the women's movements down into two parts, which she identifies as two "wings" of feminism: reformist/bureaucratic/directed feminism, and radical/collectivist/non-directed feminism. Gelb argues that, while both countries' movements embody both approaches, U.S. feminism tends more toward the reformist wing while British feminism tends more toward the radical wing. She characterizes "directed" feminism in the U.S. as having a "formal leadership structure and definite programs of action," whereas Britain's "non-directed" feminism places "greater emphasis on personal interaction, expression and articulation of feminist values, and the importance of internal democracy."[13]

Gelb locates the source of these differences—and of what she sees as the differential impact of the two approaches—in the two countries' con-

trasting formal political structures. The United States is more open to influence from interest groups, while Great Britain is more corporatist, not
as pluralist as the United States. The differences between the feminist
movements in the two countries can be attributed, she argues, to the different opportunities that follow from those state structures.

1. "Women"/The Subject-actor

In each of the women's movement studies, how the authors conceive of
the category of "women" sometimes emerges in explicit statements regarding the diversity of women's experiences and concerns. More often,
their views about who women are emerge indirectly in the issues they
identify as central to feminism. For example, authors who identify, respectively, the existence of private all-male business clubs, forced sterilization, and lesbian mothers' custody battles as central to feminism
probably imagine different—if overlapping—constituencies when they
refer to "women" or "women's concerns." Thus, the studies' conceptualizations of *domination* are embedded in their discussions of who women
are and what concerns them most.

Ferree and Hess

In their introductions to both editions of their book, Ferree and Hess
write, "Oversimplification characterizes much of what has been written
about the contemporary women's movement, both in the professional
and popular press," and they maintain that

> It is, in fact, impossible to write of the organized feminist movement
> without placing it in the context of many diverse strands of feeling and
> action. In one sense, these underlying currents are "the movement," of
> which organized feminism is only one highly visible element. This di-
> versity is our central theme.[14]

Despite their efforts to make their study inclusive, however, Ferree
and Hess's first edition in particular constructs the category "women"—
the subject of feminism—in ways that obscure important differences of
race, ethnicity, class, and sexuality, even as they acknowledge these differences at some points in the text.[15]

Ferree and Hess's second edition improves considerably on the first, not only in the goals they identify but in their conception of feminist activity and social change as well. Claiming that differences between various strands of feminism have diminished over time, Ferree and Hess concentrate less in the second edition on their four types of feminism (liberal, career, socialist, and radical), instead identifying goals without generally attaching them to any particular constituency. Among these goals are: reproductive freedom, "genuine equality" in heterosexual relationships, changes in the occupational structure and the workplace, "socially recognized personhood,"[16] sexual assault, economic justice, affirmative action, and pay equity/comparable worth. Other issues they identify as important to feminism include family policies and poverty issues (child support, the plight of displaced homemakers, and the feminization of poverty); the negative view of feminism promulgated in the media and the myth of the "postfeminist" generation; and campus hate crimes and overall campus intolerance of women, people of color, and lesbians, bisexuals, and gay men.

Some of these issues are much broader than a strict public policy focus would allow, and Ferree and Hess's greater receptivity to looking beyond policy is also evident in how they characterize social change. For example, they argue that, "For the New Feminist Movement, the major challenges of the 1980s included . . . resisting efforts to reframe feminist concerns in hostile language"[17] and that "Cultural change is the least observable but perhaps the most enduring form of transformation."[18]

The impact on Ferree and Hess's study of these broader impulses is limited, however, by some of the authors' methodological approaches and conceptual formulations. For example, Ferree and Hess rely on public opinion survey data and time series data to assess attitudes toward women and feminist issues. Ferree and Hess themselves acknowledge that such instruments may measure people's willingness to be seen as holding a certain attitude more than they measure actual attitudes. Moreover, such instruments are limited by the questions they ask, the issues they include, and the way they formulate their questions; and most questions are designed to elicit fairly simple yes–no, agree–disagree responses, inadequate for assessing complex beliefs about complicated issues.

The issues included in the data Ferree and Hess employ are: a respondent's willingness to vote for a woman for President; attitudes toward male authority in the family, men doing housework, women's activities outside the home, and sex-segregated roles in general; respondents' self-description as feminist, and their attitudes toward the women's movement (broken down into categories of white/African American, middle versus working class, and employed outside home/not); and abortion. Though Ferree and Hess acknowledge that, within the women's movement, "claims about women's exploitation 'as women' also obscured the variety of these experiences and established middle-class white women as a norm,"[19] their reliance on this type of data to discuss changing attitudes—the kind of "cultural change" to which they rightly attach great importance—could be argued to reproduce precisely this problem.

This is not to say that Ferree and Hess fail completely to represent a broader set of concerns associated with feminism, but rather to point out how their own efforts to do so are hindered by the methodology they adopt and the concepts—reflected in the survey questions—they accept. As in Ryan's study, the resulting tensions in their work are very instructive regarding the entrenched nature of old methodological paradigms.

In addition to the limits imposed by methodology, the broader political approach in Ferree and Hess's revised edition is checked by a narrower one that operates simultaneously. On the one hand, the broader perspective is evident in their statements that explicitly endorse the diversity of women's experiences and interests, such as the following:

> [T]here is always the tendency of observers to impose their meaning on events rather than to attempt to understand them from the point of view of diverse participants. . . . Our goal is to present each form of contemporary feminism in its own terms and in relation to the whole in a way that incorporates both an insider's and an outsider's perspective.[20]

On the other hand, this goal seems to recede with statements such as the following generalization:

> Jewish women, however, have attained a level of economic security and educational privilege from which most women of color remain excluded.[21]

The attention to differences in status and position within the overall category of "women," and particularly the acknowledgment of the close relationship between race and class, are laudable—the particular impoverishment of women of color is an urgent issue for the women's movement. However, no such relationship between Jewish women and a particular class position has been established empirically, and, indeed, this assertion of Jewish women's relative affluence lies far too close for comfort to classic anti-Semitic stereotypes.

A different sort of perspectival blinder is at work in the following characterization of the women's movement's evolving approach to race and class:

> It would be a mistake, however, to continue to perceive feminism in the United States today as a middle-class phenomenon. The 1970s were a period in which many other constituencies saw themselves as beneficiaries of movement goals: women of color . . . and working-class women. From their earlier position of hostility, many labor unions have endorsed feminist positions and working-class women have begun to organize on their own behalf. As a result, the racial, ethnic, and class composition of feminist activists has become broader and more varied.
>
> In addition, white feminists, confronted with a legacy of racism within their movement, have begun the long process of rethinking feminism from a more inclusive, multicultural perspective. This effort requires more than simply recruiting racial/ethnic minority women to a movement whose goals and priorities have been set by middle-class white women. Authentic inclusion demands that attention be paid to the perspectives and needs of all women, particularly the most disadvantaged.[22]

What is missing from this account is any perspective on the role that women of color have played in pushing white feminists, often over their strenuous objections, to recognize and work against their own racism. Certainly labor unions and white feminists have played important roles in rendering the women's movement more representative of women's racial and ethnic diversity. Clearly, however, feminists of color have done the most in this regard, and their work toward this end has often been vehemently resisted by unions, white women, and others. Their omission from this brief account is glaring.

Similar omissions are at work with respect to lesbians, heterosexism, and homophobia in Ferree and Hess's second edition. The examples are many: in discussing "the new grassroots direct action groups that formed"[23] in the 1980s, for example, they mention WHAM (Women's Health Action Mobilization) and note that it took its inspiration for street protests from "the radical AIDS protest group ACT-UP,"[24] but they do not specifically mention WHAM's lesbian-strong membership or ACT UP's queer orientation. They mention the Guerrilla Girls, but not the Lesbian Avengers, as other groups engaged in direct-action, discursive struggle. Likewise, their claim that "long periods of political repression and normative rigidity, as in the America of the 1980s, are inhospitable to all social movements, regardless of the issues or constituencies"[25] obfuscates the explosion of AIDS activism and queer activism that began in the mid- to late-1980s, with New York City-based groups like ACT UP and Queer Nation spawning chapters all over the world and reviving radical direct action with enormous energy and, in the case of ACT UP, enormous effect.

Another way that Ferree and Hess obscure sexuality issues involves the many instances in which the authors list points of differences among women, ranging from race to class to religion to age, yet somehow neglect to include sexuality[26]; or the sections on "Biases in Mobilization" and "Realizing the Promise of Diversity," which address race and class, but not sexuality. In addition, their discussion of feminist organizations that emerged between 1968 and 1973 includes no mention at all of any lesbian organizations.[27]

When Ferree and Hess do address sexuality as a feminist issue, as in the section, "Internal Conflict in the Women's Movement,"[28] they frame their discussion in terms that make "lesbianism," not "homophobia" or "heterosexism," the problem—a move represented by such heterocentric phrasing of movement questions as, "what degree of recognition should be given to the double oppression of homosexual women?"[29] Much of what they say in this section is important, and their second edition improves considerably on the first. Yet lesbianism, not homophobia, remains the focal point in their attempts to explain conflict; and the whole issue of sexuality is largely relegated to this section, rather than consistently attended to throughout the book.

The net result, then, of Ferree and Hess's revisions is a broadened construction of who women are, coupled with a still-constricted perspective on the implications of women's diversity.

Ryan

On the surface, Ryan's construction of "women" reflects a relatively broad range of women's experiences and concerns, in that she frequently acknowledges the presence in the movement of lesbians, women of color, and working-class women through the scope of issues she identifies as feminist. Like the other scholars of the women's movement discussed here, Ryan constructs women through a range of policy issues she identifies as central to feminist activism. Among these are the economic decline and increasing poverty women experience, especially women who head households; the ERA; abortion rights; pay equity; affirmative action; child care facilities; maternal leave; and a general lack of government social service support for working women who are mothers. Ryan also identifies racism, lesbian concerns, and pornography among the issues salient to contemporary feminism. In naming these issues, she invokes a relatively robust representation of who women are and what some of their concerns might be.

Yet Ryan's actual discussion of feminist work in these areas undermines her broader representation of women insofar as she maintains that those women most invested in these concerns (racism, class oppression, heterosexism) use them to intimidate white, straight, middle-class feminists. In this way, her concentration on intramovement struggles, which holds great potential for enhancing our understanding of why the women's movement has evolved the way it has, becomes simply a tool to promote liberal, policy-oriented activity, and, more insidiously, to dismiss the racism, classism, and homophobia which have in fact been responsible for a great deal of intramovement conflict.

Too often, Ryan's focus on intramovement struggles boils down to a question of who can plausibly call themselves the "most radical," and on what grounds. In the process, she obscures the legitimate grievances of women of color, working-class women, lesbians, and bisexual women, casting their articulations of their concerns as bids for power over beleaguered liberal, heterosexual, white, middle-class feminists. Moreover, she blames these women for the decline of "small group" feminist activity:

> Indeed, activists of this period consider the impact of antagonistic group relations to be a major cause of many women leaving the movement. . . . Within groups and between groups, charges of elitism, racism, homophobia, and classism were rampant.[30]

Ryan's treatment of sexuality approaches the issue through four main "moments" in feminism: the lesbian purge from NOW and the organization's subsequent (1971) affirmation of "the right of each person to define and express their own sexuality"[31]; the lesbian/straight splits; the pornography debates; and lesbians' involvement in AIDS activism. Ryan's discussion of the first moment—NOW's lesbian purge and its aftermath—is most notable for its liberal reduction of sexuality to a matter of rights; and for the way that Ryan allows NOW's 1971 resolution to deflect attention away from the potential consequences of the purge. Subsequent to the 1971 resolution, she asserts, the lesbian/straight splits were most volatile in the small groups, not in NOW. She does not consider the possibility that this may have appeared to be the case due to lesbians leaving NOW in favor of the small groups, where they may have felt they could get more satisfaction in their efforts to confront homophobia among feminists.

Her discussion of the gay/straight splits reflects the defensive stance of unreconstructed heterosexism in the face of a critique of the institution of heterosexuality, as do her comments on the pornography debates. This heterosexism is most evident in Ryan's discussion of divisions within the movement. To illustrate those divisions, Ryan quotes Pat Mainardi:

> The left and lesbian forces infiltrated and seized virtually every independent women's movement center and publication in the years 1969–1973, in many cases establishing the now familiar left-lesbian alliance against feminism. . . . [T]he original ideas of the radical women's movement have been suppressed. (1978: 122)[32]

While one might expect that a vision of lesbians aligning with the left to launch a full-scale (and "now familiar") attack to defeat feminism would require some explication, Ryan lets this quote stand without comment. She does the same with the following quote from an interview:

> Everybody was trashed. Different groups for different reasons at different times. Too radical, too conservative, too liberal, straight, lived with men, had boy children, etc.[33]

No mention is made of women being trashed for being lesbians. Rather, Ryan continually constructs lesbian/heterosexual splits in homophobic terms, with straight women as the victims of lesbians who perpetrated the same oppression against heterosexual women that men always had:

> As the political lesbian view spread, heterosexual women in radical groups found it difficult to defend their own lifestyle as feminist. It was common to be told that a discussion of women's relations with men was not appropriate for women's community. Married feminists were often made to feel that the problems they had in their marriages were of their own choosing since they elected to stay in those relationships. Reflecting back on this time, one woman explains heterosexual women's passivity to this assault as guilt: accepting the blame as women are taught to do, they bent under the pressure and did not push back saying "this is absurd" (cited in Hansen 1986).[34]

In Ryan's account, even the pornography debates boil down to lesbian persecution of heterosexual women:

> Because so much of the feminist anti-pornography message incorporates an anti-heterosexuality message, it contains not only an anti-male component but an anti-heterosexual female component as well.[35]

To be sure, a certain kind of lesbian chauvinism was evident in some quarters of the women's movement throughout the 1970s and beyond, and it caused substantial pain to some heterosexual women who sought to ally with lesbians in analyzing and opposing institutionalized heterosexism and homophobia.[36] However, to concentrate, as Ryan does, only on this chauvinism without any accompanying analysis of its sources in very real systems of oppression is to refuse the legitimacy of grievances about that oppression.

Finally, Ryan introduces the argument that lesbians who engage in AIDS activism thereby abandon feminism because AIDS is a men's issue. She presents Sonia Johnson's views on this matter at length, but does not challenge the equation of AIDS with men, or give any space to the argument that AIDS is a women's and a lesbian issue. By not questioning the assumptions underlying the contention that AIDS is a men's issue, Ryan obscures a number of the important realities of AIDS and AIDS activism. They include the following points:

—The link between AIDS and homophobia prompts many lesbians to work on AIDS issues.

—Many women get AIDS, HIV-positive women die faster than HIV-positive men, and women were excluded from the Centers for Disease Control definition of AIDS (which followed a model of how the disease progresses in adult male bodies). Thus women were excluded from benefits available to those diagnosed with AIDS, until AIDS activists in ACT UP[37] pressured the Centers for Disease Control to change its definition.

—The majority of cases of HIV in women are in women of color, and women of color are the fastest-growing group of HIV cases. Thus, AIDS is very much a feminist and anti-racist issue, and women and lesbians interested in working against racism and sexism in multiracial feminist coalitions have a stake in working on AIDS issues.

—Many lesbians feel that it is in their interest to work in political alliance with gay/bisexual men.

In the case of race, Ryan's discussion parallels her analysis of sexuality, in that it tends to reduce intramovement racial conflicts to guilt-tripping and one-up bids for "most radical" status. Though Ryan identifies a number of issues as central for women of color—including welfare, public housing, tenants' rights, inner-city schools, poverty, drugs, racial rates of imprisonment, unemployment, and underemployment[38]—the main focus of her discussions of race is the way women of color ostensibly intimidate white women with charges of racism. This theme lends a schizophrenic quality to her treatment of race, counterposed as it is with more anti-racist moments. In one such anti-racist moment, she acknowledges that "confrontations by diverse groups of women have broadened feminist analysis and challenged the movement into a more inclusive strategy of change."[39] In another, she refers to challenges made by women of color to the women's movement's racism in the following terms, citing Hull, Scott, and Smith,[40] and Moraga and Anzaldúa:[41]

> A recognition of similarity exists among women of color which has led to many joining together to remind the women's movement that there are different versions of what feminism means based on differences in social condition. . . .[42]

In yet another moment, Ryan observes that, "When white feminists ignore racial charges and when women of color dismiss efforts to resolve racial divisiveness, both groups lose."[43]

Yet, in many passages, Ryan casts these confrontations and challenges in much less sympathetic—and certainly less political—light. For example, Ryan refers repeatedly to the damage done by "charges of racism"; she has very little to say about the damage done by racism itself (just as she neglects a discussion of homophobia in favor of assertions about lesbian chauvinism). For example:

> The question of racism within the women's movement continues to be a confrontational and emotional issue. . . . Whereas the promotion of universal sisterhood in the 1970s downplayed racial and class oppression, the focus on difference in the 1980s heightened the potential for division among feminist women. For instance, "among feminists an accusation of racist-'n'-classist remains a surefire way to dismiss any concept, movement, or individual. It has the added attraction of working whether one gets one's facts straight or not" (Sturgis 1989: 19).
>
> The response of white women has been to feel guilty, until finally some began saying, enough.[44]

Ryan follows this passage with a quote from a woman who says "white middle class women have been guilt-tripped so much their entire life from everybody around them," including men and women of color, that "we are absolutely creeping and crawling on our hands and knees to try and get out from underneath all the guilt. And I think it's time to stop."[45] Ryan then suggests, following Robin Morgan, that white women should express their anger toward women of color. While this would certainly be preferable to white women's more common lack of engagement at all with women of color, it fails to satisfy, particularly in the context of Ryan's description of the debacle at the 1990 National Women's Studies Association conference. At that conference, a majority of the women of color walked out and subsequently left the organization:

> In the desire to address race and class concerns "NWSA set up a system that gave members of minority constituencies greater than proportional power" by allowing caucuses extra delegate voting power "based not on the numbers of their members but on whether or not they represented a group that is oppressed in the larger society" (Leidner 1991: 284). This structural component of the organization resulted in increased, and even more emotionally laden, confrontations. Eventually, white heterosexual academic women came to feel that their own needs were not being met and that they were being unfairly attacked because lesbian and women of color caucuses used "their extra power, as well as the moral force of the majority's guilt, to ensure that their wishes override all others" (ibid.: 286). At the 1990 conference a black staff member who had been fired by NWSA took her case to the Women of Color Caucus. Caucus members walked out of the conference after their demand for the firing of NWSA's executive director was refused. The hostility engendered during and after this conference led to the resignation of the entire national office staff and the cancellation of the 1991 conference (*off our backs* 1991: 6).[46]

Here, as elsewhere, we get the ostensible point of view of white, middle-class, heterosexual women, fed up with the power that women of color and lesbians supposedly wield over them. What we do not get is an account from any perspective that takes seriously the interests of women of color or lesbians.

In another passage in which Ryan places responsibility for intramovement ills on women of color, she faults them for the marginalization from the women's movement of the concerns of working-class, white women:

> . . . neglecting to look at class issues often leaves poor white women feeling alienated from women of color's demands.[47]

Finally, in contrast to her stated intention to discuss the developmental trajectory of the women's movement in terms of intramovement dynamics, Ryan obfuscates the racism within the movement when discussing the lower rates of participation among women of color:

> It is not the case that women of color are not feminists or do not believe in feminist goals, but they are making decisions about where to put their energy, and that energy tends to be on issues within their own community. As Bonnie Thornton Dill says, "sisterhood is not new to

Black women," but the "political identities of Afro-American women have largely been formed around issues of race" (1983: 134). Thus the priority for most women of color is working for the advancement of racial conditions.[48]

This passage begs the question of *why* communities of color get defined as these women's "own community" and the women's movement does not; it obscures racism internal to the women's movement and its role in keeping women of color out. Ryan acknowledges elsewhere that some women of color have chosen to work with white women in feminist groups, and she complains that media depictions of the women's movement as white and middle class obscure "those organized groups which represent the interest of women of color."[49] However, she mentions these groups only in a footnote: her readers never learn what these groups are, how they represent the interests of women of color, and what their goals, strategies, successes, and failures might be.

In all of these passages, then, Ryan's study reduces radical feminism to a bid for "most radical" status, rather than engaging with it as a far-reaching, if flawed, critique of institutionalized sexism, racism, and heterosexism, with the result that liberal feminism ends up looking like the only viable approach to identifying and addressing women's concerns. Moreover, homophobia and racism within the women's movement are dismissed, while homophobic and racist attitudes are ratified with discussions of how "trashing" of white and heterosexual women by women of color and lesbians led to the downfall of the small group sector of the women's movement. The result is that women of color and lesbians are further marginalized, represented as they are as ego-driven and destructive to women's "real" interests.

Gelb, Klein

Klein traces all major changes in women's roles and status to technological innovation (e.g., the manufacture of food and household products outside the home) and the establishment of mandatory school attendance for children, which, she says,

> . . . freed women to engage in activities other than motherwork. During this child-free period, many women, *under the guise of economic necessity,* entered the labor force.[50] [emphasis added]

For Klein, women's entrance *en masse* into the labor force was the beginning of all subsequent shifts in women's roles. However, this depiction does not capture the circumstances under which lesbians, or bisexual and heterosexual women who do not marry, enter the work force. Nor does it apply to working-class and poor women—often immigrants and women of color—whose "entry" into the labor force was simultaneous with their arrival, voluntary or forced, in this country, and in any case has been the result of economic necessity, and not simply in its guise. Moreover, many of these women have long balanced the competing demands of motherhood, marriage, and work outside the home through extended family networks, a fact elided by Klein's assumptions of a middle-class, heterosexual nuclear family structure and of a single moment in which women took up paid work.

Here and elsewhere, Klein presents women's concerns (and the experiences that ground them) as universal and essential to the condition of being female—unmediated by race, class, ethnicity, sexuality. Klein assumes a certain unity of experience and priorities among women when she claims that the central questions for feminists and for women in general include:

> Should mothers of young children work? Should the government provide day care? Should girls have the same access to sports facilities as boys? Do women have a right to reproductive choice? And are men better suited to positions of power?[51]

Klein does address other issues in her book—such as the division of household responsibility in heterosexual marriages, and sex discrimination in the workplace. She does not discuss issues of sexuality or the construction of identity; nor does she address racism, anti-Semitism, or homophobia, though for at least five years prior to the publication of her book, all of these issues had been central to feminist discourse and organizing that challenged a primarily legislative focus in women's movement thinking and politics.

Gelb builds her argument about differences in feminist approaches and their impact in the U.S. and U.K. by looking at public policy in the areas of maternity leave and child care in particular, as well as equal pay, welfare state benefits to women and children, sex discrimination on the job, domestic violence, and abortion. She also looks at such issues as sharing of housework between married male and female partners in nuclear families, sex segregation in the labor force, and male and female participation in part-time versus full-time employment. She does not address issues directly related to race or sexuality.

Though she confronts issues that enjoy seemingly broad appeal, such as maternity leave, child care, and the division of housework, her construction of these issues has to do with how they apply to heterosexual nuclear families. Given that the vast majority of the American public lives in arrangements other than heterosexual nuclear families, the fact that she assumes such conditions limits the breadth of her conclusions' applicability. For example, "progress" in the area of maternity leave means one thing for mothers who can count on a man's income as part of the household financial arrangement; it means something quite different for single mothers, or women whose female partner's income is substantially lower than the average male's. Describing "reformist feminism" as the quest for "equality through freedom" and through bringing women into the mainstream of society on equal terms with men, Gelb contrasts it to radical feminists, who, she says, organize themselves into consciousness-raising groups:

> Early on, these groups stressed consciousness-raising as a technique to develop greater self- and group awareness and, like their British counterparts, created localized, participatory projects, including day care, rape crisis centers, shelters for battered women, bookstores, and self-help health clinics.[52]

But rather than going on to investigate what radical feminists have done in the arenas she lists, Gelb criticizes the U.K. women's movement's emphasis on "women-specific" issues like abortion, rape, and domestic violence for obscuring "issues involving work and the family ('organization of daily life' issues) so crucial to change for women."[53] The directly economic issues that Gelb considers to be more important than the violence and sexuality issues radical feminists have emphasized are surely central to women's status; however, the *priority* she assigns to the former over the latter makes little sense in the context of actual women's lives, and seems to function here to dismiss radical feminism rather than to reflect women's "real" concerns. Moreover, radical feminism is not the only thing that gets short shrift in Gelb's study; her policy focus leads her away from engaging with feminist critiques of the institution of heterosexuality and feminist analyses that place race and class at their center.

2. Resistance

The women's movement studies' constructions of women and women's concerns, then, highlight relatively privileged women and their priorities. Likewise, in their construction of who *feminist activists* are, the studies emphasize these women's participation, relegating the activity of women of color, working-class women, lesbians, and bisexual women to the margins of feminist activity. In their construction of how feminists resist domination, the studies emphasize legislative over non-legislative activity.

The Agents of Resistance: Who Feminists Are

Ferree and Hess

In their first edition, Ferree and Hess's discussion of national-level organizing returns again and again to the histories, goals, and strategies of the National Organization for Women (NOW) and the National Women's Political Caucus (NWPC), while it dispenses—all in a list on one page— with the National Black Feminist Organization, the National Alliance of Black Feminists, Black Women United for Action, the American Indian/Alaskan Native Caucus, the National Conference of Puerto Rican Women, and other organizations of women of color. Some emphasis on NOW and NWPC is understandable, given the size of these organizations and the scope of their activities. However, such an emphasis need not preclude discussion of the others; moreover, the list that stands in for such a discussion appears in the context of the authors' argument that, despite the barriers that racism and classism in the movement pose to women of color and working-class women who might want to "join" it or who might "be in a position to be recruited," these women have nonetheless "been attracted to the New Feminist Movement."[54] The National Council of Jewish Women similarly appears only in lists, as do Women Employed, Women Office Workers, and 9 to 5; and there is no mention at all of national lesbian and gay organizations such as the National Gay and Lesbian Task Force or the National Center for Lesbian Rights. Thus, ironically, in their effort to belie charges that the women's movement is a primarily white, middle-class, heterosexual affair, they reproduce and perpetuate the centrality of white, middle-class, heterosexual status by ignoring lesbian organizing altogether, and by tokenizing organizing by women of color, working-class women, and Jewish women in lists of organizations—lists whose existence, they argue, proves that these women are not so marginal within the women's movement. Organizing among women of color never receives sustained attention in the first edition, but rather is mentioned in the context of the authors' refutations of charges that women of color are not interested or involved in feminism.

This portrayal of bureaucratic feminism is particularly problematic given the emphasis the authors place on this type of feminist activity— an emphasis that also effectively excludes feminist activity aimed at changing consciousness, such as feminist discourse politics.

The book's second edition, however, modifies this discussion, arguing there that changes in public policy can also bring about important changes in public consciousness, which in turn can spur people to mobilize for policy change. Moreover, the second edition presents a vastly improved treatment of organizing by women of color in particular; Jewish women's and working-class women's organizing also receives fuller treatment than in the first edition. Though none of these traditions of resistance is central to Ferree and Hess's account, each is addressed in some detail, primarily through their discussions of the activities of the organizations that they merely list in their first edition.

The second edition also reflects many of the lessons more marginalized women have brought home to their relatively privileged sisters over three decades of organizing. These lessons are expressed in the authors' recognition that, in the early years of the New Feminism, "Implicitly . . . claims about women's exploitation 'as women' also obscured the variety of these experiences and established middle-class white women as a norm,"[55] and in passages like the following:

> When the argument is reduced to a simple difference on the basis of gender rather than plural 'differences' among both men and women, there is a danger of essentializing women-ness as something distinct from the actual embodied experiences of real women, in which gender is not experienced in the abstract but in interaction with race, class, age and other aspects of the self.[56]

Even as the second edition gives much greater attention than did the first to the different perspectives and concerns of women in various circumstances, however, it continues to give short shrift to the struggles that women of color, working-class women, lesbians, Jewish women, and others have undergone to push the women's movement and its participants to acknowledge specific differences and to grasp the implications of the over-arching *fact* that difference is central to the category "women." Ferree and Hess's perspective in their second edition has clearly been influenced by these struggles; yet their account would be more accurate, and less limited by a white-centric perspective, if they were to acknowledge explicitly who and what lie behind the confrontation to which they say white feminists are now responding.

They would also do well to acknowledge *why* women of color, working-class women, and other traditionally marginalized women have found their own positions within the women's movement so problematic. Racism and classism within the movement are obscured in statements like the following:

> . . . as feminist consciousness spread to working-class communities and women of color developed critical perspectives on their multifaceted oppression, both growth and fragmentation occurred [within the women's movement]. Building truly inclusive women's organizations proved an elusive goal.[57]

Here and elsewhere in these texts, racial and class segregation are naturalized and assumed, not interrogated. That is, it is taken for granted that women of color and working-class women will necessarily form separate organizations. The social conditions beyond the movement that instill distinct concerns in distinct racial and class groups escape scrutiny, as do the racism and classism that many women encounter in the movement, and that ultimately pushes them to form organizations that also operate as buffers against this oppression. Thus the account itself subtly reproduces the kind of erasure against which the women in question have worked so assiduously during the past three decades of feminist activity—the erasure of their perspectives, experiences, and concerns, in the first instance; and the erasure of their efforts to challenge the initial erasure, in the second.

In spite of this recurring obfuscation of intramovement conflict, however, Ferree and Hess's second edition markedly improves upon the first edition's treatment of organizing activities and agendas of women of color and working-class women. Yet the same cannot be said for their approach to sexuality and the concerns and activities of lesbians and bisexual women. This approach has three basic shortcomings.

First, whereas the second edition discusses the activities of feminist organizations founded by and for women of color, working-class women, and Jewish women, it neglects to examine any organizations founded by and for lesbians and bisexual women; it also fails to note the contributions lesbians have made to the movement, and the many instances when lesbians and bisexual women have formed the core or the inspiration of various organizations and activities.

Second, as discussed earlier, the text's treatment of sexuality represents conflicts within the movement over sexual orientation issues as being primarily about the role of lesbians in the movement, but *not* about heterosexism and homophobia. Moreover, their discussion of lesbian organizing and concerns is largely confined to the one section of the book that expressly addresses the subject, rather than integrated throughout in their treatment of what feminist concerns constitute, or whom the category "women" includes.

Third, in a number of instances the authors simply omit the mention of lesbians and bisexual women or of sexuality where that mention is called for, as in these passages:

Networks are also critical in constructing a [feminist] movement that is truly diverse and inclusive. As we have seen, women of color, working-class women, young women, older women, Jewish women, Catholic women, professional women and women in unions have found it useful to form organizations that address their specific interests.[58]

It is a major achievement of the New Feminist Movement that this conception of who women are and what they want is broadly inclusive and diverse, that it refuses to separate gender from race, nationality, age, and other aspects of the human condition.[59]

The absence of any mention of lesbians from the first example or sexuality from the second, combined with a relative neglect of lesbian organizations, resistance, and concerns, leave a gaping hole in the tapestry Ferree and Hess weave to represent the New Feminism.

Ryan

Like Ferree and Hess, Ryan takes issue with charges that the women's movement is a white, middle-class women's phenomenon. Unfortunately, she too buries the names of organizations of feminists of color in a list in a footnote, and does not discuss their work. Yet Ryan argues persuasively that NOW members constitute a more diverse group than is commonly thought, in terms of both class and ideology.[60] While her arguments to this effect reveal more radical as well as liberal/moderate stances among NOW members, though, she does not attempt to argue that the organization's goals and strategies are really more radical than its feminist critics purport.[61]

Nonetheless, Ryan's work successfully represents ideological diversity among so-called liberal feminists. Moreover, she offers a unique perspective on the relationship between "non-feminist" women—or, perhaps more aptly, unmobilized women—and feminist change, when she states:

> . . . activist efforts alone rarely lead to a changed society. For the women's movement in particular, "non-feminist" women are an important component in achieving feminist goals. Indeed, the history of women's activism over the last 150 years might well be called the social movement of women rather than the women's movement . . . [62]

Here, Ryan acknowledges (if indirectly) that women who are not necessarily part of any organized feminist group can nonetheless be said to have absorbed the messages of feminism and to be implementing feminist principles in their lives, with broad social impact. This suggests a uniquely

121

broad formulation of "who feminists are" and what kinds of resistance they engage in. This formulation, moreover, is consistent with Ryan's broad definitions of feminist movement success and social change (about which more below).

Freeman, Klein

Like the other women's movement scholars, Freeman constructs feminists as a predominantly white and middle-class group of women, though she does so consciously, pointing to what she refers to as the "absence from feminist activity" of black women (in particular, black professional women) and working-class women. There is a tension between Freeman's construction of women—feminists especially—as white and middle-class, and her acknowledgment of African American women's feminist activity, however. That is, Freeman notes that "Black women have held several leadership positions within the movement, and there are separate black women's liberation groups"[63]; she also notes the formation in 1973 of Black Women Organized for Action in San Francisco and the National Black Feminist Organization in New York. She does not, however, interrupt her explanation of the absence of African American women from the movement to discuss these organizations in any detail, or to expound on black women's leadership in multiracial feminist organizations. In fact, although it is indisputable that white women have found the women's movement much more hospitable than women of color have, Freeman constructs the very absence of women of color that she purports to be reporting and explaining.[64] A fuller understanding of the racial (and racist) dynamics of the women's movement could be gained from a discussion that included why black women participate, as well as why they do not.

Freeman identifies an "older" and a "younger" branch of the women's movement. The two are distinguished by more than just the age of their members: Freeman characterizes the older branch both as having begun first (and thus being older than the small groups), and as appealing to women who were, on average, older than small group participants. The older branch, in her account, is also concerned primarily with legal and economic issues and is organized in a traditional hierarchy. This branch of the movement "started as top-down national organizations lacking a mass base," and generally "has used the traditional forms of political action."[65] In contrast, Freeman characterizes the younger branch as appealing to college-age women and young homemakers. It consisted of countless small groups engaged in a variety of activities, and had "been more experimental" than the older branch.

For Klein, feminist activists are women who develop feminist consciousness and become mobilized as a result of changes they initially experience individually—changes in their roles that relate to large-scale social changes (such as technologies that remove some aspects of "women's work" from the household) but are not understood in social terms. Thus, not only does Klein not acknowledge the role of abolitionist, civil rights, and early feminist efforts in fomenting feminist consciousness and bringing about another wave of the women's movement; she also fails to acknowledge how the most recent wave of feminism has advanced itself through its own efforts to engender and galvanize feminist consciousness. For her, the women's movement is an effect of women's consciousness, but never a creator of that consciousness. She addresses only the demographic—not political—origins of women's consciousness as women and as feminists. Thus, she writes that after the 1970 Women's Strike for Peace, "membership in feminist organizations mushroomed, and public opinion in favor of strengthening or changing women's status increased,"[66] but she does not discuss how the Women's Strike for Peace came about in the first place. Women who planned and engaged in the Strike may have initially been influenced by the effects of demographic and technological changes on their lives; but the middle step, the transformation of women's subjectivity and the translation of consciousness into group action, is precisely what Klein neglects to address throughout her study. In disregarding this step, Klein obscures the dialectic between feminist organizing and feminist consciousness, and thus fails to explain how or why women move from individual to group consciousness and then to collective action.

The Forms of Resistance: How Feminists Act

Ferree and Hess

Just as their second edition presents a fuller range of feminist perspectives and organizations than does the first edition,[67] it also offers a more nuanced analysis of the goals and impact of different types of feminist activity. Most notably, the second edition is much more careful and generous in its consideration of the intent, impact, and importance of what the authors call "cultural change." In this respect, Ferree and Hess's second edition stands alone among the women's movement studies.[68]

One finds in the second edition the broadest view and deepest understanding of the many facets of domination and resistance found in the women's movement studies:

> A more adequate account of what feminist visions have to offer would have to begin with an understanding that social control in the realm of ideas (sometimes called "ideological hegemony") and social control over the realm of action (the degrees of monopoly of coercive force) are interrelated in complex and interlocking ways. Such a model would address social power that is invisible because it is so well institutionalized, as well as the direct use of sanctions, rewards, and physical force in society. . . . From such a perspective, it seems evident that fundamental, revolutionary challenges are best mounted simultaneously against social control in both the realm of ideas and the realm of institutionalized force.[69]

Passages such as the above indicate the authors' genuine appreciation of the need to approach the study of power and resistance from a broader perspective than has traditionally been the case; perhaps what holds them back from doing so is primarily the methodological shift that such an approach would require.[70]

Both editions of *Controversy and Coalition* neglect discursive challenges, including those embodied in the autotheoretical texts, to practices within the movement that perpetuate relations of class, racial, ethnic, and sexual dominance and subordination. As these texts represent some of the most sustained and fully-developed versions of these intramovement challenges—challenges that have been ubiquitous throughout the movement and central to its approach to diversity—their omission from Ferree and Hess's study has adverse consequences for their representation of both intramovement struggles and the political nature of identity and subjectivity.

In this sense, their choice of the *types of feminist activity* they emphasize also profoundly affects their representation of *who the actors are* in feminist movements. Were Ferree and Hess to give more attention to the types of discursive politics engaged in by the traditionally marginalized women they seek to represent, their account of these women's experiences might look quite different. This work is made easier by the existence of the autotheoretical texts—extended explications of challenges to homogeneity that are accessible even to those who cannot attend many feminist events, read many of the feminist newspapers and journals, and so on. It seems unlikely, for example, that Ferree and Hess's categories of feminism—career, liberal, socialist, and radical—would remain undisturbed if they were to explore more thoroughly the implications of the arguments put forth in books they only mention—such as *This Bridge Called My Back: Writings By Radical Women of Color*—or if they were to trace the elevation of concerns about anti-Semitism in the women's movement to one of its sources—the 1982 anthology, *Nice Jewish Girls: A Lesbian Anthology*.[71] These and other books reflect debates that have been central to transformations in feminist thinking about power, gender, and resistance over the past fifteen years.

Thus, this marginalization is perpetuated not only by the authors' construction of "women" and "feminists," but also by their treatment of discourse politics, the inadequacy of which (even in the second edition, where they devote more attention to this type of resistance) has particular ramifications for women of color and lesbians, because these women have conducted their struggles against racism and heterosexism largely and of necessity in the arena of discourse and consciousness.

Ryan

Ryan's discussion of the *how* of feminist resistance is characterized by the same mix of advances and flaws. The shortcomings of her discussion of small group/radical feminism with regard to intramovement splits are discussed above. In addition, she reaches some problematic conclusions regarding the goals and effectiveness of small groups; these emerge most notably in her larger discussion of discursive politics.

Ryan's focus on discursive politics represents a major advance in the literature on the women's movement, in that both her study and Ferree and Hess's second edition take this kind of feminist activity much more seriously than did earlier studies. At the same time, this attention to discursive politics reflects how little has been done to define and specify what it might be. Most notably, Ryan's treatment of discourse politics reflects the tendency shared by all of the women's movement studies to reduce activity directed at consciousness-raising to *personal* change or empowerment, rather than seeing it as part and parcel of larger social change.[72] In Ryan's case, this reduction comes about as a result of her conflation of, on the one hand, cultural feminist activities that are almost therapeutic in their aims and effects; and, on the other hand, small group, direct-action activity aimed at changing how an audience larger than the group's participants thinks about a particular issue. Though Ryan acknowledges two distinct approaches of discursive political groups when she defines them as "small, sometimes temporary, feminist groups in-

125

volved in direct action tactics; and the various components of cultural feminism,"[73] she tends to collapse the two into the latter—cultural feminism.

This conflation leads Ryan to assert an "interactive/expressive orientation of discursive politics"[74] in which "efforts are more frequently placed in the personal and symbolic realm,"[75] and to claim that "In some sense, many of the involvements within this sector serve as an oasis from the present social/political arena."[76] Her reduction of all discursive politics to cultural feminism becomes particularly clear as she moves from discussing arena and structure to discussing goals and strategy:

> The type of expressive action found in discursive politics is geared towards achieving power within the person. The goal is the empowerment of women through a changed self-image.[77]

Contrasting this with "political activists" who "are geared to gain power for women within the system" through structural change,[78] Ryan describes the discursive politics strategy in this way:

> For expressive/interactive activists . . . [w]omen must begin on the personal level to rid themselves of internalized oppression. It is after personal change has taken place, when women begin to feel psychologically strong about themselves, that their interactive relations improve. Then they can go out and make the structural changes that are needed.[79]

What Ryan describes is a key part of cultural feminism. It is not, however, the totality of feminist discursive politics. Ryan acknowledges as much at one point:

> However, expressive/interactive groups are not formed solely for the purpose of personal contact and enrichment. Indeed, Women Rising in Resistance, a post-ERA direct action group, organized with the intention of using confrontational tactics against the present system, particularly to raise awareness of violence against women.[80]

Yet, as her only example of direct action discursive politics in her comparison of discursive politics and "political activists," this passage cannot counterbalance her overriding emphasis on "expressive/interactive activists," particularly since she manages to cast even direct action activism in terms of personal empowerment:

Zap actions, street theatre, and civil disobedience are seen as ways to get attention and psychologically empower women which lend themselves to these groups' size limitations. . . .[81]

In these and other passages, Ryan reduces small group feminism and feminism concerned with discourse to a praxis centered around symbolic self-expression and individual empowerment, with a heavy emphasis on disengagement from existing social and political structures. Ryan is not the first to make this move: indeed, all of the studies considered here that examine "small group" feminism exhibit the same tendency. The prominence of this kind of feminism—inwardly-directed and focused on individual empowerment—over the last fifteen years or so is certainly partly responsible, as is social science's tendency to see "politics" only in terms of legislation and formal institutions; if it isn't that, it must be "personal." What this dichotomy misses is the range of political activity that is concerned with large-scale social transformation of power relationships and that takes place outside the established channels of voting, lobbying, and running for office.

It is this type of feminist discursive politics that is absent from this and other studies of the women's movement, and the lacuna represents a collective difficulty in specifying what discursive politics is, how it is conducted, what its goals and effects are, and so forth. Whereas the shortcomings of Ryan's treatment of race and sexuality can plausibly be regarded as a studied ignorance of the message of by now entrenched discourses on race and sexuality, her reduction of all discursive politics to "personal transformation" activity reflects a more general lack of discussion of other kinds of discursive politics.

Indeed, Ryan associates discursive politics with small groups, yet offers as her chief example Sonia Johnson's campaign for President in 1984, an example that might fit better into the other category of feminist resistance she discusses: "political activism," which to Ryan means legislative action. (To her credit, Ryan acknowledges that Johnson's campaign represents a combination of discursive and electoral-politics strategies.) She associates legislative activity with "mass movement," though she acknowledges that some small groups can pressure local governments for change. Ryan also defines political activism as being concerned with educating the public,[82] though the forms of discursive politics that go beyond empowering women who already identify with the women's movement also make this their primary concern. And while discursive politics' "expressive/interactive" activists are at work improving their own self-image, Ryan says, for political activists,

127

the vision is to create a more humane system developed through women's input. . . . For political activists, the mission of a social movement is to change the social structure so that women, as a group, will be identified with higher valuation.[83]

The overlap between Ryan's categories, and the conflation within her category of discursive politics of inwardly-focused cultural feminism and outwardly-focused direct action, suggest that the categories themselves need to be reworked, both to take account of the fact that both discursive and electoral efforts can alter public consciousness, and to distinguish different types of activity she groups together under "discursive politics."

Finally, Ryan under-emphasizes radical feminism's important role in keeping issues of violence against women at the forefront of feminist analysis and activism. When she does discuss violence, she restricts her attention largely to pornography and to conflicts over this issue between lesbian and heterosexual feminists. Her neglect of violence as a feminist issue may well be a contributing factor to her assessment of small-group/radical feminist activity as relatively ineffective in achieving social change and as primarily directed at women's psychological empowerment.

Freeman

In spite of the earlier and very different political context in which Freeman's *Politics of Women's Liberation* emerged, her approach to feminist resistance is no less problematic and no easier to account for than the treatment of resistance and social change in the other studies of the women's movement. Even though she was conducting her research at a time when collectivist, non-hierarchical, culturally-focused feminist activity was more strongly in evidence than when subsequent studies were done, Freeman nonetheless neglects to evaluate such activity on its own terms, and privileges feminist resistance aimed at traditional targets, just as the succeeding women's movement studies do. This tendency is most apparent in her discussion of the "older" and "younger" branches of the women's movement, with which she associates NOW and small group activity, respectively.

It is in comparing and evaluating these two branches that Freeman's own prejudices become most apparent. Her comparison assesses the two branches in terms of their ideology, structure, and effectiveness. Freeman finds the "younger" branch lacking in each of these areas, though her discussion is not without complexity and, indeed, tension. That is, she does not summarily dismiss the younger branch of the movement; instead, in her *description* she acknowledges some of the strengths of the forms of resistance that she associates with this branch, only to leave those strengths unmentioned and unexplored in her *evaluation*.

In distinguishing between the older and younger branches of the women's movement, Freeman insists that it is inaccurate to characterize the former as reformist and the latter as revolutionary. Yet she goes on to describe in detail the radicalizing effects the younger branch has had on the older—NOW in particular. Freeman makes a connection between NOW's expanded agenda, its increasing youth, and its turn toward radicalism in the early 1970s. She writes that since its inception, NOW

> has consistently moved in a more radical direction. . . . By its fifth convention in the fall of 1971, NOW was ready for a major expansion of concerns and numerous resolutions were passed giving a feminist position on a multitude of subjects—such as the war—not directly related to women.[84]

Though Freeman does not acknowledge this, in order for NOW to undergo such a shift, there must have been a substantial number of women—presumably from the "younger branch" that was influencing NOW in this direction—who did view the war as being directly related to women's lives. In failing to acknowledge this difference in perspectives, Freeman obscures the politics of the younger branch and claims a consensus on the question of which issues are in fact "directly related to women"—a consensus which, in reality, did not exist. She continues:

> This move was anticipated by the original Statement of Purpose, NOW's early support of the guaranteed annual income, and its concern with women in poverty. Nonetheless, it was a major break with the past. . . . In its 1973 convention, NOW was even following the lead of the younger branch of the movement in taking positions favoring the decriminalization of prostitution; the investigation of "fundamental questions concerning the structure of society premised on profit and competition"; and setting up further task forces on such topics as older women, women in sports, and rape. It also resolved "that a major organizational effort be mounted immediately within NOW on behalf of the needs of *all* minority persons, and that . . . actions be undertaken toward elimination of structures, policies, and practices that contribute to racism within NOW."[85]

Freeman asserts that structure and style, more than ideological approaches, distinguish the two branches from each other; but while she argues that it is a mistake to construe the younger branch as being more radical and the older as being more reformist, she also argues that the role of the younger branch vis-à-vis the older one has been that of ideological vanguard, pushing the older branch (and NOW in particular) in increasingly radical directions. She writes, "Although there is no sharp ideological distinction between the older and younger branches of the movement, the latter does operate as an ideological vanguard" of the movement, and she credits this branch with NOW's changing position on lesbian rights.[86]

Thus, Freeman herself attributes these radical, anti-racist, anti-homophobic, broad approaches to power and politics to the younger branch of the women's movement. In view of this fact, her relatively negative evaluation of the younger branch's small groups, out of which these broadly subversive, relatively class- and race-conscious initiatives emerged, is problematic. This negative evaluation emerges from Freeman's assessment of the younger branch in terms of its structure and political effects.

Freeman describes the structure of the younger branch's small groups as reflecting a "conscious lack of hierarchy." These groups are organized democratically, with no leadership positions and no internal hierarchy. Their relationship to each other is highly informal; this branch of the movement is "decentralized, segmentary, reticulate," and there is generally little coordination between small groups. As Freeman writes, the younger branch is all mass base and no national organization.

The older branch of the movement, on the other hand, is all national organization and no mass base. Discussing NOW as exemplary of this branch's style of political activism, Freeman characterizes it as traditionally structured along hierarchical lines of power and responsibility. Though she discusses at length the problems NOW encounters in coordinating its various chapters, due to a lack of middle-level structures to coordinate the national office with local chapters, she concludes that "Despite these problems, NOW manages to function rather well because its members make up for its organizational deficiencies."[87]

Freeman is unclear about the relationship between structure and ideology. At some moments she argues that they are related, as when she writes: "The way an organization is structured in the beginning 'loads the dice' not only for its goals, but also its strategy of how to attain them."[88] She also argues that the different structures of the older and younger branches of the movement grew out of the differing experiences of their members. The implication—no doubt a sound one—is that the various feminist contingents had different experiences of both domination and resistance[89]; these experiences led to different ideologies about how best to effect change, and these ideologies were expressed in distinct organizational structures.

A substantial part of Freeman's discussion, though, is taken up with refuting the notion that structure and ideology are mutually imbricated. Other evidence she offers, however—including her own argument that the small groups operate as an "ideological vanguard" for the movement and as such have affected the structure of NOW and other "older branch" organizations—seems to indicate that structure and ideology are intimately related. Her assertion, for example, that the radicals left NOW because they disagreed with its structure rather than its ideology begs the question of why it was the *radicals* who left, and why those who opposed a hierarchical structure did so from a common *ideological* position.

Small groups choose their structure based on their goals—and they choose their goals based on their ideological understanding of domination and resistance. Freeman critiques the structure of the small groups as inefficient, but in doing so she is evaluating them not on their own terms, but on the terms of the older branch. A non-hierarchical organizational structure is inefficient if the goal is to interact with institutions—such as policy-making ones—that respond only to traditional, hierarchically-structured interest groups. On the other hand, a non-hierarchical structure is effective if the goal is to resist the domination that takes place within hierarchies, to empower women from all backgrounds and levels of experience, and to effect a fundamental change in how people work together, so that such work takes place on a fully cooperative basis. The small groups know their structure isn't the most "efficient" in a traditional sense; they consciously opt for a different structure because of the gains they see as being possible within this structure, and because of the flaws that inhere in the standard one. That is, their ideology about the sources and manifestations of domination, and thus the appropriate forms of resistance, expresses itself in their organizational structure, which could be said to be quite efficient, measured in terms of its own agenda for resistance.

Freeman seems to acknowledge that the two branches she identifies have different ideologies and agendas; but she ultimately evaluates the younger branch's success in terms of the older branch's goals. Her definition of politics includes the goals, targets, and strategies of the older branch with its focus on traditional political institutions, but not the younger branch, with its focus on broad-based cultural change. For the older branch, "politics" means political office and public policy; for the younger branch, "politics" means power relationships wherever they exist and however they manifest themselves.

Klein, Gelb

Klein's inattention to feminism's own continuity, its relation and debt to other social movements, and the processes through which women come to engage in collective resistance results in a depiction of atomized individuals acting alone. In her analysis, feminist consciousness is something that individual women acquire *as their individual situations change*—not in relation to other women, as a group. Group consciousness emerges because many women go through the same changes individually; but not because women interact with and learn from each other.

This aspect of Klein's argument relates to her emphasis on the perception of, and support for, feminism in the mainstream of American society. Klein writes:

> The success of political protest depends on public support for ending the problems faced by women. In order to gain this endorsement, however, the public must accept the legitimacy of the group's political tactics as well as its grievances.[90]

For Klein, feminism's "real gains" rest on mass appeal; she does not address gains made by smaller numbers of committed women, gains that lead to other mobilizing efforts that result in mass mobilization of support for feminist goals and tactics, or the kinds of changes that are the cumulative effect of women's resistance at the level of daily life practice (itself an effect of women's subjectivity). That is, Klein looks only for the presence of mass support; she does not examine the feminist organizing that precedes and creates such support. Nor does she look at feminist activity that would *appear* to be individual, but is collective in both its origins and effects.

Gelb's primary concern is with the forms of feminist political activism that have been most salient in the U.S. and the U.K. (and to a lesser extent Sweden), which she divides into reformist/bureaucratic/directed feminism and radical/collectivist/non-directed feminism. Her chief concern, she says, is "To analyze the impact of women's movements on the political process and in helping to structure policy alternatives and outcomes."[91] This agenda makes clear at the outset her public policy bias, such that she sets out to evaluate non-policy-oriented feminist activity in terms of its public policy impact at the level of national government. With this combination of goal and strategy, she cannot help but find non-policy-oriented feminism wanting. One failing she identifies in this type of feminism is that it is characterized by insistence on ideological purity and a reluctance to work with groups espousing different viewpoints. This type of feminist politics is decentralized and locally based, largely lacking a national political presence and impact. Fragmentation as well as enthusiastic commitment to sectarian (feminist) views typify this model.[92]

As do Freeman, Ferree and Hess, and Klein, Gelb characterizes her project in broad terms, yet executes one that is in fact a good deal narrower. While she describes her work as a study of "reformist" and "radical" wings of feminism in the United States and the United Kingdom, what she investigates is primarily the reformist/institutional wings in each country. Though she claims the radical/non-institutional wing is more influential in Great Britain, she does not investigate it in much depth at all, and spends even less time on this wing of feminism in the United States. Despite her argument that "non-institutional," collectivist feminism prevails in Great Britain, Gelb's study focuses on those elements in British feminism that mirror the institutional forms of U.S. feminism, and she minimizes the differences between the two movements. Were she to focus on those differences, she would necessarily elaborate a deeper discussion of collectivist/decentralized feminism—including discursive politics—in both countries.

Gelb's construction of feminist resistance shares many of the same attributes of Freeman's and Ferree and Hess's discussions, including her division of feminism into two camps, one that is institutionally focused and one that is not; and her general lack of attention to the latter, coupled with her negative assessment of it when her discussion does center on it.

Gelb focuses on institutional feminism's impact on public policy, but not on discourse and subjectivity. Given that she also claims to be interested in measuring changes in public attitudes, her omission of "non-institutional" feminism that focuses on consciousness and ideology, and her lack of attention to the changes in discourse and consciousness wrought by institutional feminist activity, obstruct her efforts to gain a clear understanding of the origins of such change. Where Gelb does investigate "radical/non-institutional" feminism, she evaluates it on the terms of "reformist/institutional" feminism (as do Freeman and Ferree and Hess). Her contention that the radical/non-institutional wing of feminism is less effective than the reformist/institutional wing stems from the tensions in her discussion of social movement success.

Gelb's assumptions that women form a coherent group and thus that it is possible to identify "universal goals related to all women"[93] also affect her conceptions of feminist change, in that she assumes that local, single-issue-oriented action is inferior to national action without considering the reality, borne out by the trajectory of the women's movement, that the needs of women—and thus the strategies they employ—are tremendously diverse. Some goals call for a strategy of national action; others do not. Moreover, women who have been marginalized in national organizing efforts are more likely to engage in local organizing activity. What is clear here is that Gelb prioritizes national action directed at changing public policy, and marginalizes feminist resistance and change on the level of cultural consciousness and norms, neglecting the relationship between the two.

3. Success/Change

Ferree and Hess

The shift in Ferree and Hess's revised edition toward a greater appreciation for broad cultural change is apparent in the successes they attribute to feminist resistance:

> Feminist cultural and entrepreneurial groups . . . see their efforts as producing change in a dimension that complements rather than competes with the direct action of other organizations. Through an ongoing system of consciousness-raising, they sustain "oppositional cultures that embody values, practices, and meanings derived from concrete struggle" (Taylor and Rupp 1993). In addition, by changing the language with which women name their experience, and by fostering social networks in which alternative definitions can be reaffirmed, cultural groups practice what Katzenstein . . . calls "discursive politics."[94]

The authors' continuing partiality toward policy change, however, is apparent in passages such as the following:

> In a democratic society, the ultimate success of a social movement depends on the ability of its organizations to use and manipulate the political system. Otherwise, members continue to be without a voice in policy making, and movement issues continue to be perceived as irrelevant or illegitimate. To the extent that it succeeds, however, the movement is transformed into an "interest group" participating in institutionalized political processes.[95]

Thus, feminist success, according to Ferree and Hess, can best be measured in legislative change and in the extent to which the women's movement has been transformed into an interest group, recognized by and working within liberal political institutions. This view implies a notion of power that is distinctly liberal: if success is measured by legislative change, that is because domination of women takes place primarily through legislative channels, emanating outward from a formal, centralized legal authority.[96] And if the index of success is a movement's transformation into an interest group that engages in electoral politics, then extra-organizational activity, and discursive politics aimed at challenging hegemonic ideologies, may be irrelevant.

Nonetheless, the extent to which they have incorporated cultural change into their second edition's vision of what constitutes feminist success is striking, as exemplified in their statement that "Cultural change is the least observable but perhaps the most enduring form of transformation. . . ."[97]

Ryan

Like Ferree and Hess's second edition, Ryan's study offers an expansive view of women's movement success and of social change. In addition to changes in legislation and other formal policies (such as hiring practices), Ryan also sees the need for a broader transformation of the informal practices and the discursive paradigms that shape people's lives at all levels. This broad view is most evident in her claims that

> One of the lessons to be learned from the early women's movement is that mobilization of people is not enough; social movements must also mobilize sustaining ideas,[98]

and that

> The feminist reaction to men's lack of commitment was to *change the social environment* so that women could live independently if they chose to or were forced to do so.[99] [emphasis added]

Ryan ends her book with the observation that

> The hard part of dedicated social movement involvement lies in the recognition that it is the persistent tapping—sometimes a hammer, sometimes a feather—that leaves a mark. And it is through this process, a series of marks, that *a new cultural reality is born.*[100] [emphasis added]

Yet Ryan is not unconflicted in her support for the form of politics—diversified and discursively-oriented—that is most concerned with bringing about the broad cultural change she endorses in these passages. In fact, she argues that what is needed for the women's movement to be successful is a unifying issue to keep the movement mobilized. In the first wave of feminism, suffrage functioned as the unifying issue; in the second wave, the Equal Rights Amendment fulfilled that function initially, as have reproductive rights and especially abortion more recently. Ryan treats these issues as primarily legislative ones (although one could certainly argue that their success or failure is rooted in cultural paradigms); her argument reveals a legislative bias in her view of movement success. It also reveals a persistent desire for the sort of feminist "unity" that has evaded those who have sought it and enraged those whose differences have been suppressed in the quest for it. Indeed, Ryan argues that such unifying issues render women's differences less important than they seem to be when women pursue diverse goals in a variety of feminist groupings. Certainly the splits within the movement—based not on "charges" of racism, classism, homophobia, and so forth, but on the "isms" themselves—have demonstrated how destructive her argument in favor of a single unifying issue can be when put into practice.

Freeman

The difference in the two types of feminism (bureaucratic and collectivist) that Freeman identifies is at the heart of her conclusion that the movement's younger branch has been politically ineffective compared with its older branch. Freeman writes,

> . . . diffusion of ideas [with which she credits younger branch] does not mean they are implemented; it only means they are talked about. . . . [The younger branch's] debates, disputes, and ideas provide food for feminist thought. Its segmented oligarchies and service projects restrict its activities to politically innocuous ones.[101]

Indeed, Freeman even asserts that members of the "younger branch" are not actually political activists; nor are they more radical then their older/reformist counterparts. Rather, "the most typical division of labor is that those groups labeled 'radical' engage primarily in educational work and service projects, while the so-called reformist groups are the political activists."[102]

Clearly, Freeman's definition of politics is a good deal narrower than the one employed by the feminists who engage in "service projects" as a way to articulate new choices for women's lives and to empower women to consider those choices. Freeman casts these activities as emphasizing "personal" change. In contrast, the ideology that emanated from the small groups that engaged in them is one that emphasizes fundamental "sea changes" in the way that women and men think about women. For example, a battered women's shelter is not simply a haven for women fleeing abuse from the men in their lives; it is, through its existence and its activities (which often include community education), a source of changing consciousness for the community as a whole. It is a public statement that battering exists (thus shattering the isolation surrounding victims of domestic violence); that it is unacceptable and unnecessary; that women have alternatives to male violence; that these alternatives are, by and large, created by other women; and that women are changing their relationship to a social system that tolerates and even condones violence against women. The implications of such a "service project" are deeply political and transformative, as they strike at the very heart of male domination of women. Feminist legislative changes can have some of the same ideological and discursive effects, in that besides mandating specific practices, they constitute public statements that women enjoy a certain status under the law.

However, Freeman ultimately adopts a narrow definition of political activity, and she evaluates that activity in narrow terms (e.g., neglecting the discursive effects even of policy change). She also reduces changes in collective consciousness to "personal change." Therefore, she is unable to see the work of the small groups (and the discursive effects of bureaucratic feminism) as political, and radically so, as it gets at the "root" of male domination of women, by focusing attention on the social conditions that make violence against women seem commonplace and acceptable. Looking through the lens of traditional social science theory and method, Freeman sees small group activity but fails to evaluate it *on its own terms*. She writes,

> Fortunately, the younger branch is not the sum total of the women's liberation movement. There exist some national, somewhat centralized organizations capable of coordinated political action. It is these organizations that usually develop the ideas fermented by the small groups. While it is likely true that NOW and other national organizations would not be as innovative without the ideological pressure these groups provide, it is also true that their new ideas would have few avenues for implementation if it were not for NOW.[103]

The "avenues for implementation" Freeman has in mind are traditional avenues of policy change and electoral politics. What gets obscured in this

analysis is that the small groups do have their own avenues of implementation, and that their influence on NOW is actually evidence of this fact.
In privileging engagement with formal institutions through electoral politics as the singular effective strategy for feminists, Freeman closes down
her own exploration of the women's movement, consigning a large part
of it to inferior—even irrelevant—status without ever examining it on its
own terms. That feminists whose targets are societally hegemonic ideologies and daily practices fail to have a direct, immediate impact on governmental policy is beside the point; Freeman's charge is analogous to
criticizing women politicians for failing to alter power relations between
heterosexual partners so that men pay more attention to women's sexual
pleasure or participate more fully in child care; or for failing to bring
about more complex and positive media images of lesbians.

Klein

For Klein, feminist consciousness results not from the dissemination of
feminist ideas, but in technological innovation and a decline in fertility:

> The shaky foundation for women's lives collapsed when fertility
> dropped precipitously in the 1960s. Mothering, the linchpin of female-
> ness throughout the century, became less central to women's lives.
> Motherhood took on a new perspective when older mothers found
> themselves suddenly free of primary child-care responsibilities and
> when younger women found school and work more attractive than
> early marriage and family responsibilities.[104]

The materialism of this argument is appealing—after all, ideas are produced by material relations/conditions. Yet, the reverse is also true—i.e.,
that changes in material relations can often be attributed to changes in
ideas and paradigms. For example, the tremendous advances, and then re-
cessions, in women's reproductive rights since the late 1960s have been
grounded not in substantial material changes, but in profound ideological
shifts. Klein's argument obscures the ideological sources of ideas: in her
account, feminist organizing is always the product, never the generator, of
feminist consciousness. Moreover, though technological change was extremely important (particularly, perhaps, in the area of birth control),
Klein's reduction of feminist consciousness to an effect solely of technological and demographic change takes it out of the context of other social
movements. This is highly problematic, as feminism has, in both its first
and second waves, followed on and drawn from anti-racist social move-

ments. But Klein gives neither the abolition nor the civil rights movements more than passing mention. Interestingly enough, neither does she have much to say about the roots of contemporary "bureaucratic" feminism in mainstream politics.

Gelb

Like the other women's movement scholars, Gelb's approach to movement success and social change is somewhat schizophrenic. On the one hand, she acknowledges a variety of forms of social change. On the other, she pursues a narrow exploration of policy change: her subsequent conclusions about the success of the two "wings" of the women's movements neglect altogether the category of changes in social consciousness. In defining social movement success, Gelb writes:

> Definitions of what constitutes social movement 'success' may vary. 'Success' may refer to legitimization of a group's goals, change in individual or group consciousness, and/or change in public policy outcomes involving redistribution of social goals and changes in power relations (Jenkins 1983, 544). For some, political access for hitherto excluded groups constitutes 'success.'[105]

Elsewhere, she argues that

> Success may also refer to the mere fact of survival, and/or the creation of alternative sources of power through the development of new organizational forms (Rowbotham 1983: 136). It is evident that the movement in each nation has succeeded in different terms, partially because of different goals and the systemic factors that constrain political activism.[106]

Yet Gelb ultimately—and without explanation—opts for definitions of success other than "change in individual or group consciousness." She assumes without reflection that the group's goals are "retarded" by making the transformation of the consciousness of group members a central goal.[107] Her reluctance to examine the changes in consciousness that can plausibly be attributed to what she views as a largely ineffectual movement in Britain is also evident in her assertion that the British women's movement has "a huge distance to go in terms of reaching even a fraction of women in the U.K."[108] Gelb cites the movement's hugely successful mobilization for abortion rights (1979) and against nuclear power (1982), yet she does not allow these mobilizations, which reflect the widespread dissemination of feminist consciousness, to inform her characterization of the movement as practically ineffectual.

Gelb—like the other women's movement scholars—obscures radical/collectivist feminist efforts to effect changes in social consciousness. Also like Freeman, Ryan, and Ferree and Hess, Gelb does not categorically dismiss such change. She is certainly aware that some feminists place consciousness change high on their political agendas, yet she does not produce a sustained discussion of cultural consciousness; nor does she allow for the possibility of feminist success in this area once she has exempted it from her study. For example, though she argues that British feminism has been successful in effecting "consciousness and lifestyle transformation," she bemoans its failure to coordinate nationally, rather than concentrating on local projects, and she ultimately concludes that "the movement's main contribution may be simply its survival."[109] Nor does she examine the impact on "consciousness and lifestyle transformation" of institutional feminist activity.

4. Method

Ryan

Ryan's methodology is the most comprehensive of the studies, if nonetheless problematic in its emphases and omissions. She draws the information for her study from primary documents, participant observation in liberal, socialist, and radical feminist organizations, and interviews.

Unfortunately, though Ryan's sources are broad and varied, they do not represent the perspectives of women of color, lesbians, bisexual women, and working-class women. These omissions are particularly consequential for her discussions—central to her analysis—of splits within the movement over race and sexuality.

Ryan's participant observation included her involvement in NOW, the New American Movement (which merged with Democratic Socialist Organizing Committee to become Democratic Socialists of America); the Congressional Union and a splinter group, A Group of Women (which she describes as a group that arose to introduce civil disobedience into the ERA campaign); her attendance at national Women's Gatherings; and her participation in civil disobedience.[110]

Participant observation, of course, has the advantage of putting the researcher in a position to see the minute workings of organizing, and to assess what works and what does not, how, and why. However, it may also have the disadvantage of lending an air of "objectivity" to one person's preferences for certain agendas and strategies. If not counteracted, this can be particularly acute in cases in which the participant-researcher cannot viably participate in identity-based groups whose identity she does not share (e.g., women of color organizations for the white researcher, lesbian/bisexual organizations for the heterosexual researcher, and so on). In these cases, it is incumbent upon the researcher to seek out perspectives she misses due to the necessary partiality of her participation. If she does not, she runs the risk—as Ryan's study illustrates—of perpetuating the hegemony of traditional viewpoints.

According to Ryan, her interviews were the main source of information for her study. Here again, though, while she carefully selects interviewees based on her criteria that they be long-term activists, leaders, or well-known theorists, and that they jointly represent "the broad spectrum of ideological perspectives and activist strategies,"[111] her analyses do not, for the most part, reflect the typically marginalized perspectives of women of color and non-heterosexual women; occasionally but not consistently, they reflect the views of working-class women.

Ryan's research benefits from the exceptional breadth of experiences and sources on which she draws. Her study's potential is limited less by her methodology than by her neglect of key perspectives.

Freeman

Like the other authors, Freeman neglects to consider the full impact of feminist challenges to hegemonic ideologies. This neglect can best be explained by the limitations that standard political science theory and method impose on her approach to the women's movement. Freeman acknowledges these limitations in her introduction, only to ignore their implications for the conclusions she draws throughout the rest of her book. She writes (quoting and agreeing with Gerlach and Hine):

> 'a successful movement is the point of intersection between personal and social change' and as such often makes use of but is not exclusively restricted to the political institutions of our society. *Although the element of personal change is often the most significant,* this book will be primarily concerned with social change of a concrete and tangible nature. This is partially because *personal change is very hard to measure,* and partially because I want to look at change as it has been manifested in public policy on the federal level.[112] [emphasis added]

Freeman's designation of social change in the realm of daily practice as "personal" is symptomatic of her overall view of power, which does not consider challenges to hegemonic ideologies as political and fundamental. Her point that it is difficult to measure is sound—but it begs the question of political science's bias toward things measurable.

As in Gelb, Ryan, and Ferree and Hess's first edition, Freeman's study does not acknowledge this work as fundamental to an expanded understanding of the complexities and multiple mechanisms of domination facing women, and thus to a transformed agenda for resistance, which seeks to effect change at the foundations of society. Rather, she miscasts it as "personal," and dismisses it not as wholly unimportant, but as difficult to measure. She goes on to conduct her study and draw her conclusions without regard to it, with the result that the conclusions she draws are distorted.

One problem, then, with Freeman's and other studies of the women's movement is their reliance on definitions of "politics," "change," and "success" that have been developed and applied in the context of studying a particular type of change (legal/policy) in a particular arena (formal institutions). This reliance is due in large part to social science's bias toward studying phenomena that are easily measured. Its consequence is that it exempts from study large sectors of the women's movement and feminist activity. Along with adopting the women's movement maxim, "The personal is political," meaning that power relationships exist at every level of daily life, researchers of the women's movement must also develop an awareness of, and methods for analyzing, efforts to effect social change that take place at the level of daily practices and hegemonic ideologies.

Klein

Klein's emphasis on mass support also leads her to discount a great deal of local/non-electoral feminist organizing as less important to the women's movement's success. In measuring the success of feminist resistance, Klein states: "Women's activism is here measured by the number of events aimed at changing women's traditional status per year from 1890 to 1980."[113] In fact, however, she adopts a method that focuses only on *national* events leading to *electoral* change. She justifies excluding local events on the grounds that "Since the women's movement is a broad-based effort at political change, the main events are national in scope."[114] But a case could be made that the strength of the women's movement stems precisely from its diffusion throughout society, its mix of local, grassroots, and national interest-group activism. Feminism's success in changing women's status can be attributed in large part to the cultural changes that result when feminists everywhere raise questions about women's traditional roles, as well as when they link feminism with other movements for social change. Yet Klein explicitly excludes these forms of feminist agitation from consideration, stating that

> Women have been visibly active in such movements as progressivism, the peace movement, the student movement, and the socialist movement, but their central concern in participating in these movements was not to change women's status or to assert their rights. Such activities are therefore not included.[115]

Klein's exclusion of women's organizing in other social movements ignores the fact that much of this organizing has taken the form of feminist agitation within those movements to make them more responsive to women's concerns and receptive to women's contributions. Her exclusion of such organizing seems particularly ironic, given the origins of some strands of feminism in other social movements of the 1960s. Klein's method obscures the pervasiveness of feminist activity—yet it is precisely this pervasiveness that enables the far-reaching, cultural changes required to transform women's roles, status, and subjectivity. Her method also obscures the relationship between the women's movement and other movements—most importantly, the civil rights movement, to which the women's movement owes a great debt. The resulting portrayal of feminist organizing privileges those forms of feminist activism that take place within specifically feminist, formally organized groups; this portrayal thus also conceals, especially, the feminism of those women of color who do their primary organizing in communities of color and organizations of color that are not solely or explicitly feminist.

Finally, Klein conveys a narrow view of feminist organizing and change by concentrating on the emergence of a "women's vote" in the 1980 presidential election as the culmination of women's movement activity. Klein sees feminist power as manifesting itself not in cultural production, but in a common voting pattern among women—a form of power whose applications are important yet limited. Her focus on a women's vote as the expression of feminist efforts obscures other forms of feminist resistance as well as feminist concerns associated with manifestations of domination that take place outside the arena of public policy and elections.

Even within the arena of elections, Klein's focus on the women's vote is problematic. Klein identifies a *feminist* vote that emerged in 1972, when "women's equality was an important priority in shaping the votes of both men and women." What she finds politically significant, however (for reasons that remain unclear), is the emergence of a *women's* vote:

> In 1972 when men and women voted on the basis of concern for sex equality, there was a feminist vote but no women's vote. By 1980, the size of the feminist constituency had expanded and become part of a larger women's vote. This women's vote reflects a difference in men's and women's perception of what is best for the country and what is best for women. It provides women with a new political resource that can force politicians to take women and their concerns seriously.[116]

Not only is it problematic, for all of the reasons discussed above, that Klein seems to want to put all of the eggs of feminist change into the basket of presidential elections; it is also puzzling that she should accord so much significance to the emergence of the women's vote in the 1980 presidential election. In this election, the women's vote manifested itself negatively: that is, fewer women than men voted for Reagan, the candidate who won despite women's lesser support. Though this lesser support might suggest a *potential, future* force of women voters, Klein's optimistic pronouncement that women have *now* been provided with "a resource that can force politicians to take women seriously" would seem unwarranted at the time of her study. Moreover, it is not clear why Klein accords greater significance to a women's vote than to a specifically feminist one.

Ferree and Hess, Gelb

The traditional tools of social science are inadequate for identifying, let alone evaluating, the changes that result from feminists' efforts to transform hegemonic ideologies. Ferree and Hess and Gelb rely on opinion polls to gauge changes in "public opinion," but such polls are inadequate to gauge many changes in consciousness for a number of reasons: because opinion polls circumscribe possible responses by delimiting the questions in the first place; because they are designed to measure effects, but not processes, of change; and because hegemonic ideologies, and challenges to them, by definition operate subconsciously as well as consciously, and are likely to resist being captured by opinion polls precisely to the extent that they have become ingrained in public consciousness. In short, Ferree and Hess, Gelb, and other social scientists have relied on opinion polls and other rough methods to do the work that can only really be done well through theoretical inquiry, given the ideological nature of both discursive politics and its targets.

Ferree and Hess are not unaware of some of the drawbacks associated with public opinion polls. In their second edition, they offer the following caveat and disclaimer:

> Although polling can be an important means of tapping cultural shifts, especially when they are emerging and still contested, many cultural beliefs are so taken for granted that no polling organization would ever ask about them, nor would variation in answers be found if they did.[117]

Ferree and Hess are conscious of some of the potential pitfalls in the research they do. They are also more successful than some of the other scholars of the women's movement in approaching their goal of representing the women's movement in its diversity:

> . . . there is always the tendency of observers to impose their meaning on events rather than to attempt to understand them from the point of view of diverse participants. . . . Our goal is to present each form of contemporary feminism in its own terms and in relation to the whole in a way that incorporates both an insider's and an outsider's perspective.[118]

Gelb, on the other hand, having adopted traditional political science's emphasis on public policy, is unable to consider more fundamental manifestations of power and feminist challenges to them.[119] In a reflection of her theory of power, Gelb's methodology is to measure membership in formal feminist organizations, assess policy changes in government, parties, and unions, and explore changes in public attitudes through opinion polls. This methodology precludes accurate assessment of the efficacy of feminists concentrating on cultural transformation—through discursive struggle—many of whom explicitly reject formal organization (as a replication of damaging power hierarchies) and a focus on public policy (as a misidentification of the nature and locus of the most pressing forms of women's oppression, or as unable to alleviate these forms of oppression because they lie outside the realm of what is legislatable).

5. Conclusion

The foundational studies of the women's movement incline toward traditional targets of political influence and traditional strategies for exercising such influence; they view women in essentializing terms; and they employ a theory of domination and resistance, and a method for exploring and evaluating domination and resistance, that perpetuate the centrality in feminism and in social science of subjects who enjoy privileges based on skin color, class, education, sexual orientation, and ethnicity. The net effect of these theoretical and methodological flaws is to marginalize women who are usually marginalized, as well as to obscure the discursive aspects of women's oppression and feminist responses to those aspects.

Social Movement Theory 5

Some social movement[1] theorists and women's movement scholars are beginning to acknowledge that a social movement's success in securing fundamental social transformation may best be indicated by the degree to which the movement's ideas become an integral part of a culture, influencing people's world views and their individual and collective actions. In general, however, this remains a minority view. Despite growing acknowledgment among scholars of the need to assess social movement success in terms of both policy change and more fundamental transformation, social movement theorists and scholars of the women's movement continue to assert that social movement success is indicated by the degree to which movement organizations become part of the policy process, working within that process to influence legislation and other social policy. Yet this is but one form of success; it is not the only—or even the most far-reaching—form. For students of the contemporary women's movement, then, the question remains: why do the women's movement studies fall short of representing and exploring feminist activism in all its complexity? Why, in particular, do they so often ignore the discursive activities aimed at effecting radical change in dominant ideologies?

The answer to this question lies in the studies' liberal theoretical underpinnings, and the methodologies that follow from them. The studies are theoretically grounded in liberal constructions of power and domination, resistance and social change. A look at the history and development of social movement theory helps to illuminate the reasons contemporary studies of the women's movement conceive of power, domination, resistance, and social change as narrowly as they do.

Prior to the 1960s, the study of collective behavior was grounded mainly in variations of "frustration-aggression theory," which emphasized grievances or deprivation as the root cause of collective action. Deprivation could be absolute or relative, but it was assumed to be the engine of social movement activity.[2] Another approach that was popular at the time was "malintegration theory," the premise of which was that protest can be explained in psychological terms, as aberrant, irrational, or anti-social behavior.

In the 1960s, according to Mayer Zald, the study of social movements continued to focus on the question of what motivates action, but expanded to entertain theories that explained protest activity as the result either of socialization (e.g., "red diaper babies"); of a broad cultural shift away from the apparent social consensus of the 1950s; or of the emergence of a protoclass of students, who, facing increasing credentialism and blocked mobility, experienced and acted with a high degree of solidarity.

Although these refinements in theories about the motivation behind action were more nuanced than what they supplanted, they left many questions unanswered, including why some apparently aggrieved groups do not engage in collective protest; what other conditions might be necessary for collective action; what resources are available to movements and how they are organized; and what the role of the state might be in assisting or quelling social movements.[3] These questions—and the search for their answers—formed the basis of "resource mobilization" (RM) theory as it emerged in the late 1960s.

Resource Mobilization Theory

The publication in 1965 of Mancur Olson's *The Logic of Collective Action* signalled a shift away from the conventional focus on participant attitudes and on case studies that described movement structure but not much else. Drawing on rational choice theory, Olson posited participation in collective action as something to be explained in terms of actors' rationality, though his definition of rationality is famously narrow. Indeed, Olson's critics fault him for representing people exclusively as atomized, self-maximizing individuals. Olson's "free rider" concept— the ostensible paradox of collective action that grows out of the assumption that people will not contribute toward collective efforts to realizing social goods if they can reap the benefits of those goods without participating—was the heart of his reconceptualization of the actor as rational, and has prompted both criticism and theoretical refinement.

The break with traditional behavioral approaches to the study of collective action that began with Olson's book solidified in the late 1960s and 1970s with the advent of "resource mobilization theory," which retained the rational actor of Olson's work but placed that actor in an institutional context and made those institutions (including social movement organizations) the focus of study. According to the theory's architects, social movement activity can be explained as the product of an increased flow of resources from elites to social movement organizations (the agents of movement activity). By placing actors within an institutional context—indeed, by defining movements' main actors as institutions/organizations—RM theory sought to factor into the study of social movements the pressures and incentives that structure the political/institutional context in which the rational actor acts.

In their groundbreaking work on resource mobilization, John D. McCarthy and Mayer Zald[4] introduced a focus on social movement organizations. Although their approach almost entirely neglected the goals, successes, and failures of movements, as well as the role of the state, other RM theorists would come to address those concerns. In the meantime, McCarthy and Zald inaugurated the study of social movements as organizations or institutions, coordinating the actions of a mass base.

Grounded in liberalism (and its elision of difference), RM theory posits homogeneous subjects/actors who mobilize similarly, in similar contexts and for similar reasons, irrespective of differences in privilege or oppression. If these homogeneous subjects find themselves the targets of domination, it is exercised via the formal policies of institutions—such as laws or hiring practices. Likewise, if they resist, they do so within institutional contexts, in order to change these policies.

RM theory casts both domination and movement activity to resist that domination in institutional terms—government and other policy-making institutions on the one hand, social movement organizations on the other.[5] Recently, some RM theorists have increased their attention to grass-roots mobilization, "recruitment networks,"[6] "counter movements," and other factors that shape social movement activity and social change.[7]

RM theory represents an advance over earlier approaches to the study of collective action in several respects. First, contrary to "frustration-aggression" and malintegration theories, RM theory conceptualizes social movements as political rather than mainly psychological phenomena. Relatedly, participants are seen as rational, not irrational, actors, motivated to act by incentives.[8] This is an advance over the view of protest as the hallmark of irrationality and antisocial behavior. Second, RM theory has led to a fuller understanding of the "micromobilization" processes that prompt people to act, and of the importance of recruitment networks.[9] Work grounded in RM theory has responded to Olson's "free rider" problematic with an understanding of selective incentives and the role of solidarity in people's decisions to participate in social movements.[10]

Third, RM theory sees mass action as a phenomenon characterized by organization and planning, emphasizing the role of social movement organizations in coordinating protest. This in turn enables a much greater understanding than psychological theories offer of how people become mobilized to participate, why collective action takes the forms it does, and why particular strategies are chosen. The importance of this approach, which underscores the conscious planning of social movements, is apparent when one compares, for example, the common myth that Rosa Parks acted alone with the reality that the Montgomery Bus Boycott was the result of months of planning by African Americans connected through formal and informal networks, and of failed negotiations with the city's white leaders, who were warned in advance that their inaction would lead to a boycott.

Fourth, RM theory attends to the larger political/policy context in which movements operate. This attention aids analyses of why some movements are more successful than others in affecting the policy process. Moreover, it helps to explain why movements tend to cluster: openings in the political opportunity structure that one movement helps to create lend themselves to exploitation by another.

Finally—and crucially—by taking collective action seriously, and treating it as a choice open to those who share common grievances, RM theory acknowledges a legitimate role for people in shaping public policy beyond simply voting. Protest is seen as *political* activity, and analyses of the workings of social movement organizations help to demystify the origins, goals, and methods of collective protest activity.

For all its strengths and improvements on traditional approaches to the study of collective action, however, RM theory's assumptions ultimately limit its applicability. These limitations have prompted prolific critiques and theoretical innovations. First, theorists working within the RM paradigm have identified its shortcomings, refined its assumptions, and illuminated new lines of theoretical inquiry. Second, Steven Lukes and then John Gaventa provided an early and important departure from established assumptions and methods for the study of collective action, problematizing some of RM's simplifying assumptions. And third, a strain of social movement theory has emerged that focuses on so-called "new social movements" and is preoccupied with the meaning-creating functions of social movements, as well as the relationship between movement participation and identity.

RM Theorists' Critiques

Criticism from within RM theory has focused on its "free rider" concept and its emphasis on "rationality";[11] its emphasis on resources such as money and access to elites to the exclusion of consciousness and framing;[12] and its narrow definition of success. For the purposes of this study, the most critical shortcoming of RM theory is its tendency to focus on institutions. That tendency has limited its view of social movement success by defining it in terms of the growth, longevity, and professionalization of social movement organizations. Those familiar with the civil rights, student, feminist, lesbian/bisexual/gay, and AIDS activist movements will recall that significant conflict has arisen within these movements over the investment movement organizations sometimes develop in soft-peddling their challenges to a political system in which they hope to gain membership and status. That is, social movements' effectiveness can often be *compromised*—not advanced—when they conform to the requirements of acceptance by traditional political institutions, particularly if the movement relies on direct action tactics to pursue its goals. Or, in the words of one activist, "You can't go out for drinks with someone in the evening and then chain yourself to his desk the next morning."[13]

In sum, then, RM theory's advances over earlier approaches to the study of social movements are important and substantial. They have not, however, proved sufficient, as subsequent theoretical endeavors attest. And while early critiques of RM theory accepted its liberal assumptions, more recent challenges have been more thoroughgoing. The first wave of critiques of RM theory that praise it for taking grievances as a given neglect to explore its limited view of what constitutes grievances. That is, grounded as it is in a liberal paradigm that privileges policy, and actors acting in policy arenas, RM theory neglects to consider differences in *types* of grievances, and the different types of political activity they spawn. These provocations were taken up first by Lukes and Gaventa, and then by the New Social Movement theorists.

Lukes and Gaventa

Steven Lukes

Steven Lukes's work is important here because it is probably the earliest significant effort from within political science to reconceptualize the workings of power in terms broader than the traditional, liberal conceptualizations that assume a political system that is uniformly open to challengers. Theoretically, Lukes's approach to power bridges RM and postmodern paradigms, sharing some of the assumptions of both liberal approaches to power (in that he views domination as largely conscious[14]) and postmodern approaches (in that he moves beyond the strictly conscious dimensions of subordination).

In *Power: A Radical View*,[15] Lukes seeks to expand accepted notions of power, positing a "third dimension" of power, beyond the first and second dimensions articulated within political science. The first dimension of power, he argues, involves the ability of one party to make a second party do something they would not otherwise do; it is consciously and overtly coercive. The second dimension involves the ability of one party to control a political agenda by ensuring, through coercion or manipulation, that the second party's interests do not find a place on that agenda. The exercise of this type of power is perhaps less direct than the first dimension, but it is nonetheless conscious and overt. Both of these models of power, Lukes says, posit two actors engaged in a conflict over their interests, in which one actor emerges victorious.

Lukes's contribution is a third model of power, one that addresses those situations in which no conflict is apparent because one party has been able to shape another party's *desires*. In such cases, the first party need not manipulate or coerce the second party directly; the exercise of power has taken place at the level of shaping and identifying interests, so that the first party has been able to convince the second that the latter has an interest in an outcome that is, in the end, favorable to the former (and unfavorable to the latter). What is noteworthy about this conception of power is that it does not assume that the exercise of power is necessarily visible, nor that the subordinated party is necessarily conscious of being subordinated.

John Gaventa

John Gaventa operationalized Lukes's theory in his study of the political economy of coal mining in Central Appalachia from the late 19th century through the 1970s. If a single study could revolutionize a discipline's theory of power and its methodologies, this study would have revolutionized political science. Instead, RM theory continued to hold sway long after the publication of Gaventa's book. Even now, as New Social Movement (NSM) theory challenges some of RM theory's assumptions and complements it in other ways, Gaventa's work is largely overlooked. This is perhaps precisely because it demonstrates that many of the aspects of domination that NSM theory characterizes as "new," and attributes to the "age of information" or other contemporary phenomena, operated with deadly precision in the 19th century—and, moreover, in the traditional realm of social movement study: labor movements.[16]

Gaventa's study illustrates the mechanisms and effects of dominative power exercised in Lukes's third dimension—in this case, the construction of coal miners' self-defeating subjectivity by a powerful coal company utilizing public and private institutions as well as myths and symbols. In addition, his study points to the key role played by *consciousness* in mobilizing resistance. When the workers lacked a critical consciousness of their oppression by the coal company, they failed to challenge the company even when the opportunity arose. Consequently, the company retained its power over the workers, despite a long moment in which its actual institutional power had diminished.

Gaventa's discussion of failed strike attempts in the 1920s in the Cumberland Gap region indicates that consciousness alone is insufficient for resisting domination if one's opponent controls all of the key institutions. The fact that the coal company controlled economic, political, and social institutions in the region when the workers *did* strike enabled the company to put down the strikes, regardless of the strikes' grounding in the growing conscientization of a subjugated work force. Nonetheless, consciousness is key, and what is so interesting about this study (and what was so innovative at the time it was published) is its acknowledgement and investigation of hegemonic power that shapes not only the explicit political agendas but also the subjective reality of the dominated subject/actor—an aspect of power relations that RM approaches typically do not address.

For Gaventa, the thing to be explained was acquiescence. This guiding focus already put him at odds with established paradigms. Marxist and classical democratic theories, he notes, both assume that people who are oppressed will invariably act to counter that oppression. Conservative theories of democracy argue that quiescence amidst inequality signals satisfaction with the existing system, supports decision-making by the few, or at least facilitates social stability.[17] In seeking to understand why a group of people who are systematically dominated fail to challenge that domination, Gaventa argues, we need to think about power differently. In contrast to first-dimension analyses that blame miners for a "lack of civic responsibility" or "their deficient culture," and second-dimension analyses that see the region as the victim of neglect and broken promises by the institutions that affect it—both the mining company and local government and union institutions—Gaventa proposes an analysis of coal miners' apparent passivity that is grounded in a third-dimension conception of power. This analysis sees inequality as created and enforced "not only through institutional barriers but also through the shaping of beliefs about the order's legitimacy or immutability."[18] The three dimensions of power, Gaventa says, work symbiotically, each reinforcing the others so that domination exercised along one dimension enables, and is enabled by, domination exercised along the others.

Gaventa argues that we must also understand the direct and indirect mechanisms of power. Direct mechanisms the mining company employed were largely discursive: distorting information ("selling" the industrial order by associating it with conspicuous consumption); degrading the local culture and values of mountaineers both through the media and in local, informal conversation; directly appropriating local culture (e.g., by giving Appalachian names to places of work and British names to new hubs of development and of social and consumer activity); and directly appropriating socializing institutions such as schools, churches, and government.[19]

By analyzing such cultural and discursive phenomena, Gaventa (as Lukes before him) had already gone beyond what political science generally considered to be the relevant mechanisms of power. He went even further by attaching a *political* importance to the psychological ramifications of the indirect mechanisms of power's third dimension. These mechanisms include the way the powerless lower their demands, or adopt attitudes of "extensive fatalism, self-deprecation, or undue apathy"; and their greater susceptibility to "the internalization of the values, beliefs, or rules of the game of the powerful as a further adaptive response." Denied participation, Gaventa argues, the powerless "might not develop political consciousness of their own situation or of broader political inequalities."[20]

Lukes's third model of power represents an important contribution to discussions about what comprises politics. Gaventa's operationalization of Lukes's view of power, and specifically his case study's illumination of the subtle workings of domination upon a group's collective consciousness, is an equally important contribution. Yet there is still more to be said about power.

Lukes and Gaventa both address power relationships in which at least one party is conscious of having an interest in dominating another party, and acts consciously to control the other party's actions (through controlling its desires). But what of those situations in which there is no party that can be identified as orchestrating the exercise of power that is taking place? In order to tease out the workings of large-scale social divisions (or what Foucault calls "major dominations") along lines of gender, race, class, and so on, it is necessary to move beyond Lukes's and Gaventa's focus on individual actors and discrete events. Cultural contexts—structures of power that affect everyone in a given society, though in different ways—and "sea changes" in those contexts require an analytic model that goes beyond Lukes's third model of power. The same can be said for arenas of political and social struggle beyond that of public policy. While Gaventa's work concerns mainly policy change, his conceptualization of the "indirect mechanisms" of power can be used to elucidate the workings of "major dominations" on oppressed people. What is needed to round out that analysis is a conceptualization of the ways in which those on the powerful side of these large-scale social divisions often participate *unconsciously* in the domination of others, following an insidious script that both dominator and dominated have internalized and conform to without conscious consideration. Radical feminism began the work of exposing the indirect mechanisms of power as they operate on women's consciousnesses; later work on identity construction (such as autotheoretical writings, as well as postmodern theoretical work on identity) has taken up this project, in some cases extending the notion of unconscious participation in domination to articulate the processes by which dominative identities are constructed. This work has also revealed the complexities of agency and choice for people whose identities in some sense *depend on* their subordination.[21]

Finally, where social movements and the systems they seek to change are concerned, Gaventa's work provides the important insight that the three dimensions of power (and we could add others) work symbiotically. Rather than one arena or dimension being the "real" locus of power, he suggests, different dimensions reinforce each other; moreover, when power falters and loses its hold at one level, often its exercise at other levels can "hold the line" for the powerful until they reestablish their hegemony where they had temporarily lost it. And though Gaventa focuses on traditional channels for protest—labor union organizing and litigation—his insight can also assist us in linking resistance at multiple levels of domination. It can, for example, spur us to look at how changes in social paradigms of thought reinforce and are reinforced by legislative and policy changes—and how, much more frequently, legislation and policy work to preclude both the consolidation of power and the creative leap necessary to mounting effective challenges to the dominant order. This promises to be a much more fruitful approach to the study of resistance than those that claim (as some of the women's movement studies do) that legislative or institutional efforts are the only practical or effective ones.

New Social Movement Theory

Just as RM theory placed actors in an institutional context, New Social Movement (NSM) theory places them in a social context—that is, within networks of social alliances and obligations.

NSM theory differs from RM theory in three key respects: first, in its conceptualization of actors/subjects; second, in its attention to "micromobilization," or the face-to-face interactions that contribute to social movement participants' mobilization; and third, in its attention to what Mueller[22] calls the "generation of oppositional meanings."

The Actor/Subject

Whereas deprivation theory constructed protesters as irrational and impulsive, and RM theory constructs them as rational, self-maximizing actors united through shared interests and available resources, NSM theory makes the construction of identity and subjectivity, at both individual and collective levels, a primary focus.

At the level of *individual identity*, some NSM theory has replaced RM theory's rational individual (whose rationality is indicated by a self-maximizing, individualistic approach to gaining access to the most public goods with the least amount of effort) with an actor embedded in social relations that instill obligation, and that can spur one to join in collective action.[23] This actor is conscious of her/his connections to and interdependency with other people and, in the case of anti-nuclear and environmental movement participants, her/his dependence upon the natural environment.

NSM theory, expanding on RM theory's attention to micromobilization, looks more deeply into the relationship between micromobilization and identity construction. Both Melucci and Mueller[24] agree that actors' identities are constructed, and their mobilization prompted, through "submerged networks"—"micromobilization" based on "face-to-face interactions"—and that these submerged networks operate beyond public view.[25] In its emphasis on the identity-creating and -affirming aspects of social movement activity, however, much NSM theory posits actors who participate in social movements for the primarily psychological (rather than political) purpose of gaining affirmation of their identities.[26]

With regard to *collective identity*, some NSM theorists view it as fairly seamless and resilient,[27] while others view it as fragmented and tenuous, arrived at through negotiation, and always subject to renegotiation.[28] Others, such as Carol Mueller, strike a middle ground.[29] Despite their differing conclusions, the attention these theorists give to collective identity and its construction by social movements is fairly representative of NSM theory, and constitutes an advance over approaches that take collective identity as a given. The feminist autotheoretical texts thematize and perform these conflicts over identity and intramovement relations, providing very specific and detailed accounts of the sometimes coercive aspects of collective identity construction and articulating alternative subjectivities. Even more important, the feminist autotheoretical texts insist on the *political* nature of both collective and individual identity—in contrast to Melucci and other NSM theorists, who psychologize it.

Insofar as NSM approaches embed their actors in social relations, world economies, and global environments, they represent an advance over RM theory's atomized rational actor who works from the narrowest of material self-interests. Yet much NSM theory amplifies psychology to the exclusion of politics. The psychological benefits movement participants enjoy are taken to be the sole or primary motivating factor in their participation.

This can be attributed to a conflation of identity and individual psychology. New Social Movements—particularly (in the United States) the feminist, anti-racist, lesbian and gay/queer, ethnic, and disability rights movements—organize people along lines of identity. This is not, however, because these movements *provide* identity or even see identity affirmation as their primary task, though they do engage in processes of identity construction and affirmation designed to counter the negative impact of oppression on the basis of those identities. Rather, NSMs organize people along identity lines because members of a given identity category—women, African-Americans, Latinos, gay people, disabled people—tend to share some common experiences of oppression, and a common desire (if manifested in differing agendas) to create change at a social—not just individual—level.

The main question these movements ask themselves, then, is not "Who am *I*?" as Melucci[30] or Gamson[31] would argue, but "Why are *we* oppressed because of who *we* are?" and "How can we change this state of affairs?"

There are some NSM theorists who do not reduce identity to individual psychology. Eyerman and Jamison, for example, see social movements and their participants as "cognitive actors,"[32] conscious of their place in history and intent upon redefining history through effecting fundamental transformation of social identities.[33] However, even the actors in their account remain in some ways two-dimensional. The actor of NSM theory has a stable and internally coherent identity; fragmentation takes place at the level of the movement as a whole, and is apparent in participants' disagreements. (This is one area in which identity theory, grounded in postmodern views of the subject, can move forward from where NSM theory leaves off.)

NSM theory's usefulness is limited to the degree that it casts participants in new social movements as simply embarking on a "quest for identity"—a formulation that depoliticizes these movements. NSM theory becomes more useful to the degree that it acknowledges both the political aims of NSMs and major political inequities that characterize the context in which they arise.[34] Where NSM theory breaks down, moreover, feminist appropriations of postmodern theory, as well as feminist theories of identity, can pick up, expanding our understanding of the collective nature of identity construction and the political nature of identity contestation.

Domination/Resistance: Micromobilization and Face-to-face Interactions

Some NSM theorists (as well as some other critics of RM theory) who do acknowledge large-scale domination emphasize the role that cultural codes and paradigms play in securing that domination, and locate resistance in those realms as well. Joseph Gusfield's distinction between "linear" movements (such as labor movements and unions) and "fluid" movements (the NSMs) represents one NSM formulation of resistance (and therefore domination) that takes place at the level of interpersonal relationships and localized encounters *as well as* at the level of public policy:

> Fluid movements . . . imply *changes in how values and realities are conceived,* [and] they occur outside or in addition to organized and directed action. They may involve contention with others and with alternative meanings and constructions. Yet, they are less likely to be drawn into such collective actions as strikes, boycotts, pickets or demonstrations. *They occur in the myriad actions of everyday life:* in micro and less public acts. It is harder to identify success or failure.[35] [emphasis added]

Gusfield sees the activities of the women's movement as exemplary of the way "fluid" movements operate at multiple levels:

> The women's movement and feminism occur in more than the organized efforts at constitutional amendment, equal rights legislation, and

affirmative action. They also involve relationships and interactions between men and women in micro and even intimate relations. The
movement occurs in the multiplicity of events where a conception of
women's rights and gender justice have become issues.[36]

Resistance, for Gusfield and some other NSM theorists, is aimed at shifting the "frames" through which people interpret the meaning of an action (e.g., abortion) in relation to other actions and issues (such as
self-determination or murder). Such framing also has the potential to shift
people's identity and their understanding of their own actions. As Gusfield acknowledges, "In this form, change has a significant ideational
component. . . ." Moreover, the mere presence of a movement calls into
question the area of life that the movement contests, and thus challenges
commonly-held norms: "Alternatives now exist where choice and contention were absent."[37]

Alberto Melucci is another NSM theorist who—at some moments,
if not others—appreciates the connections between ideology, identity,
and domination. His description of how domination is exercised through
the construction and manipulation of individual identity is positively
Foucauldian, right down to the disembodied dominator. Individually and
collectively, he says, people are given more and more "information resources" to define themselves and their lives; yet these processes of definition are increasingly subject to

> a diffuse social control that passes beyond the public sphere to invade
> the very domain where the sense of individual action takes shape. Di-
> mensions that were traditionally regarded as private (the body, sexuality,
> affective relations), or subjective (cognitive and emotional processes,
> motives, desires), or even biological (the structure of the brain, the ge-
> netic code, reproductive capacity) now undergo social control and ma-
> nipulation. The technoscientific apparatus, the agencies of information
> and communication, and the decision-making centers that determine
> policies wield their power over these domains. Yet, these are precisely
> the areas where individuals and groups lay claim to their autonomy,
> where they conduct their search for identity by transforming them into
> a space where they reappropriate, self-realize, and construct the mean-
> ing of what they are and what they do.[38]

Like Foucault and theorists working on the politics of identity (see chapter 6), here Melucci beautifully draws our attention to these little-theo-
rized sites of domination. However, just as his formulations of collective
resistance are restricted by his reluctance to move from the individual to

the collective level—i.e., he psychologizes new social movements by casting them as a group effort to define individuals' identities—this formulation of domination suffers from being confined to a focus on the *individual* impact of the social and political forces that construct identities.

Yet Melucci distinguishes himself from Foucault and Deleuze and Guattari on the grounds that he sees a possibility for resistance whereas, he claims, they do not. Melucci attributes a "one-dimensional" view of power to Foucault, Deleuze, and Guattari, arguing that they view power as "the construction and administration of subjects." Melucci, on the other hand, sees both powerful organizations attempting to define the meaning of reality *and* networks of actors using those organizations' same resources "to define reality in novel ways."[39] The means of domination become the means of resistance, even if the site of resistance remains not only psychological but primarily individual.

Melucci does emphasize ideological and linguistic/symbolic sites of domination and resistance, although he assumes an opposition between resistance at those sites and resistance "in the political system."[40] However, despite his views about how power and domination operate, he ultimately tends to psychologize resistance. He casts social movement activity not as resistance to domination and as struggle to change power relations, but as a quest for identity, and—in the case of the women's movement—for acceptance by others.

His individualizing and psychologizing takes the form that Laraña, Johnston, and Gusfield's does, in that he locates new social movements in a larger social and political context—the "information society"—which he claims produces uncertainties and ambivalences that require "the search for identity, the quest for self"[41]:

> . . . the potentially limitless extension of information increases the margins of uncertainty for the entire system. . . . Uncertainty affects the meaning of individual action. . . . The individual answer to the question, Who am I? becomes problematic. . . . The search for identity becomes a remedy against the opacity of the system, against the uncertainty that constantly constrains action (Pizzorno 1987).[42]

Melucci essentializes women—the subjects of the women's movement—by positing a unitary "female" experience and characterizing certain movement activities as "female." In so doing, he offers a peculiarly contradictory treatment of "difference," at one moment recognizing the importance for contemporary social movements of challenging suffocating norms of conformity, at another attributing to all women a singular "difference," a unitary way of being. In all of this, moreover, he reinscribes women's marginalization by uncritically embracing language that continues to place constructions of maleness at the center:

> For women, the profound memory [sic] of subordination and entrap-
> ment in a body "other" than that of the dominant culture make a
> struggle for emancipation an important, and quantitatively perhaps the
> most significant, component of the movement's action. Collective ac-
> tion by women, however, is structured not only on the campaign for
> equal rights but also for the right to be different. . . . Being recognized
> as different is perhaps one of the most crucial rights at stake in postin-
> dustrial systems. Granting recognition to women entails accepting a dif-
> ferent outlook on reality, existence in a different body, and a specific
> way of relating to others and to the world.[43]

Melucci assumes that the "outlook on reality," bodily existence, and "way of relating" from which women ostensibly differ requires no specification or attribution; the assumption is that it is exclusively male, and universal in the sense that we all know what it constitutes. Women, meanwhile, clamor for recognition of their—again, supposedly obvious—"differ-ence."

Melucci's retreat into "difference theory" (he draws on Carol Gilli-gan, among others) in his discussion of women's movements leads him away from politics and power struggles, and even away from the work of transforming cultural codes that he elsewhere posits as central to NSM agendas (e.g., as when he argues that movement participants seize the very means of domination—information and communication—that have been used against them to "resist or even overturn" dominant and op-pressive cultural codes). It also leads him away from his own claims about the fractured nature of collective identity, as when he posits "a different outlook on reality" and "a specific way of relating to others and to the world." His acceptance of "difference" discourse leads him to such state-ments as, "Women rely on the female form of communication. They know it is different from male communication." Moreover, Melucci con-structs women's movement activity in terms that render it apparently in-effectual. Women's collective resistance is characterized, he insists, by a

> cultural overproduction within the [women's] movement, a symbolic
> wastefulness that contains a profound ambivalence. "Female" activities
> within the movement consist of pointless meetings, writing for its own
> sake not for the market, apparently aimless communication, and time
> spent in ways incoherent with utility and efficiency . . . the duplication
> of the same activities by a myriad of groups, with complete disregard

161

for economies of scale, are all aspects that the dominant masculine culture judges as "senseless." Nevertheless, it is this waste that breeds innovation. . . .[44]

In contrast to these profoundly problematic claims, Melucci makes
the sound and valuable observation that the women's movement and
other NSMs are "eminently communicative in character"[45] and thus—in
their emphasis on symbols and information—unrecognizable to policy-
focused analysts. When Melucci runs aground, it is precisely because he
remains rooted in individualistic, psychologizing assumptions about the
goals of NSMs; he has not linked the parts of his argument in such a way
that his observations about the nature of domination (pervasive throughout society, exercised via language, symbols, and cultural narratives) illuminate the *social* and ultimately *political* nature of identity construction.
This is also the problem with the social science studies of the women's
movement, in that they tend to portray feminist activity that is primarily
discursive or ideological in individualizing, psychologizing terms. Here,
postmodern identity theory and the feminist autotheoretical texts can
fill in.

The problem with Melucci's work is not that it focuses on psychology. To the degree that it casts psychic domination as a social and political process, his work is enormously useful and political in its implications.
Rather, the problem is that Melucci does not distinguish between the
dominant and the disempowered groups, and he does not adequately account for "major dominations," social schisms along lines of
sex/class/race/sexuality, in his discussions of domination and resistance.
Certainly the processes Melucci describes, by which individual identity is
structured and manipulated, affect all in a given society. However, they do
not affect everyone in the same way, because the interests that create and
are represented by these mechanisms of power are those of only some
people, set against the interests of others. By identifying contemporary
domination with processes that he posits as universal, Melucci implies a
society very different from ours—i.e., one in which the powerful have
joined the ranks of the dominated, with everyone equally subject to a
nameless, faceless power.

The general tendency in NSM theory to psychologize identity and
movement participation becomes clearer when NSM theorists discuss
movements' activities and goals. Just as they are inclined to overemphasize
social movement actors' psychological needs, and social movements' psychological benefits, NSM theorists also typically depoliticize movement
goals and strategies, in the sense of not viewing them in terms of power
relations. Their focus remains primarily on the *internal* workings and goals

of social movements. It is not surprising, therefore, that NSM theorists generally do not concentrate on the nature of domination. Some NSM theorists define social movement success in terms of group process; many neglect entirely the matter of social conflict and power outside of the group.

Conversely, some NSM theorists attempt to cast inwardly-focused activity that emphasizes self-transformation as political, movement activity. One example is Verta Taylor and Nancy Whittier's discussion of lesbian feminist communities, in which the authors promote the notion that "collective self-transformation" by itself constitutes political activism:

> . . . radical feminism gave way to a new cycle of feminist activism sustained by lesbian feminist communities. These communities socialize members into a collective oppositional consciousness that channels women into a variety of actions geared toward personal, social and political change.[46]

This statement would be unproblematic were Taylor and Whittier to provide examples of what kinds of "social and political change" lesbians are socialized into by lesbian communities; yet they limit their examples to national cultural events, such as music festivals, which are explicitly designed to be internally-focused, insular events. In limiting their focus to what some scholars have labeled "cultural feminism"[47] and ignoring the surge of lesbian activism in the 1980s that is more connected to gay/queer movements than is lesbian feminism, Taylor and Whittier arrive at a description of lesbianism's relation to politics that ultimately negates politics—not because it emphasizes the importance of consciousness and self-transformation, but because it begins *and ends* with these.[48] Like some other NSM theorists, Taylor and Whittier reduce a movement—lesbian feminism—to its psychological effects. The fact that the authors valorize the solipsism they construct—as opposed to NSM theorists who criticize it—matters little. The effect in Taylor and Whittier's case is to mistake the personal for the political; the effect in the other NSM theorists' cases is to mistake the political for the personal.

It is noteworthy that few NSM theorists speak in terms of these movements' "grievances," let alone domination and resistance. Laraña, Johnston and Gusfield[49] explicitly argue that grievances are irrelevant or, at most, secondary to NSMs' primary, identity-oriented activities and goals. Noting that "the support and identity-affirming functions of feminism and gay rights groups are well known,"[50] the authors assert that these movements are driven by a "quest for identity," which they characterize as a "youthful activity."[51] They contrast these movements with other NSMs, particularly environmental ones, for which, they assert, "grievances have a more important place in group formation."[52] In this way, they reduce feminist and gay movements to a psychological quest for identity.

Yet, ultimately, the ostensibly more grievance-based NSMs fare no better: even the environmental movements, supposedly driven by a genuine concern about the human impact on the natural environment rather than by a youthful psychological imperative, are really acting out that quest, according to these authors. For these activists, "the NSM perspective tells us that identity quest co-occurs as a displaced (or unconscious) but nevertheless fundamental raison d'etre of group formation."[53] Even movements whose grievances—"threats to the ozone layer, nuclear proliferation, or saving the whales"—are "so distant from everyday life that they can only remain immediate through their ongoing social construction and reassertion in the group context" rely on especially tight group cohesiveness to drive them. "In rational choice terms, identity defense and affirmation provide the necessary counterbalancing selective incentives where the more practical payoffs of the movement are small."[54]

Where collective resistance is concerned, Melucci and Mueller posit submerged networks operating beyond public scrutiny to articulate identities and agendas prior to more public mobilization. As the autotheoretical texts make clear, however, some of the activity of submerged networks takes place not in face-to-face interactions but through other channels (such as publishing) designed to reach more than one person at a time; moreover, these identity-constructing and mobilizing efforts are deliberately conducted publicly, both in order to "spread the word" more efficiently and, more important, in order to promulgate a discourse about women that emphasizes diversity. This reflects a different political agenda than what Melucci and Mueller emphasize. They represent the process of forging collective identity as a process of coming to a consensus (however loose or tenuous) as to "who women are." In contrast, feminist discourses that emphasize diversity reject the notion that such a consensus is a necessary precursor to effective political action. In fact, these discourses insist, such apparent unanimity cannot be achieved without excluding or obfuscating some of the inevitable differences that render "women" a category whose coherence is a matter of linguistic convenience and construction more than of any real homogeneity.[55]

Another problem with NSM theory is that it does not typically engage with the complexities and dilemmas of resistance such as those that Foucault and the Haug collective[56] explore in their discussions of the pleasures (as well as pains) of submission and the dynamics of oppressed people's active participation in their subordination. It is these pleasures and these dynamics that can make resistance so difficult and tenuous—and that can explain quiescence. Again, other theoretical enterprises can aid our understanding here. Gaventa describes this phenomenon in his study of coal miners; Foucault and the Haug collective go even deeper into investigating the complexities of power and pleasure, subordination and resistance in their work on sexuality and, for the Haug collective, women's subjectivity. (See below.)

Some NSM theorists are beginning to explore the links between structures of domination, consciousness, and resistance. Aldon Morris is one who has suggested this as a fruitful direction for research:

> . . . an important research agenda is to explore the interlocking nature of relevant systems of domination and the varieties of consciousness that flow from them, with a view to understanding how they affect collective action.
>
> This kind of conceptual and empirical research is currently being undertaken by scholars working in the black feminist tradition. . . .[57]

Social Change: The "Generation of Oppositional Meanings"

NSM theory generally conceptualizes social change in terms of individual identity and collective consciousness, though particular theorists working within this paradigm may focus on only one or another of these.

As discussed above, NSM theorists who address identity tend to construct it in individualistic terms and to represent movement goals concerning identity in terms of support for individual lives, rather than connecting a movement's focus on identity to larger political goals of effecting fundamental social transformation—e.g., changing the possibilities for women's subjectivity and the social organization of gender. Here, it will suffice to say that these theories' construction of social change retains, tacitly, a public-private split even as it appears to transgress it. For Melucci, for example, the construction of collective identity takes place as a movement's "invisible process," beyond public view; for him, and for Laraña, Johnston, and Gusfield, movements embody participants' "quest for identity," a search for the answer to the question "Who am I?" This focus elides movements' efforts to pose and answer these questions in collective terms, and to affect the larger society by challenging the way power relations are exercised, and domination is secured, through the construction of identity.

NSM theorists who approach social change through the concept of collective consciousness, on the other hand, see change in terms of the transformation of cultural codes, language, and consciousness. Gusfield, for instance, formulates NSMs' strategy and impact in terms of their framing effects (see quote above). Similarly, Eyerman and Jamison contend that "The cognitive praxis of social movements is an important source of new societal images and the transformation of societal identities."[58] They argue for movements' role as cognitive actors:

> The forms of consciousness that are articulated in social movements provide something crucial in the constitution of modern societies: public spaces for thinking new thoughts, activating new actors, generating new ideas, in short, constructing new intellectual "projects."[59]

Likewise, Snow and Benford's theories of "collective action framing" emphasize the importance of a movement's "interpretive schemata" that organizes "objects, situations, events, experiences, and sequences of actions," assigning them meaning and importance within an overall world view.[60] Framing is integral to collective action because it provides an interpretive grid through which actors and potential actors can understand and represent social phenomena in ways that suggest and support social change activity. For them, creating collective consciousness that enables people to question the status quo and seek alternatives to it is a key function of social movements.

Aldon Morris, like Melucci, articulates the relationship between consciousness and *social,* rather than simply *individual,* processes. Drawing on Gramsci, he writes:

> Hegemonic consciousness is always sustained by public institutions that are meant to attend to the general welfare: the government, schools, the media, and a host of lesser institutions presenting themselves as representative of the society as a whole and intent on benefiting the broadest range of people. In short, hegemonic consciousness is a ruling consciousness because it is rooted in and supported by the most dominant and powerful institutions of a society. Its organizational expression enables it to wrap itself in institutional garments bearing labels proclaiming its universality.[61]

Unlike Melucci and most other NSM theorists, however, Morris places the discussion of social movements' function of creating consciousness around social inequities in the context of social stratification by race and gender, as well as class—the traditional focus of social movement studies:

166

[T]here are systems of human domination other than class that are real and objective. . . . Hill has argued that it is a crucial mistake for labor scholars to reduce race consciousness to class consciousness. . . . Other systems of domination have been similarly ignored.[62]

Morris notes that African American feminists are engaged in the project of exploring interlocking systems of domination. Thus, he moves beyond the privatizing implications of Melucci's and others' undifferentiated conception of consciousness—i.e, the notion that we are all affected similarly by processes of psychic construction and manipulation, and thus seek autonomy through constructing an individual identity for ourselves. Instead, Morris not only acknowledges the different ways that consciousness is constructed, depending on one's position within various social hierarchies; he also points to an intellectual tradition that has been the site of a good deal of intellectual work around analyzing and transforming those phenomena.

In sum, NSM theory adds a great deal to the study of social movements, and works as a much needed corrective to resource mobilization theory's emphasis on institutions and material resources. It moves beyond the liberal paradigm, acknowledging as social and imbued with power relations those dimensions of life that liberalism relegates to the realm of the personal. It also attends to social movements' concern with identity, even if it typically casts that attention in individualistic terms. NSM theory recognizes the permeability of public-private boundaries, and draws attention to oppressive psychic processes that originate in the social organization of language and symbols and that function through insidiously powerful mechanisms. The best of NSM theory renders these processes and mechanisms explicitly political.

Yet NSM theory's approach to domination and resistance ultimately remains inadequate for understanding contemporary social movements, including the women's movement, because of its much more frequent tendency to empty these movements of political motives and effects, casting them instead in terms of individual psychology. With regard to the study of the women's movement, this tendency is particularly problematic as it corroborates, rather than challenges, the similar assumption the women's movement studies make about discursive feminist activity. With regard to sexism, this tendency is disturbing: despite the value of some theorists' incisive descriptions of the social forces and processes of identity construction, their restriction of their examination of identity to its individual effects too easily implies the old anti-feminist canard, "It's all in her head"—particularly when combined with their reticence about the "major dominations."

NSM theory often recapitulates the problematic characterization of social movements as primarily psychological. Though NSM theory's representation of the psychological aspect of movements is less pathologizing than that of malintegration theory—and its emphasis on cultural production is progressive—it misses the point when it returns to the primarily psychological understanding that characterized early theories of social movements. Emphasizing emotional and psychological needs, and the ways that some social movements ostensibly fulfill those needs for their participants, obscures the fact that many so-called "new social movements" are fundamentally concerned with large-scale power imbalances that permeate every aspect of society. This concern with power is what renders these movements political; to the extent that their political concerns and motives are eclipsed by analyses that focus on individual psychology, their very character is misconstrued.

Postmodern Critiques: Power and Subjectivity, Domination and Resistance

6

A s the preceding chapter argues, social movement theory has yet to come to terms with the kinds of domination and resistance that preoccupy some major constituencies within the women's movement. Consequently, scholars who look to social movement theory to identify key aspects of feminist analysis, agendas, and activities find little in this body of work to help them articulate and understand feminist analyses of subjectivity and identity and their relationship to feminist politics. Even the work in NSM theory that concentrates on identity generally fails to link it to politics in the way feminism does, and to treat feminist activity in these areas as *political* activity.

Scholars of the women's movement would do better to look to feminist theories of identity and subjectivity that draw on theoretical enterprises grounded in "postmodern" theories' insights and provocations.

Power

Postmodern social theories[1] have emerged in response to various shortcomings in liberal and structuralist theories of power, politics, identity, and subjectivity. Postmodern feminist theories typically emphasize a non-essentialist conceptualization of identity, and, relatedly, strategies for resistance based on coalition (at the collective level) and on local disruptions of cultural norms (at the individual level). Postmodern feminist theory forms an epistemological counterpart to feminist discursive politics (in its emphasis on the construction of subjectivity through language) and particularly the feminist autotheoretical texts. Social scientists and others who seek to understand the contests over difference and strategy that have been taking place within the women's movement will be aided in their efforts by becoming acquainted with the terms of current debates surrounding postmodern theories of power, identity, subjectivity, and resistance, and these theories' feminist appropriations.

Rethinking Power: Michel Foucault and Sandra Lee Bartky

Liberalism assumes a coherent self, endowed with rationality and an understanding of universal laws, and acting in accordance with its innermost essence, reflected in its will. Postmodernism, on the other hand, assumes a constructed subject that partially embodies, and enacts, conflicting social injunctions stemming from competing social institutions and processes that influence the subject's desires and agency. Contrary to some structuralist theories, postmodernism generally holds that the influence of these social forces is not total: the subject has some latitude with respect to them. And contrary to liberalism, this view holds that this latitude is limited: subjects cannot wholly circumvent these forces—and, moreover, this latitude stems not from some essential will, expressed through the subject's actions, but is itself a product of multiple, competing discourses through which the subject makes sense of her world and her actions within it. And whereas social science theories grounded in liberalism locate power in a central authority and prescribe a strategy for change based on appeals to this authority for "rights" (in order to free the subject to act according to her essence), postmodern theory concerns itself with "webs" of power, localized networks and shifting points in the social terrain on which power is exercised.

Here, I use the work of Michel Foucault and Sandra Lee Bartky to articulate the major premises of postmodern and postmodern feminist theories of power. Foucault's discussion of the deployment of sexuality provides an example of the kinds of localized couplings of incitement and prohibition that he argues characterize the exercise of power. This discussion is grounded in the postmodern notion of power as dispersed, operating at all levels of society. Bartky's discussion of the disciplining of women's bodies is an example of feminist appropriations of Foucault's theory and method, and of the convergence of feminism's and postmodernism's analyses of forms of domination that draw their support from cultural norms rather than from centralized institutions of formal authority.

While there is some dispute as to whether Foucault's theories should be classified as modern or postmodern, his relation to either of these categories is less important than his critique of liberal, juridical notions of domination and resistance. Foucault has been cast as both modern and postmodern. Though he didn't refer to himself as postmodern, according to David Couzens Hoy,[2] his thinking is neither modern nor anti-modern (in the nostalgic, neo-conservative sense). It is, rather, postmodern in its decentering of both the subject and the locus and workings of social power.[3]

Likewise, Bartky straddles theoretical boundaries, mixing postmodern insights with provocations more redolent of radical feminism. Indeed, few if any theorists could be said to be "purely" postmodern—particularly if one accepts the postmodern premise that such stable, seamless purity does not exist. The point here is to illuminate insights that have emerged from a body of thought that is most often called "postmodern" and that typically has these insights in common.

Michel Foucault

In volume one of *The History of Sexuality*,[4] Foucault critiques a "juridical" conception of power which defines power's workings in terms of prohibition only and which locates it centrally, as an overarching structure. This model of power suggests that the ability to compel obedience resides in a centralized authority: "In Western societies since the Middle Ages, the exercise of power has always been formulated in terms of law."[5] Foucault identifies the origins of the juridical model of power in the monarchic societies of the Middle Ages, and he argues that it continues to hold sway in contemporary society because it is through this model that power makes itself palatable: ". . . power is tolerable only on condition that it mask a substantial part of itself. . . ."[6]

The notion of power as something that is imposed from above and takes the form of prohibition leaves open the possibility of subverting structures of domination simply by doing what one is told not to do. Using sexuality as an extended "case study" for how power actually works, Foucault counters this notion of resistance, arguing that key to power's functioning is its ability to incite behaviors ("what one is told not to do") so that they then become "relay points" through which power is exercised and expanded. He articulates a "strategic" model of power, arguing that power is exercised at multiple sites, often by no one agent in particular; and furthermore, that domination is not always simply a matter of being prohibited by an authority from doing what one wishes to do, but rather often involves incitement to act in ways that hold some pleasure for the actor at the same time that they secure her subordination. Foucault claims that "We have been engaged for centuries in a type of society in which the juridical is increasingly incapable of coding power, of serving as its system of representation. . . [but it] is this juridical representation that is still at work in recent analyses concerning the relationships of power to sex."[7] He argues for an alternative analytics of power, a strategic model rather than a juridical one, in which power is seen not as emanating from a central point, but rather as being produced by local and unstable relationships. These relationships far exceed legal, juridical ones, and in his account include medical, psychiatric, pedagogical, and family relationships. Power is not something that exists elsewhere and is imposed upon us from without; rather, it comes into being from moment to moment in our daily lives.[8]

In addition to his focus on the location of power within a wide range of relationships, Foucault's strategic model of power is also concerned with the mechanisms by which power makes itself felt and reproduces itself within these relationships and others. Foucault's discussion of the mechanisms of power, how power and pleasure enhance and reinforce one another, revolves specifically around what he calls the "deployment of sexuality," i.e., the way that sexuality works as a "relay" through which both power and pleasure increase their magnitude and reach. For Foucault, the primary mechanism by which the mutual enhancement of power and pleasure takes place is the transformation of desire into discourse through the imperative of the confession—the incitement to speak about sex and desire, and to submit one's desires to the scrutiny of ever-more intricate discourses concerned with the meanings about the self that such desires ostensibly reveal. The confession, Foucault says, is itself pleasurable in a way; it also creates more and more sites at which both power and pleasure can operate. This transformation of desire into discourse is a *social*, as opposed to a *natural*, act; moreover, its success typically requires the participation of the subject. Foucault argues that this participation takes the form of confession to an authority, be it a religious, family, pedagogical, medical, or psychiatric authority. (We could expand this list of authorities to include the informal narratives of "locker room talk," those fictions against which men—and women?—measure their sexual adequacy; the ubiquitous "quizzes" in popular teen and women's magazines that claim to reveal sexual truths via responses to multiple choice questions; and so on.)

Foucault's larger point about sexuality is that it is socially constructed: children's masturbation, for example, becomes a "problem" only as the result of a social process by which certain practices are isolated, defined, and problematized, and remedies are prescribed. Likewise, a class of "perverts" known as homosexuals arises through the same sort of social process. This process of the social construction of (and intervention into) sexuality is enmeshed in power and domination. Yet power and domination cannot simply be contrasted to, and resisted by, either persisting in problematized behavior (since power's increase of itself relies on such persistence); or emphasizing pleasure (because subordination and pleasure are so often intertwined as well).

Though Foucault's concern is to critique theories of sexuality that subscribe to the juridical model of power, his strategic model of power is also useful in examining theories of hierarchies based on gender, race, class, ethnicity, and so on.[9] Indeed, many feminists explicitly employ his critiques in their work. By examining how power and domination work in their own lives, many other feminist authors have arrived at conclusions similar to Foucault's, without necessarily coming into contact with his works and ideas. This is the case with the autotheoretical texts, insofar as they focus on power's multiple workings at the local level. A reading either of Foucault, or of feminists drawing on Foucault's insights, or even of radical feminist theories of sexuality, beauty, or language,[10] makes clear that the juridical model of power and domination is inadequate in explaining power, domination, and resistance in the lives of members of marginalized groups.

Sandra Lee Bartky

Bartky appropriates Foucault's analysis (in *Discipline and Punish*) of the production of docile bodies to investigate the disciplining of women's bodies. Though Bartky criticizes Foucault for being "blind to those disciplines that produce a modality of embodiment that is peculiarly feminine,"[11] she takes up his focus on disciplinary practices directed at the body to investigate the production of feminine bodies, and to "probe the effects of the imposition of such discipline on female identity and subjectivity."[12] This project maintains Foucault's phenomenological approach and applies it to practices directed specifically toward women while focusing less than Foucault does on historical context.

Bartky's discussion is seriously limited by the fact that it centers around only the most common, hegemonic constructions of femininity operating within white, affluent, U.S. culture. Within these confines, though, her analysis is a good example of the type of feminist inquiry into power that postmodern insights facilitate. Bartky reports such precise and relentless prescriptions for women's bodily control as the injunction to avoid expression of strong emotions, because "an expressive face creases more readily than an inexpressive one"[13]; and women's magazine articles on how to get in and out of cars in such a way as to appear graceful and modest while not missing the opportunity "for a certain display of leg."[14] She also draws on empirical information to illustrate the production of differences between men's and women's bodily experience—for example, differences in touching and movement that mark women's inferior status in social and workplace situations.[15]

Based on these and other observations about the disciplining of women's bodies—their hair, skin, weight, shape, diets and exercise programs, posture, movement, and gaze—Bartky concludes that the disciplinarian enforcing these practices and standards is "everyone and yet no one in particular." She seeks to expand our understanding of power's locus beyond even what Foucault proposes, arguing that understanding how power can be institutionally *unbound*, as well as institutionally bound, is crucial to understanding the subordination of women:

> The absence of a formal institutional structure and of authorities invested with the power to carry out institutional directives creates the impression that the production of femininity is either entirely voluntary or natural.[16]

The practices to which women are subject and which produce feminine bodily experience profess, Bartky argues, an aim and nature that is radically distinct from their actual, covert effects. The lack of identifiable agents of enforcement thus masks the fact that injunctions to "be feminine" serve the interests of female subordination.[17]

Bartky, like Foucault, explains the tenacity of these types of domination in terms of the construction of subjectivity and identity, such that the targets of disciplinary practices receive pleasure from complying with them. Women gain a sense of mastery and security when they prove themselves able to achieve prescribed standards of femininity. It is this combination of the form of power—cultural dictates, as opposed to legal ones—and the incentives for subjects to participate in their own subjection, that renders insufficient (though not extraneous) resistance that takes the form of legal challenges to centralized authorities. Different strategies of resistance, both individual and collective, and different constructions of the subject, are necessary to bring about fundamental social change.

Lukes's and Gaventa's discussions of power (examined in chapter 5) illuminate the inadequacy of standard models of power employed in political science research. Foucault, Bartky, and others go even further than Lukes in their discussions of power to address "normalizing" cultural dictates that are perpetuated through a number of institutions and less concrete "relay points," yet have no discernible origin. Common to both Lukes's model of power and postmodern thinkers' focus on discourse, however, is a conviction about the limitations of liberal institutions of government to ameliorate a wide range of social problems.

Identity and the Subject

Early Feminist Analyses: The "Universal" Female Subject

Feminism has consistently challenged the central position in liberalism of the white bourgeois male subject. Insofar as these feminist challenges accept uncritically the notion of a coherent subject, and the similarity of individual subjects to each other, however, they have sought to displace the male subject with a female one. (The feminist activities with which the women's movement studies are concerned are prime examples of this challenge.) Thus, for example, some strains of feminist discourse throughout the first fifteen years of the contemporary women's movement, and still to some degree today, have sought to articulate "women's socialization" and "women's experience," and to identify "women's issues," in terms that would be universal to all women.

Early feminist strategies initially responded to the ostensibly "universal" subject (that was, in reality, based on a male model) by constructing a supposedly universal female subject. This subject was constructed to represent experiences, desires, and political interests that some women saw as being common to all women. (Chapter 4's discussion of the women's movement studies illustrates how tenacious and problematic this notion of a universal female subject and a unified set of women's concerns can be.) By definition, feminism is a political movement advanced on behalf of "women." Who "women" are, and what constitute "women's interests," however, has been the subject of controversy since the movement emerged. Some women—typically those who found themselves on the "wrong side" of racial, sexual, class, ethnic and other social divisions—challenged the "universal" female subject of earlier feminist formulations as representative of only a small, relatively privileged sector of the female population.

Initially, these challenges to a singular privileged female subject took the form of articulating multiple—yet still ostensibly unified—female subjects. One classic example is the Radicalesbians' 1970 construction of the lesbian figure:

> What is a lesbian? A lesbian is the rage of all women condensed to the point of explosion. She is the woman who, often beginning at an extremely early age, acts in accordance with her inner compulsion to be a more complete and freer human being than her society—perhaps then, but certainly later—cares to allow her. These needs and actions, over a period of years, bring her into painful conflict with people, situations, the accepted ways of thinking, feeling and behaving, until she is in a state of war with everything around her, and usually with herself.[18]

175

These formulations had the important effect within the women's movement of unsettling accepted constructions of "women" and "feminism," and underscoring the presence and contributions of, for example, lesbians and women of color in the women's movement. They also allowed feminists to describe and analyze certain experiences in ways that have proven extremely insightful, if incomplete and in other ways problematic. However, like the exclusionary feminist constructions they sought to challenge, these formulations retained the impulse to define a stable subject position to represent all members of a certain category. Insofar as they joined the debate on the given terms that the goal was to identify what being a woman, a lesbian, a woman of color was "really" about, feminists found themselves competing in an impossible contest to produce a figure whose identity and experience could represent all women, or, alternatively, those women whose ultimate marginality gave them the clearest perspective from which to build a feminist agenda.

Each archetype ("the" lesbian, "the" working-class woman, etc.) was assumed to carry a unified set of experiences and a cohesive political analysis and agenda for change. This was based on several assumptions, including the assumption that women with similar experiences will have similar identities and vice versa; the assumption that women's experiences and identities bear a direct, knowable, and definable relation to their political postures; and the assumption that, therefore, women need only find other women like them and join with them to pursue their (inevitably) common goals. Related to this notion is the idea that certain women, by virtue of having identities or experiences that are particularly marginal in relation to hegemonic constructions of women and femininity, embody the "most radical" subject position and evince the most subversive politics.[19]

Margaret Small exemplifies this notion in her claim that

> Lesbians are objectively outside of the reality which heterosexual ideology explains. Therefore, they have the potential for developing an alternative ideology, not limited by heterosexuality.[20]

In "A Black Feminist Statement," The Combahee River Collective echoes this conception of the relationship between identity/subject position and politics:

> We realize that the only people who care enough about [Black women] to work consistently for our liberation is us. . . . This focusing on our own oppression is embodied in the concept of identity politics. We believe that the most profound and potentially the most radical politics come directly out of our own identity, as opposed to working to end somebody else's oppression.[21]

They conclude:

> In her introduction to *Sisterhood is Powerful*, Robin Morgan writes: "I haven't the faintest notion what possible revolutionary role white het-erosexual men could fulfill, since they are the very embodiment of re-actionary-vested-interest-power."
>
>   As Black feminists and lesbians we know that we have a very definite revolutionary task to perform and we are ready for the lifetime of work and struggle before us.[22]

In these analyses, identity and subject position (one's position within the overall social structure) are one and the same; moreover, they determine one's politics. The Collective's important point that no movement to date has made central the liberation of black women is thus coupled with the assertion that none will, save one comprised of black women. The effect of this statement, then, is paradoxical: on the one hand, it calls attention to the continuing marginalization of black women in progressive move-ments for social change; on the other hand, it suggests that such margin-alization is inevitable, and thus exempts progressive movements (other than those in which black women are central) from responsibility for combatting such marginalization.

Postmodern feminist theories of identity and of its relation to the po-litical follow—and respond to—these earlier formulations of the relation-ship between identity, subjectivity, and power. They propose a different conception of subjectivity than that which dominates the universalizing discourses of both liberal feminism and these early analyses.

Postmodern Feminist Theories of Subjectivity and Identity

Postmodern feminist theories generally argue that we do not create freely—based on individual, unhindered choice—the language through which we construct and understand our circumstances and our options for altering them. Rather, as subjects we are the sites of competing discourses that carry with them various and often contradictory possibilities for ac-tion. Chris Weedon[23] distinguishes this poststructuralist understanding of subjectivity from a liberal humanist one. The latter, she says, assumes that individuals choose freely how to live, based on their individual conscious-nesses (from which their knowledge of themselves and of the world de-rives). In contrast, poststructuralism holds that knowledge is constructed discursively. In any given situation, multiple discourses operate—and often compete—to provide subjects with an understanding of their situations and options for action. For example, a teenager contemplating her sexual desire for a female friend may find herself caught between discourses that construct that desire variously as a sin, a "phase," something to be embarrassed about, something to celebrate, something that will lead her to engage in illegal behavior, and so on. Individual subjectivity—the teenager's understanding of her situation, the meanings she assigns to her desire, and the actions she sees as being available to her—can be seen as a product of the competition between these various discourses. This competition will yield different results at different moments, depending upon the teenager's access to various discourses, and on the relative strength of these discourses within the overall array of discourses surrounding her.

Of course, the discourses to which we are subject, the options to which we have access, are grounded in the historical and political circumstances in which we find ourselves. To talk of women's identities and agency as if they are all constructed by the same constellation of discourses, emerging from some common experience associated with femaleness, is to ignore the variety of material circumstances and discursive incitements facing women in diverse situations. Similarly, to talk of any one woman's identity or affiliations as if they were fixed and complete is to ignore the process by which particular aspects of an individual's identity are animated by various discourses and potential subjectivities as the individual moves through her life, from circumstance to circumstance.

Chandra Talpade Mohanty writes of this phenomenon, and of the historical and political necessity of constructing women's identities and affiliations as partial, provisional, and fluid. Women's contextual affiliations—along lines of gender or sexuality, with communities of color, as immigrants, and so forth—create what Mohanty refers to as a politics of location and the "temporality of struggle." Locating herself in relation to these concepts, Mohanty writes:

> In this country I am, for instance, subject to a number of legal/political definitions: "third-world," "immigrant," "post-colonial." These definitions, while in no way comprehensive, do trace an analytic and political space from which I can insist on a temporality of struggle. Movement *between* cultures, languages, and complex configurations of meaning and power have always been the territory of the colonized.[24]

Mohanty likens her process of moving between cultures, languages, and circumstances to what Caren Kaplan calls "a continual reterritorialization, with the proviso that one moves on." As one moves on from one situation to another, one's affiliations are engaged or disengaged—based on the varied components of one's identity, such as "third-world," "immigrant," "white," or "lesbian"—depending upon the exigencies of the new situation.

In an article Mohanty co-authored with Biddy Martin, the authors explore the contextual nature of identity and subjectivity, and their relation to political alliances, in Minnie Bruce Pratt's "Identity: Skin Blood Heart."[25] Pratt's discussion of her own relationship, as a white, Southern, Christian-raised lesbian, to the forces of racism and anti-Semitism centers on the complex workings of identity and power; she illustrates the fact that one's status as "victim" or "perpetrator" is never seamless or secure. As a result, Martin and Mohanty argue, through Pratt's essay,

> "The system" [of dominative power] is revealed to be not one but multiple, overlapping, intersecting systems or relations that are historically constructed and recreated through everyday practices and interactions, and that implicate the individual in contradictory ways.[26]

This view of power is consistent with Weedon's argument that the discourses (and the possibilities for subjectivity they offer) to which individuals are subject often work in competition with each other.

The results of the competition among available discourses are, Martin and Mohanty argue, often contradictory, leading subjects to act in ways that contrast with the liberal notion of individuals acting freely and consistently. An excellent discussion of this phenomenon is provided by Frigga Haug and the other members of a socialist feminist collective based in Hamburg and West Berlin.[27] The collective's project is to analyze the ways in which sexuality gets constructed through socialization processes. Their aim is to undertake a "historical study of the constructed nature of feminine sexuality"[28]; their focus is the intersection of the internalization of oppressive standards with the pleasure inherent in succeeding in one's efforts to attain those standards. The collective members developed their theories through what they call "memory work": that is, they individually and collectively wrote, analyzed, and rewrote stories about events in their own lives that had to do with the sexualization of their bodies. They chose this method of analysis in order to learn "how individuals make certain modes of behaviour their own, how they learn to develop one particular set of needs as opposed to certain others. . . ."[29]

Through this method, the collective develops an argument that has important implications for feminist theories of women's subjectivity: rather than accepting a passive-subjugated/active-liberated dichotomy, the collective members argue that what often looks like liberation, because it involves conscious choice, initiative, and agency on the woman's part, is actually part of the process by which women's subordination is secured. Women

know from their experience that *skill* is involved in conforming to prevailing rules and orderings. Among other things, we take pleasure in acquiring and endorsing the requisite skills. . . . The subjective feelings of
happiness and satisfaction accompanying our manipulation of systems
of rules are thus more than an illusion, a product of the "imagination"
of individual women; they are a practice through which both sexual ordering, and the oppression within it, are reproduced.[30]

Moreover,

the competence demanded of women in the observance of rules is so
elaborate that the effort and pleasure involved in attaining it conceals
the subordinating character of the process whereby women make
themselves "slavegirls."[31]

The collective thus adds to other feminist analyses of internalized oppression, moving the debate on from the dichotomous positions of, on the
one hand, woman as passive victim of oppressive standards, mired in false
consciousness; or, on the other, woman as active and therefore freely
choosing and liberated. The collective's analysis also constitutes a rejoin-
der to those who would argue that women who actively participate in
their own subjugation have chosen a masochistic path freely.

These passages begin to elucidate the contradictory pressures on
women, the differing and contesting requirements involved in the construction of femininity, and the latitude for acting within or against the
standards associated with femininity. Moreover, they illustrate the complex relations between pleasure, domination, and subjectivity, and the role
of discourse in all of these, that postmodern theories articulate.

Identity Theory, Autobiography, and the Women's Movement

Elsewhere in this book, I have made the case for the importance of autotheoretical texts to the women's movement and to scholars studying that
movement. But mine is not the first work to do so: there is a growing body
of literature that focuses on women's autobiography, much of it from the
perspective of the questions raised by postmodern theories. This literature,
which has been crucial to my own thinking about autotheoretical works,
is likewise important for social scientists who seek to understand the way
feminism has approached identity and subjectivity as political matters. This
literature on women's autobiography acknowledges the central role in the
women's movement of autobiographical narratives, and explores the polit-

ical meanings of these constructions of the self. It is distinct from the theoretical works discussed above: those works examine identity and its relation to social structures in general and often abstract terms, while the growing body of "identity theory" is grounded in the very autobiographical articulations that are emerging from the women's movement.

The varied works within this literature on identity raise questions about how to read and interpret personal narratives at a variety of levels of nuance and complexity; and what disciplinary and other boundaries keep scholars from looking at personal narrative in our work. The issues this literature raises that are the most relevant for this study have to do with the reader's relationship to the text, and with the political uses of autotheoretical work. Regarding the first issue—concerning the relationship of the reader to the text, whether the text facilitates or disrupts the reader's identification with the narrator/author, and with what political implications—Nancy K. Miller suggests that autobiography need not posit a "universal" experience. However, she also suggests that for her, the power of autobiography lies in its capacity to evoke the reader's identification with the narrator.[32] Joanne Braxton, even more than Miller, insists on autobiography as the medium through which commonality—in the case of the texts she looks at, the "commonality of the black woman's experience"[33]—is expressed through similar "motifs, images, archetypes, uses of language, and patterns of narrative movement."[34]

These works reflect an "identity politics" approach to women's narrative—one that echoes the rhetorical moves of such movement manifestos as The Combahee River Collective's "A Black Feminist Statement" and the Radicalesbians' "woman-identified woman." Such approaches should not simply be dismissed as reductive. As the Personal Narratives Group editorial collective points out, to the degree that autobiographical texts do evoke identification, they can be useful tools for social change:

> Even in our world of printed facts and impersonal mass media, we consciously and unconsciously absorb knowledge of the world and how it works through exchanges of life stories. We constantly test reality against such stories, asserting and modifying our own perceptions in light of them. The significance of these exchanges for women in clarifying social realities and challenging hegemonic oppression has often been profound. Contemporary political movements have capitalized on life stories in their efforts to transform society and women within it. In the course of the Chinese Revolution, women came together to "speak bitterness," recounting lives of pain and persecution at hands of patriarchal families. In the contemporary Western feminist movement, consciousness-raising groups allowed women to tell each other about their experiences, doubts, and anger—without fear of judgment or punish-

ment. . . . These exchanges and the knowledge they impart about emotional and physical well-being, communal values, aspirations, or power become part of our reality. They are as true as our lives.[35]

In contrast, some other works on women's autobiography approach it from a set of assumptions, grounded in postmodern and poststructuralist theory, about the ambiguity and multiplicity of meanings to be found in personal narrative. Mohanty and Martin's piece on Pratt's essay, "Identity," discussed above, is one example. Martin's work on lesbian autobiographies is another: Martin observes that, in the writing of Cherrié Moraga and other contributors to *This Bridge Called My Back,*

> There is no attempt to specify the relations between gender, sexuality, race and ethnicity in the abstract; Moraga and other contributors instead address the question of relations and priorities by examining how they intersect at historically specific sites.[36]

Here, Martin draws attention to the autotheoretical texts' illumination of the provisional, partial, and shifting nature of identity and political strategy, arguing that "such attention to detail, rather than to coherent life history, succeeds in illuminating discontinuties between past and present" which in turn expands the possibility for future change.[37]

Diana Velez also brings a postmodern skepticism about identification to her reading of autotheoretical works. Specifically with regard to "heteroglossia" or the mixing of languages (e.g., English and Spanish) in some of these texts, Velez argues that the effect—often intentional, and at any rate politically important—is to disrupt some readers' identification with a text, to underscore *performatively* differences an author may be working to articulate *thematically.*[38]

The other notable achivement of this work on identity is its examination of the uses to which the women's movement has put women's autobiographical accounts. This literature generally posits two chief effects of these accounts. First, they illuminate the specifics of domination as it operates in the quotidian realm of women's lives:

> Personal narratives of nondominant social groups . . . are often particularly effective sources of counterhegemonic insight because they expose the viewpoint embedded in dominant ideology as particularist rather than universal . . .[39]

Second, they provide models of resistance, revealing "the reality of a life that defies or contradicts the rules." In this way, the authors argue,

"Women's personal narratives can thus often reveal the rules of male domination even as they record rebellion against them."[40]

The autotheoretical texts, then, are important sources for social scientists seeking to understand women's domination and resistance; and this body of theoretical work on identity, and specifically on the construction of identity through autotheoretical writing, can help researchers to grasp the nuances embedded in the texts, as well as to look below their surfaces. These and other discussions of what feminist autotheoretical texts, as well as to look below their surfaces. These and other discussions of what feminist autotheoretical texts reveal about the construction of identity and imply for a poloitics of difference and coalition can be profoundly useful to social scientists who seek to understand how the feminist movement as a whole has conceived of these issues and integrated them into feminist practice.

Universality, Specificity, and Movement Unity

Postmodernism's critique of the notion of universality furnishes the insight that feminism operates on behalf of women, but cannot be said to do so as long as it responds to the supposedly "universal" male subject of liberalism by attempting to establish a counterpart, "universal" female subject. Postmodern theory asserts a decentered subject—that is, multiple subjects, all articulating partial (and shifting) experiences and situations, none representing all or being the subject of universal truths. The assertion of a coherent group of subjects—"women"—on whose behalf feminist agendas can be pursued results inevitably in exclusion. While efforts finally to capture all women's differences in identity, experience, and situation must ultimately fail, they nonetheless suggest a coherence among women even as they fail in securing that coherence. For Judith Butler,[41] this inevitable open-endedness need not be cause for worry, but rather can be seen as productive. Postmodern feminism recognizes the inevitable incompleteness of any effort to include all women within a certain discourse. When Butler says that the incompleteness of "women" in feminist discourse and politics is not cause for alarm, it is because she expects that agendas will be formulated by coalitions and will be fluid and responsive to people and political issues not anticipated at the outset.

At the same time, there is a logic to the repeated, often indirect assertions of "women" as a category that makes sense for feminism—including for postmodern feminist theory—even as those making the assertions seem to be arguing more directly for a lack of coherence of the category. This logic has to do with the need to illuminate the deep, cross-cultural, and transhistorical embeddedness of sexism, even while attending to its different manifestations and mechanisms over space and time. It also has to do with the fact that women are constituted as a category in many arenas (including legal ones), even if women would constitute themselves differently, and even as contradictions abound in the ways that legal and other institutions categorize women.

Feminist Critiques of the Postmodern Construction of the Subject

The premise of postmodern feminist theory—that women do and do not constitute a group—is regarded with suspicion by some feminists who believe that decentering the subject, throwing open the question "who is woman?" and recognizing the impossibility of a comprehensive answer, can only signal the demise of feminism as a movement that seeks social change on behalf of women.

Some feminists are critical of postmodern constructions of the subject, and they call for adhering to a politics based on universalizing constructions of "women." One such critic of feminist appropriations of postmodern insights is Nancy Hartsock:

> Somehow it seems highly suspicious that it is at the precise moment when so many groups have been engaged in "nationalisms" which involve so many redefinitions of marginalized Others that suspicions emerge about the nature of the "subject," about the possibilities for a general theory which can describe the world, about historical "progress." Why is it that just at the moment when so many of us who have been silenced begin to demand the right to name ourselves, to act as subjects rather than objects of history, that just then the concept of subjecthood becomes problematic?[42]

Christine Di Stefano shares Hartsock's reservations about postmodernism and its usefulness for feminists, arguing that a feminist appropriation of postmodernism

> would make any semblance of a feminist politics impossible. To the extent that feminist politics is bound up with a specific constituency or subject, namely, women, the postmodernist prohibition against subject-centered inquiry and theory undermines the legitimacy of a broad-based organized movement dedicated to articulating and implementing the goals of such a constituency.[43]

The alternative offered by advocates of a feminist appropriation of postmodern theory—coalition politics based on shared opposition to domination—is unlikely to be tenable, Di Stefano argues. Writing of coalition politics, or political solidarities based on shared opposition, she argues:

> Another problem is that "robust" solidarities of opposition (rather than of shared identity) may be psychologically and politically unreliable, unable to generate sufficient attachment and motivation on the part of potential activists.[44]

Di Stefano locates the epistemological appeal of the postmodern decentering of knowledge in its distinctiveness from epistemologies that have been bound up in domination. While this may be the source of postmodernism's appeal for some, its decentering of knowledge and its fracturing of the subject is not simply a new theoretical trend, a philosophical effort to think in ways that escape age-old relations of domination. Rather, these theoretical gestures reflect emerging articulations by marginalized "others" of their lived experience of fractured identities and their relation to domination and resistance.

It is no accident that some feminist theorists who find postmodern insights about identity and resistance persuasive have turned their attention to the political reflections of Pratt, Moraga, Audre Lorde, and other authors of autotheoretical writings.[45] In their article on Pratt's essay and the construction of identity, Martin and Mohanty argue that

> The exposure of the arbitrariness and the instability of positions within systems of oppression evidences a conception of power that refuses totalizations, and can therefore account for the possibility of resistance.[46]

This formulation suggests a potential for certain kinds of resistance that is closed down by the structuralist and totalizing impulses in both the women's movement studies and rejections (like Hartsock's and Di Stefano's) of the postmodern feminist decentering of the subject. This potential for resistance derives from the fact that, if one's position within the social structure is constructed, unstable, and partial, one retains some degree of latitude and mobility in one's position and actions. And if, as Judith Butler argues, change comes out of variations on the repetitions that constitute gender (or other) identities, then the concept of latitude with respect to one's subjectivity is crucial for theorizing resistance.

Di Stefano's objection that coalition politics may be unreliable implies that the identity politics (cohesive, concerted political action based on stable, shared identities) it seeks to supplant is stable. It seems clear, though, that one reason postmodern theory has emerged at all is that such notions of shared identities, and the solidarity they are supposed to engender, are breaking down as politics based solely on identity breaks down. As Linda

J. Nicholson and Nancy Fraser write, ". . . the practice of feminist politics
in the 1980s has generated a new set of pressures which have worked
against metanarratives."[47] Postmodern epistemologies of fractured identities surely reflect the schisms plaguing social movements whose demands
for cohesion on the basis of identity and experience conflict with their
members' understandings of their lived experiences, the relationship between their identities and politics, and the lack of coherence in each.

What can we make of this debate? For one thing, the arguments advanced by critics of postmodernism echo those made in the women's
movement studies in accordance with liberal assumptions about what
politics consists of, and what success means for a social movement.

In this sense, criticisms against postmodernism launched by Hartsock, Di Stefano, and others can be seen as injunctions for feminism to
conform to the course laid out by other social movements. This is a
course from which feminism has already diverged, and, according to Butler (and others), with good reason. Both the implicit ideals constructed by
the women's movement studies and the more direct injunctions to political conformity issued by critics of feminist appropriations of postmodern
theory reinforce as normative ideals more traditional, policy-focused
forms of feminist activity directed at centralized authorities. These ideals
and injunctions also cut against the grain of important developments
within the women's movement. These developments include the greater
emphasis on coalition, the proliferation of groups that constitute themselves around multiple identities and combine a new understanding of the
political nature of identity and subjectivity with coalition politics.

Resistance

Postmodernism and Individual Resistance: Bartky, Butler, and "Anonymous"

Given their view of power as dispersed throughout society, exercised and
resisted at innumerable local points, postmodern theories generally call
into question a political strategy based primarily on securing rights for
those who lack them. Bartky articulates the inadequacy of prevailing,
rights-based forms of resistance:

> Liberals call for equal rights for women, traditional Marxists for the entry
> of women into production on an equal footing with men, the socializa-
> tion of housework, and proletarian revolution; neither calls for the de-
> construction of the categories of masculinity and femininity. . . .
> Femininity as a certain "style of the flesh" will have to be surpassed in the

direction of something quite different—not masculinity, which is in many ways only its mirror opposite, but a radical and as yet unimagined transformation of the female body.[48]

Bartky imagines this "transformation of the female body" to be a matter of nonparticipation in the aesthetic standards and disciplinary practices she critiques. Pick up the lipstick, she warns, and you put down the revolution. In this moment of trying to conceptualize resistance, Bartky lets go of her earlier, more complex (and more "postmodern") observations regarding the pleasure and sense of identity some women gain from striving to achieve feminine ideals: "The harshness of a regimen alone does not guarantee its rejection, for hardships can be endured if they are thought to be necessary or inevitable."[49] Bartky's "just say no" strategy of resistance can be quite powerful, but its appeal may be limited for reasons she herself points out.

On both an individual and a collective basis, direct opposition is a powerful strategy. Women's nonparticipation in practices that discipline their bodies—and other practices that secure their subordination—can go a long way toward lessening the effects of those practices on their own lives and on the lives of other women for whom they provide a model of resistance to counter the ubiquitous models of compliance. But forgoing these practices can also mean denying oneself certain forms of pleasure and power; thus, there are other paths to change which we would also do well to recognize and encourage. Bartky's earlier insight about the seductiveness of disciplinary practices for their targets is important: it is unlikely that large numbers of women will easily give up habits that give them a sense of pleasure and competence.

Judith Butler calls our attention to another possibility for social change, one that is based on her argument that gender constitutes repeated performances of gendered behavior, performances that vary both between subjects and for an individual subject over time. The implication of this formulation of gender, Butler argues, is that variations on the repetitive performances that comprise gender can unsettle established gender norms. On this view, one need not necessarily put the lipstick down to subvert gender norms: alternatively, one can combine it with other behaviors—such as cross-dressing, acting or speaking in "unfeminine" ways, and so on—that upset the coherence of the performance.[50]

An example of the variation and incoherence (in terms of traditional gender performances) that Butler writes about can be found in the sartorial practices of this anonymous contributor to *OUT/LOOK: National Lesbian & Gay Quarterly*, in an article on "S/M Aesthetic":

> I am hardly ever mistaken for a man. . . . Apparently my gender as well as my sexual orientation and my sexual tastes are getting across quite

well. Even when I "femme out" in a black dress or leather bodice and skirt, I am usually with women who are identifiably butch—or I actively try to retain some item of apparel (like the motorcycle jacket) or retain some key piece of my appearance (like the short hair or weapons) that tells the straight boys the tits are not for them. . . . If we all have to *look* heterosexual to be safe on the streets, who cares how many gay rights laws are passed or how long ago they repealed the laws against sodomy?[51]

Neither Bartky's form of resistance on the one hand nor Butler's and the anonymous writer's on the other constitute, in themselves, formulae for liberation. However, they do both constitute resistance to manifestations of domination that go beyond legal and policy forms. And while the studies of the women's movement give a sense of how crucial to women's lives legal and other institutions are, and how important it is for women to seek to change them, the insights offered by Foucault, Bartky, and others underscore the importance of looking beyond electoral politics and policy outcomes to analyze ideological forms of domination and resistance.

Postmodern Feminist Theory and Collective Feminist Resistance

Critics of postmodern theory say that it has waged such a vociferous battle against coherent subjects and metanarratives that it is no longer possible to act on behalf of women, nor to illuminate the major social divisions with which feminism is concerned. Certainly, some incarnations of postmodern theory could be seen to subvert not only totalizing conceptions of the category "women," but radical politics as well. On the other hand, there is no need to accept this form of postmodern theory as the only legitimate one. Linda Nicholson and Nancy Fraser's notion of a qualified postmodernism offers an approach to postmodern theory's insights other than a wholesale acceptance of its most far-reaching—and, for feminism, potentially undermining—claims. Fraser and Nicholson argue that postmodern feminist theory can retain "large historical narratives [and] analyses of societal macrostructures" such as sexism. At the same time, postmodern feminist theory must be nonuniversalist: to the extent that it is cross-cultural, it must be comparative, with an agenda of illuminating contrasts rather than constructing "covering laws." Moreover, postmodern feminist theory must

> tailor its methods and categories to the specific task at hand, using multiple categories when appropriate and forswearing the metaphysical comfort of a single feminist method or feminist epistemology.[52]

Like Butler, Fraser and Nicholson see feminist practice as "increasingly a matter of alliances rather than one of unity around a universally shared interest or identity."[53] Unlike Di Stefano and Hartsock, they see this state of affairs not as something to be argued for or against, but rather as a social and political reality to be reckoned with.

Whereas Di Stefano assumes that identity politics is stable and reliable, Butler questions whether this can ever be the case, and whether an insistence on unity of identities or experience is necessary for feminist politics or inimical to it. In taking issue with feminism's adherence to liberal models of subjectivity, Butler writes, "By conforming to a requirement of representational politics that feminism articulate a stable subject, feminism thus opens itself to charges of gross misrepresentation."[54] Butler points out that feminism is a political movement that is assumed to act on behalf of a category of subjects, "women." Yet, she argues, it is less and less clear who these women are, and efforts to articulate the privileged subject of feminism inevitably exclude. She writes of the "embarrassed *et cetera*"[55] (present also in this book) that feminists append to lists of women's differences, an *et cetera* that signifies the "illimitable process of signification," the never-finished task of articulating women's differences from each other, the conditions structuring women's identities and lives, and categories of women that hold some political salience. This *et cetera*, she argues, underscores the impossibility of ever completing the list, of ever capturing women's diversity once and for all. Butler concludes that this is a "problem" for feminism only as long as feminists continue to expect and assume some essential truth about women, an articulable sameness that binds all women together and can thus function as the foundation for feminism.

Butler argues that "the reconceptualization of identity as an *effect*, that is, as *produced* or *generated*, opens up possibilities of 'agency' that are insidiously foreclosed by positions that take identity categories as foundational and fixed."[56] This is because, she says, agency "is to be located within the possibility of variation on"[57] the regulated process of repetitions that generate the subject. That is, identity is not given, but rather is constructed through repetitions that may have many variations; therefore, it will be impossible finally to list all of the possible identities that can describe "women." Moreover, change can be made not through unearthing a repressed essence, nor through creating something entirely new and unconnected to that which preceded it, but rather through variations in the regulated repetitions that structure our lives. Thus, the impossibility of ever completing the list and displacing the *et cetera* can be seen as indicating not feminism's "incompleteness," but rather its potential for an openness and fluidity necessary to match the fluidity of subjectivity. Feminism is called upon not to anticipate, account for, and incorporate all differences, but rather to respond to variations in the construction of identities as well as to encourage such variations to move in feminist directions.

As in Nicholson and Fraser's argument, the political implications of this construction of women's subjectivity point to a new kind of coalition politics, whose terms may not be clear at the outset. Butler writes,

> The insistence in advance on coalitional "unity" as a goal assumes that solidarity, whatever its price, is a prerequisite for political action. But what sort of politics demands that kind of advance purchase on unity? Perhaps a coalition needs to acknowledge its contradictions and take action with those contradictions intact. Perhaps also part of what dialogic understanding entails is the acceptance of divergence, breakage, splinter, and fragmentation as part of the often tortuous process of democratization. The very notion of "dialogue" is culturally specific and historically bound, and while one speaker may feel secure that a conversation is happening, another may be sure it is not. . . . Is the premature insistence on the goal of unity precisely the cause of an ever more bitter fragmentation among the ranks?[58]

The contributions of postmodern theories of subjectivity have to do with their recognition of the possibilities for identity's fluidity, as well as its continual construction in the nexus of cross-cutting discourses (and discursive exercises of power). These points are particularly important to an understanding of how consciousness is transformed and new options for action become available to a given subject. Postmodern theories of subjectivity can enable a richer understanding of the process by which subjects come to be mobilized on behalf of feminist change—richer, that is, than an understanding that posits static subjects whose identities either are or are not engaged by a given movement or discourse, rather than constructed by it.[59]

On the question of feminist resistance, then, these feminist theorists suggest that the unity required for collective political action can be premised on a collective recognition of the inevitable limitations, and thus necessary fluidity, of any political analysis or agenda for action—rather than being premised on securing uniformity of group members' identities or perspectives, which can only take place through coercive means. This approach to difference finds its movement counterpart in Moraga's and Pratt's work, and other feminist autotheoretical texts and the debates they reflect, as well as in direct action activism aimed at changing the world by changing the way people think.

Social Science Methodology　7

Far from encouraging our ability to think creatively about discovering the truths in personal narratives, our academic disciplines have more often discouraged us from taking people's life stories seriously. Disciplines have mainly done this by elevating some kinds of truth—the kinds that conform to established criteria of validity—over others. Generalizations based on these elevated Truths become norms which are rarely challenged for their failure to consider or explain exceptions. This elevation and generalization serve to control: control data, control irregularities of human experiences, and, ultimately, control what constitutes knowledge. Considered in these terms, the truths in personal narratives cannot stand the tests to which they are subjected, i.e., the tests of verifiability, reliability, facticity, or representativeness. Using such a limited definition of Truth admits only one standard at a time for the perception and interpretation of a small segment of a complex reality. While such a conception may be "safe" in its claim to meet any challenge to its scientific validity, it inevitably excludes certain experiences that require understanding. As appealing as it may be to some to carry out this Cartesian division of the world into discrete and knowable parts, the cost is high. It is devastating for those whose experience, history, and perceptions—whose truths—are obliterated.

—Personal Narratives Group

This book has argued that social movement studies in general, and studies of the contemporary U.S. women's movement in particular, need to revise and expand their theories of power; and that, concomitantly, they need to consider methodologies and bodies of knowledge not typically used in social science. Chapter 6 offers a detailed discussion of how social science might look at power differently, while chapters 2 and 3 look at "data" on activism that social scientists might use in studying the women's movement and feminist social change. In chapter 6, I discuss postmodern theory's approaches to power and argue for social science to adopt such theories so as to broaden the scope of what counts as "social/political." Here I turn my attention to the status of "science" in social science.

Social scientists have long been reevaluating the hold that positivism once had on their disciplines, acknowledging the status and impact of values on social science. This process has sometimes led social scientists to search for ways to "correct" for values that they identify as entering into a body of research. Operating within this strategy, some feminist social scientists have adjusted for androcentrism by changing their subject of inquiry—looking at public policy specifically designed to meet women's needs, for example, or examining a whole set of factors related to women's experience in order to gauge women's social and political position (such as Klein's examination of fertility and divorce rates, labor force participation among women, and so on). Changing the subject of social science inquiry to include questions and sources of data that are immediately and specifically relevant to women has yielded a great deal of very useful empirical information about some aspects of some women's lives, and further inquiry in this direction is needed. It is also important, however, for the researchers undertaking such work to examine any claims to objectivity (or comprehensiveness) they may be tempted to make. Linda Alcoff underscores the dual necessity of social science's empirical work and its political underpinnings when she writes that the emancipatory potential of feminist social science is contingent upon the premise

> that women's liberation from her universal position of subordination is at least possible. No amount of ethical reasoning will help if this first premise is proved false. And so the impetus for a large amount of empirical research appears to be primarily and unmistakably political.[1]

Acknowledging the political importance of a specifically feminist social science calls into question claims to objectivity. It also calls into question the wisdom, and the possibility, of making objectivity a goal of social science research. That is, for feminist social scientists to take seriously the values that motivate their research entails a revision of accepted approaches to the standards of objectivity by which social science is often evaluated.

If feminist social scientists acknowledge the necessary role of values in *motivating* their projects, they will be led to acknowledge the inescapable presence of values *throughout* those projects. That is, it seems that acknowledging the necessity and legitimacy of a feminist agenda for social science would entail not a rejection of feminist social science as "biased," nor a paradoxical argument that politically-motivated research can nonetheless be "objective." Rather, it will entail the recognition that, in Alcoff's words, "values are not obstacles [to truth], but are actually constitutive of truth."[2] In this view, truth is constructed discursively; it does not exist in some pure form outside of its construction—which, of course, shifts cross-culturally and transhistorically. The implication of such a model of truth for social science is that researchers will need to examine the discourses and political agendas that motivate their projects and lead them to ask certain questions in certain ways. Social scientists will have to examine (often implicit) claims that some questions and subjects of inquiry, and some methods and types of data, are universally appropriate to social science, while others are necessarily off limits.

Alcoff raises the question of whether such a view of social science's approach to truth (i.e., that values are constitutive of truth) and thus its methodology succumbs to "radical relativism." With regard specifically to feminist social science, she argues that the status of women's experience in social science provides insights into whether or not this is the case. In my discussion of the autotheoretical texts, I make a case for how researchers can approach women's accounts of their own experiences, and their analyses of those experiences in larger political contexts, in a way that avoids the relativism of simply taking each account at face value, by consciously locating those accounts historically and politically. This methodology is consistent with a theory of power premised on the notion that subjectivity is constructed through language, and that people's identities, affiliations, and actions are therefore the products of discourses that emerge and compete at specific historical moments and social locations, in response to specific political and historical provocations. Relativism threatens our work if we embrace the anti-analytic notion that social scientists need to correct the exclusion of women from social science inquiry (or its androcentric treatment of their concerns) by embracing, uncritically, their own representations of their desires, concerns, and experiences. We can guard against this relativism by locating accounts of women's experience in the context of social relations and discursive/power struggles, and evaluating them in terms of their implications for those contexts and struggles.

This process of contextualizing and analyzing women's accounts is easier in the case of the autotheoretical texts because the authors do much of this work themselves, providing the researcher with a lot of information about the forces operating in the authors' lives. Even if she disagrees with how the author represents herself in one of these texts, the researcher has a good deal of information from which to formulate her critique. In addition, simply insofar as the texts constitute a written, extended, reflective account, the authors provide ample material from which the researcher can tease out and investigate the texts' tensions and inconspicuous meanings.

Using autotheoretical texts as data makes a place for people's understanding of their experience to enter into social science in a new way; it also enables the researcher to link individual lives to cultural ideologies and those ideologies' influence on the formation of people's subjectivity. This method is viable for some types of inquiry (into the women's movement, and/or into the impact of some feminist discourses on the lives of women from different backgrounds and positions within the social structure). However, this method also depends on people having the time, capacity, and impetus to reflect on their own lives, locate them within social discourses, and represent that process publicly for researchers to see. There are countless reasons that not many people will be moved to do this. However, it is not necessarily the case that, in order to formulate general claims, researchers would have to have access to large numbers of such accounts; general (though always provisional) claims can be made on the basis of small numbers of accounts as long as the researcher locates them within cultural narratives. Moreover, one need not rely on first-person accounts to study the construction of subjectivity, or *only* first-person accounts; one can look at dominant discourses and common actions. But all of this requires, first and foremost, an acknowledgement that social science is more social than scientific, and that educated speculation reveals at least as much as rigid empiricism does—even if we are accustomed to the illusion that empiricism alone can yield generalizable conclusions about how people act in a given situation. Rigid empiricism is a vestige of positivism, and seems more rooted in method than in the actual workings of power and human activity.

In adopting an approach that examines power relations by looking at discourses and the construction of subjects, and the methods this approach implies, social scientists will have to reconsider several of the standards and requirements by which work within their disciplines is often evaluated. Among these are: empirical measurement; proving one's argument conclusively (rather than engaging in open-ended speculation where appropriate); establishing direct cause-and-effect relationships; and separating out variables from each other, treating them one at a time.

It is important to note that some social movement theorists, and most of the authors of the women's movement studies discussed in chapter 4, recognize that there is an aspect of social movements that is difficult to measure because it has to do with what Snow and Benford refer to as "the signifying efforts of movements,"[3] what Freeman and Gelb have called "personal transformation," and what I have referred to as cultural "sea changes" and "fundamental social transformation" brought about through discursive struggle. However, the women's movement studies neglect that side of the movement, despite their momentary acknowledgment of its importance. One reason they do so is because the methods developed within social movement studies do not lend themselves to the study of discursive struggle. In order for them to look at that neglected aspect of feminist activity, researchers need to change their ideas about power to include the power of signifying. The methods must necessarily have an empirical base; however, it appears likely that the imperative to *measure* change, and, along with it, to prove direct cause-and-effect relationships, from the outset restricts the social scientist's attention to certain aspects of social relations that are quantifiable (in order to measure them) and isolable (in order to prove direct cause and effect). But many types of social transformation result from the cumulative impact of many different kinds of resistance. The differences between women's circumstances now and what they were forty years ago are the result of legal changes (which are relatively easy to measure) but also of culture-wide discursive changes that bring about (and are themselves brought about by) changes in people's subjectivity, *as well as* legal changes

Related to the difficulty of measuring certain forms of change is the way that standard definitions of what constitutes "social change" exclude some important phenomena. This is true of definitions of "collective action" as well. Researchers should look for evidence of collective action that is not visible as such when standard methodologies are employed. In chapter 1, I give the example of women leaving abusive male partners— actions which, on the surface, appear to be individual, but which can be traced to a collective shift in discourses about male violence against women, as well as the existence of institutions that provide support to women who leave abusive men. These actions, considered together, amount to collective resistance. It is collective both in terms of the large numbers of women now leaving abusive partners, and in terms of the origins of the resources, both discursive/ideological and material/institutional, that enable women to undertake this action.

Changes need to take place as well in what counts as legitimate "evidence." In looking for sources of evidence of discursive shifts, the changes that engender them, and those that result from them, researchers must continue to draw on empirical evidence, but they must expand the accepted categories of "evidence" to include phenomena that are not measurable. One way to examine feminist changes that are brought about discursively, I have argued, is to look at feminist presses and the autotheoretical texts. There are doubtless other ways as well, and certainly many of the women's movement studies incorporate some degree of attention to the unmeasurable, even if they do so within fairly standard notions of where "real" power lies.

Given that it seeks to understand large-scale change brought about by shifts in available discourses, this kind of project requires a variety of approaches to looking at language and representation. For example, researchers could examine a broad spectrum of media representations (including popular entertainment, mass visual media, as well as news media, literature and music, and language use in formal and informal settings), looking for shifts over time in how certain groups of people (e.g., African-American women), life situations (e.g., homosexuality, or single parenting), exercises of domination (e.g., rape), and resistance (e.g., women killing their abusers) are portrayed and responded to. One could set trends in media representations (which embody a variety of competing discourses) against trends in people's actual situations and trends in legal sanctions. These could be viewed in light of people's perspectives on their own options, in order to describe the discursive struggles taking place and the different factors that might influence the success of particular discourses.

In looking within social movements, a researcher could talk to long-time activists about how they perceive their goals and analyses to have shifted. In-depth interviews could yield some information about the activists' perceptions of the sources of their shifts in perspective; this information could then be coupled with that gleaned from other sources (e.g., movement publications, speeches, cultural artifacts that embody and reflect discursive struggles that define the terms of debate at a given historical moment, etc.) in order to locate the individual perspectives in context.

The ability to advance general claims is important, as I have argued in earlier chapters, and social science's goal of making supportable, general claims is crucial to understanding the workings of power and the large-scale social divisions that operate throughout society. Social scientists employ a variety of methods to ascertain the connections between individuals and overarching social forces—for example, case studies of organized groups of people (social movement organizations, for example, or other formal associations); opinion polls; and interview data. Each of these methods has its uses. Opinion polls and questionnaires, for example, reach large numbers of people (with little depth in assessing their subjectivity/beliefs/actions/desires, etc.). Interviews reach fewer people but provide greater depth in assessing their views and actions.

There are three major problems with opinion polls and interview and questionnaire data, however. First, they can miss fundamental shifts in social norms precisely because those shifts are so fundamental. That is, one of the characteristics of cultural "sea changes" is that they are often sufficiently gradual and widespread to mask themselves and go undetected by the majority of people. When they are more obvious, newer, less complete, and thus more visible, the contests between such transformative discourses and those of the status quo may be difficult for any one person to grasp, and thus are unlikely to be reflected in opinion polls, which comprise an aggregate of individual perceptions. Examining culturally-produced discourse may be a much more effective approach for illuminating shifts in public attitudes.

Second, taken alone, data from interviews and opinion polls can sacrifice the insights made available by looking at the specificity of people's experience of domination and resistance. Third, they can too easily shape respondents' questions to the researcher's agenda in ways that are not obvious in the researcher's presentation of evidence and conclusions.

Coupling interview and questionnaire data with other information about discursive competition to place that data in context (as described above) goes a long way to circumvent the first problem. Certainly a researcher could interview someone or give them a questionnaire, and collect information about what discourses they have been influenced by—what religious, ethnic, and geographical discourses, what historical moment in terms of the society's politics and popular culture. This general information could supplement specific information about the individual respondent. In other words, the researcher could obtain some information directly from interviewees, as well as from sources of influence they indicate. This would enable the researcher to do some of that work of locating a life in relation to discourses, but not to usurp that role completely from the subject. Some of the information about the discourses and ideologies that the person has been influenced by comes directly from her, but the researcher maintains control over interpreting those discourses and their effect on the respondent. There are many sorts of questions that would benefit from being researched in this manner. Such a method could be useful, for example, in determining why some women become feminists while others do not; why some women who hold feminist beliefs will not call themselves feminists; and so forth.

Though this is a more involved process, the information that it would yield and the claims that it would enable would be much better supported than those produced by simply taking interview and question-naire data alone. Conducting open-ended interviews and coupling ques-tionnaires with open-ended, follow-up interviews, also vastly enhances the value of the data they produce. (Many social scientists, of course, al-ready do this.) Opinion polls do not lend themselves either to open-ended questioning or follow-up interviews, unless undertaken with those requirements in mind. They are thus particularly susceptible to the second and third problems with these methods (to which interview and ques-tionnaire data are also susceptible). That is, in addition to the limitations on the detail and richness of the accounts these methods make available, the questions formulated by the researcher can profoundly influence the responses, both in terms of how the questions formulate an issue (and limit the available responses), and in what they convey to the respondent about the researcher's own views and agenda.

In order to address this methodological shortcoming, researchers need to breach another tradition within social science—that is, the con-vention of masking one's relation to the subject of inquiry. Just as Cher-ríe Moraga's discussion of the legend of Malinche in Mexican and Chicano culture is informed by the fact that she is Chicana, a woman, a lesbian, well-educated, and a feminist, among other things, my own read-ing of her work is informed by the fact that I am Anglo, a woman, bisex-ual, a feminist, and well-educated, among other things. It is also informed, for example, by my lack of knowledge about Christianity, so that there are, no doubt, aspects of Moraga's writing that remain obscure to me because of their implicit references to Christianity. The differences between us of race, ethnicity, sexuality, religion, and a host of other fac-tors influences my interpretation of her text. In alerting my readers to those differences, and the possible lacunae or tensions in my analysis they may produce, I may make it easier for them to discover the sources of those lacunae and tensions and assess their political implications.[4]

In other words, if social scientists were to emphasize not only the sit-uatedness (within historical and political contexts) of their subjects of study, but their own situatedness as well, they would enhance the inter-pretation of their own methods and conclusions, and facilitate the con-textualization of their own efforts. This would entail a serious commitment to the notion that values are indeed constitutive of truth, and the rejection of implicit as well as overt claims to universality or to-tality of perspective, or even to local but "neutral" perspective. This emphasis on the researcher's own situatedness will help to ameliorate some of the shortcomings particularly of interview and questionnaire data, as well as other kinds of data and analyses, all of which necessarily bear the mark—whether or not it is visible to others—of the researcher's own agenda and perspective.

I have begun here to identify some directions social science research could take to bring its methods into closer alignment with notions of power as dispersed (as well as centralized), truth as constructed, and individuals' subjectivity as central to politics and collective action. Clearly, not all social scientists accept these premises. However, if those who do accept them begin to assess their implications for research methodology, and put their conclusions into practice, the result could be the beginning of a major transformation of social science research.

Last Words/Words First   8

I came to feminist politics in the context of a (largely academic, largely white) lesbian and feminist community that was most heavily influenced by radical feminism.[1] This meant that early on, I learned to analyze women's subordination in terms of consciousness and the material aspects of psychic oppression—aspects that radical feminism emphasizes—as well as in terms of the legal, economic, and physical sanctions imposed on women by men. It also meant that I came to analyze women's oppression through a set of narratives that constructed women's experience of gendered domination as being roughly similar, regardless of differences among women of race, class, and ethnicity. The discourses around oppression based on race and class that were the most salient for me at the time posited these phenomena as "extra" forms of oppression added to—not constitutive of—the original form, sexism (which was, therefore, constructed through white and middle-class women's experiences—those groups being the least marked in hegemonic discourses on race and class). My encounters with liberal feminism reinforced an additive approach to different forms of domination.

That is, liberal feminism assumes that the composite gendered position that has emerged from discourses controlled by white, middle-class, heterosexual women is fixed and neutral. It assumes that this "neutral" gendered position—with its attendant political agenda—is a norm, onto which "deviations" from the class, race, and sexual norms embedded within it are added and must be explained—in contrast to the "neutral" position, which requires no explanation. The effect of constructing as neutral the gendered position of women who, with respect to other hier-

archies of domination (such as racial, class, and sexual ones), occupy privileged positions, is to normalize those privileged positions and exempt
them, too, from scrutiny. This is what Joan Cocks calls liberal feminism's
"near-total lack of imagination, an inability to think past every received
habit of thought and practice except one."[2] Radical feminism did the
same, frequently with the exception of sexuality—i.e., lesbian realities
were much more represented in the radical feminist discourses I encountered. However, the analyses of sexuality, and specifically of heterosexism,
which were the most salient for me and those around me tended to reduce heterosexism and homophobia to a function of sexism.

Certainly, heterosexism and homophobia are agents of sexism, but
they cannot be reduced to effects of gender domination any more than
racial, economic, or ethnic oppression can. I became aware of the limitations of radical feminist discourses on the relationships between various
forms of oppression only gradually, although there are several incidents
that stand out in my memory as moments when I consciously noticed
that my analysis was shifting. On one occasion, a friend offered me a
postcard to tape to the door of my office on campus, where I worked for
the student association at the university from which I got my bachelor's
degree. The front of the postcard carried a quote from a feminist thinker
(whose name I have long since forgotten) claiming that sexism is the root
of all other forms of oppression. I recall reading the postcard and decid-
ing not to put it on my door because I did not, any longer, believe what
it said. I remember that moment as one of disjuncture between what I
had previously internalized and what I was coming to believe. My perspective and analytical framework were shifting as a result of the new
writings being published by women of color that I, a white woman, was
reading in my Women's Studies classes; the efforts to forge a coalition between white feminists and women of color on campus of which I was a
part; and the debates emerging in the women's movement (and being
conducted through movement publications) particularly, at that moment,
on issues of anti-Semitism and racism within the movement.

On another occasion, riding the bus home, a friend, an African-
American woman, asked me why I was a feminist, and what I thought
feminism was. As I tried to explain to her what I believed in, awkwardly
articulating various pieces of an analytic framework that addressed a variety of forms of oppression, I found myself becoming confused about why
I called what I believed in "feminism." Nearing my stop, and noting the
puzzlement on her face, I concluded that perhaps "feminism" was an in-
appropriate term, since I was interested in much more than the forms of
oppression that constituted the narratives of "women's experience" that
I had internalized (and which, as I have noted above, tended to separate

gender from other social phenomena, and to view race, class, and so on as "additive"). And yet I knew that wasn't what I meant either, that there was a reason to call what I believed "feminism." Now, I might dispel my friend's puzzlement by noting the wide variety of feminisms, and the fact that the discourses whose competition was reflected in my own seemingly contradictory statements came to me through the women's movement and through writers and activists who called themselves feminists. At the time, though, I simply was struck by the incompatibility of the view of gender as the "primary contradiction" (and its resolution as the one which would resolve all other contradictions) with the view that, as another friend of mine so aptly stated it, "if you fight only one 'ism' at a time, the others will come around and bite you in the ass."[3]

Thus, my early engagement first with radical feminism and then with writings by women of color, Jewish women, and some white lesbians (almost all of these authors were lesbians) presented me with tensions whose articulation I encountered later in postmodern and poststructuralist feminist thought, particularly in their discussions of the interactive constitution of oppression and the political importance of language and identity, and their emphasis on coalition politics. I address these strains of thought in detail in chapter 6. My readers might notice there a tendency on my part to valorize postmodern and poststructuralist feminist thought, and to treat them (despite my overt claims to the contrary) as discourses which resolve the tensions I have encountered in liberal (as well as radical) feminism. They might choose to understand that tendency as the assertion of an entrenched humanist discourse that assumes coherence, teleology, and closure—one to which the discomfort of earlier disjunctures might make me particularly susceptible when presented with the option of a different framework. Alternatively, readers may not choose to read any valorization of postmodern feminist theory in this way; or they may not see it at all. Nonetheless, this information about the various discourses that have influenced my thinking, sketchy though it is, may aid readers in unearthing and contextualizing the tensions in my own work.

My relationship to feminism, then, has been influenced by charges in my understanding of issues of "diversity" among women, the relationships between different forms of oppression, and the construction of the female subject in several of the forms of feminism I first encountered. What also needs to be addressed here is my frustration with liberal feminism and how that frustration influenced my early allegiance to radical feminism, and later, to those parts of postmodern and poststructuralist feminism, that emphasize language and consciousness.

When I first encountered it, radical feminism's stress on consciousness, language, and symbols, and the ways they shape women's psyches, provided me with an exceptionally powerful tool: a framework through which I could understand in political, collective terms experiences I had assumed were personal, individual. The phenomenon of "clicks," often associated with the CR groups of the late 1960s and early 1970s, has been written about widely. Most women who engage seriously with feminism can tell of many moments when they experienced these epiphanies, and I was no exception, particularly when it came to understanding key experiences I had had: with sexual harassment; with the body image problems so many women struggle with; as a lesbian and later as a bisexual woman; and so on. I came to see more clearly the ways that social forces influencing me psychically came to have a tremendous impact on my life in eminently tangible ways. On the one hand, oppressive discourses had led me to accept responsibility for the egregious and ongoing sexual harassment I had encountered at an earlier workplace. On the other hand, liberatory feminist discourses enabled me to come out as a lesbian in such a way that I could embrace and affirm that identity.[4] I was fascinated (and still am) with the power that discourses can exert over an individual's subjectivity and over collective consciousness and action.

I was (and am) less fascinated with legal/formal impediments and incitements. The degree to which I tend to dichotomize, to excess, consciousness/discourse and formal institutions (most evident, perhaps, in chapter 4's discussion of the women's movement studies) reflects my impatience with formal institutions' inability to grapple with psychic oppression and its material consequences—and with what I see as liberal feminism's stake in those institutions.

In particular, first as a lesbian and later as a bisexual woman, I have felt as though liberal feminists have often ignored the very significant pressures which keep queers like me, and others who are marginal to liberalism's privileged subjects (white, propertied heterosexual men, and those who can approximate them most closely in their dealings with liberal institutions), in line, or which make stepping out of line quite costly indeed.

Another incident comes to mind: my friend Cris and I are sitting in a campus lounge, engaged in a three-hour long argument with a mutual (then heterosexual) friend, Kathy, who wants to become a constitutional lawyer. The debate comes to revolve around freedom of speech, one of a number of rights that Kathy claims protects us all because it appears in the Bill of Rights. Cris and I, lesbians, object vehemently. "Go outside," we say, gesturing to the part of campus where students are hanging out in the spring sunshine. "Go out there and yell 'I'm a dyke' and see how far the First Amendment will protect you." This on a campus like any other, where queer students are harassed daily, are subject to violence, are vilified in bathroom graffiti, are mostly ignored by the student government and university administration. The assumption that legal codes are sufficient to protect us, or are even primary among our concerns, seems ludicrous to us. Cris speaks of a lover whose parents threw her out of their house when she was sixteen because they discovered her affair with a girlfriend. We both speak of the countless, "small" forms of domination we experience in the course of every day which take their cumulative toll, leaving us weary, fearful, angry.

Kathy's insistence on the power of the First Amendment, and the Constitution generally, to protect all people equally reflected, for me, the more general liberal feminist claims that government institutions can be made to work to the benefit of the people these institutions have at other times excluded. There is substantial evidence that these claims are true, in part. However, there is also substantial evidence of the profound limitations of these institutions' responsiveness to traditionally marginalized groups, as I discuss in chapter 1. Moreover, these institutions and the power they wield do not account for all forms of domination. Battles must be waged in other arenas as well. For some, the stakes in those other battles may seem more pressing at times.

So I am critical of liberal feminism's focus and priorities; they are not always very close to my own. And yet, liberal feminist agendas of economic and legal change are indispensable to what I envision as a just society. If I formulate my critiques too reductively—readers can judge for themselves—it is perhaps because I fear that engagement with liberal governmental institutions on their own terms reinforces those terms, and reproduces the marginality of all of us who continue to be shortchanged by those institutions—queers, women, people of color, poor and working-class people, those whose religion or ethnicity, or other conditions of existence, place them outside the perceived American "mainstream."

I am also critical of how social science studies of the women's movement privilege liberal feminist strategies in their discussions of feminist resistance. I myself have benefitted immeasurably from others' resistance to hegemonic discourses, whether that resistance has taken the form of teaching, speaking, private conversation, published writings, graffiti in public places, notes scribbled in the margins of library books. I have also engaged in, and witnessed, a wide variety of resistances. Some of these involve contending with government institutions—for example, working on a county-wide ordinance to establish the civil rights of non-heterosexuals in a community where I had lived for six years, or organizing against the New York State Department of Corrections to protest its regressive prison AIDS policies. Others have to do with working to change people's consciousness—such as plastering public places with stickers printed with safe sex information, or picketing a book shop whose Women's History Month display featured *Sports Illustrated* swimsuit calendar images, and engaging passersby in conversation about it. Again, my critique springs from my concern that, insofar as they ignore these types of resistance, social science studies of the women's movement miss the chance to capture the movement's complexities (and thus the complexities of the domination the movement combats); and my concern that these studies perpetuate the notion that the only effective or legitimate forms of resistance are those that also reinforce the workings of governmental institutions. I do not believe that this is always in the best interests of those who are ill-served by those institutions.

My critique of social science also comes directly out of my experience as a graduate student of political science—or, as Cornell likes to call it, Government. Though one of my undergraduate majors had been political science, I had concentrated most of my intellectual and critical energy in women's studies (my other major). It wasn't until graduate school that I really had to come to terms with political science as a discipline.

Doing so was no easy task. I spent countless hours in seminar rooms feeling as though I were asking all the wrong questions. One seminar in particular featured weekly battles royal between the two professors—separated by gender, ethnicity, nationality, and tenure status, not to mention political perspective—who co-taught it. I sat transfixed as they lobbed verbal grenades over the seminar table while hapless graduate students ducked the line of fire. Years later, I can't remember what they argued about; but my memories of the power struggles that weekly rocked that room are vivid.

By the end of my first year in graduate school, I was convinced that I should transfer to another discipline, one in which I would be asking the "right" questions. I interviewed faculty in various departments, searching for an intellectual home. In the end, I decided to stay in Government, not because I had reconciled myself to its paradigms, but because I couldn't face another first year of grad school—the one I had endured had been much more than enough. It wasn't until long after that that I realized that "intellectual home" is probably an oxymoron, as long as one retains one's critical edge: if you're comfortable, you probably *aren't* asking the right questions.

So I remained, counted my blessings that I didn't have to run more than one regression in my entire graduate career, and put together a great committee of faculty who were, for the most part, as critical of the mainstream of social science as I, and who always encouraged me in the directions I wanted to take. It was a story with some rough moments, but it had a happy ending.

A postscript to my earlier search for an intellectual home came later in my graduate career, when I worked with other grad students and faculty on a study designed to determine what factors hindered students in the department from completing their PhDs. The findings that emerged were fascinating: among other things, we discovered that women students, students of color, queer students, and those whose major field was political theory were much more likely than other students to feel constrained both by disciplinary boundaries and by our program's specific requirements (e.g., the high percentage of one's total courses that had to be taken within the department). I fit into three of these four categories. Suddenly, what I'd been feeling as a first-year student had a context and a structural—not just individual—explanation. (Okay. Quantitative research can be good for some things—though the truly rigorous would no doubt argue that our sample was too small for our findings to be statistically significant.)

One last trip back to the seminar room. It's a different seminar, taught by a professor so unencumbered by the imperatives of rigorous social science that he's actually assigned a novel. The discussion meanders through the subject of Latin American coups and revolutions before it smacks up against The Big Question: how does genuine, fundamental social change come about?

By this point, I have begun to trust that I am asking some of the right questions and, occasionally, coming up with some pretty good insights. And I have been thinking about The Big Question a lot lately. So I hazard some comment, no doubt clumsily articulated, about how people can become free only to the extent that they are able to imagine ways of living that facilitate that freedom.

Heresy. It's as if Hegel's ghost has walked in and sat down at the seminar table; backs tense, shoulders hunch, brows knit on scruffy male Marxists throughout the room. No one says anything out loud, though I hear plenty of under-the-breath muttering. Then the chimes in the bell tower begin their evening din, the group disperses, and I never get to explain what I mean, and the relationship of my argument to historical materialism.

So I wrote this book instead, to try to begin to focus attention on the *material* reality, the *material* consequences of psychic oppression. If, as I believe, the scruffy Marxists' objection was that what we are able to imagine, let alone realize, for our lives is first and foremost shaped by material circumstances, then I think they're right. But there's much more that needs to be said, because there is enormous heterogeneity in how people

207

who find themselves in basically the same material circumstances actually live their lives. Why does one gay teenage form an anti-homophobia group in her middle school while another joins the legions of gay teens who commit suicide every year?[5] Why do some battered women leave their batterers while others cling to them? Why do some African Americans embrace their colors and communities while others adopt the isolating and ultimately untenable strategy of becoming "model minorities"? What leads one Asian American to speak out in favor of multilingual education and another to become the head of the nation's "English only" movement? Why does one laid-off steel worker get angry at the company, while another gets angry at "Mexicans," and a third gets angry at herself? Why do some whites organize against racism, some men against sexism, some heterosexuals against homophobia, while others say, "that has nothing to do with me"?

It's the old idealism/materialism debate. Options for change are, of course, strongly influenced by economic, legal, policy, and other material considerations. However, economic or policy change is not, in itself, sufficient to bring about lasting social change; nor does it *determine* the course of social change. Policy change, even when far-reaching, does not guarantee much of anything without an attendant shift in perspective. A case in point is the (truncated) institution of the "Great Society," which offered relief from misery to millions of people. But without a fundamental shift in perspective—one that says our country and our Constitution are about "providing for the general welfare" because everyone is entitled to dignity, freedom from poverty, and protection from the worst that market forces can wreak—policy changes are all too easily reversible. Hence, the "Great Society" was first eviscerated by incomplete and inadequate implementation, and then destroyed altogether by the Southern Strategy, Reaganomics, and the Contract With America. So we come to a point where contemporary U.S. politics is profoundly and fundamentally shaped by the right's war on human freedom, well-being, and dignity. And this is not only a policy, but also a *discursive*, war: people accept the savagery of the new right's agenda only to the degree that they reject the humanity of its victims.

The flip side is that any given economic and policy environment yields a tremendous variety of social arrangements. What people do with what they have, the choices they make within those given economic and policy environments, is strongly influenced by norms, expectations, customs and traditions, and other intangibles. Structural, fundamental material changes come about when ideologies, expectations, and norms—the grammar through which we make sense of our world—are transformed. Many activists know this. And many social movements count on it.

Notes

Chapter 1

1. Ben Anderson, *Imagined Communities: Reflections on the Origin and Spread of Nationalism* (London: Verso, 1983).
2. These join earlier class-based critiques which, though just as fundamental, have been less successful in working their way into our political culture and imagination.
3. Ellen Willis, "Toward a Feminist Sexual Revolution," in *No More Nice Girls: Countercultural Essays* (Middletown, CT: Wesleyan University Press, 1992).
4. Women's movement activists and feminist theorists often identify liberal feminism with the National Organization for Women, the National Women's Political Caucus, and other organizations engaged in electoral politics.
5. Diane Macdonell, *Theories of Discourse: An Introduction* (Oxford and New York: Basil Blackwell, 1986), 19.
6. Uday S. Mehta discusses these aspects of liberalism in his article "Liberal Strategies of Exclusion," *Politics and Society*, December 1990.
7. Michel Foucault, *The History of Sexuality, Volume I: An Introduction*, trans. Robert Hurley. (New York: Vintage-Random House, 1980).
8. Celia Kitzinger, *The Social Construction of Lesbianism* (London; Newbury Park, CA; Beverly Hills, CA; New Delhi: Sage Publications, 1987), 196.
9. Supreme Court Justice Powell, *Regents of the University of California v. Bakke*, in Toby Kleban Levine, et al., eds., *Eyes on the Prize: America's Civil Rights Years: A Reader and Guide* (New York: Penguin, 1987), 258.
10. The Court actually posits race as the "sole" criterion in quota systems. It must be pointed out, however, that even in quota systems such as that employed by the UC Davis admissions committee, race is a *definitive* criterion

(in that some seats in each entering class were reserved for students of color) but not the *sole* criterion, in that, for example, successful completion of a college-level pre-med program is also a requirement—one that should, but does not, lay to rest objections that students admitted on this basis are "unqualified."

11. *Bakke*, in Williams, *Eyes on the Prize*, 256.

12. Nancy Fraser, "Women, Welfare, and the Politics of Need Interpretation," in *Unruly Practices: Power, Discourse, and Gender in Contemporary Social Theory* (Minneapolis: University of Minnesota Press, 1989).

13. Eleanor J. Bader, "Court Gives Kids To Abusive Dads," *New Directions for Women* 17; 1, 20.

14. Ibid.

15. Ibid.

16. Ibid.

17. Meryl Hooker of the National Gay and Lesbian Taskforce, private conversation, June 1996.

18. Chapter 5 includes in-depth readings of two autotheoretical texts: Cherríe Moraga, *Loving in the War Years: lo que nunca pasó por sus labios* (Boston: South End Press, 1983); and Minnie Bruce Pratt, *Rebellion: Essays 1980–1991* (Ithaca, NY: Firebrand Books, 1991). Other feminist autotheoretical texts include: selections from Evelyn Torton Beck, ed., *Nice Jewish Girls: A Lesbian Anthology* (Watertown, MA: Persephone Press, 1982); Audre Lorde, *Zami: A New Spelling of My Name* (Trumansburg, NY: Crossing Press, 1982) (originally published by Persephone Press); selections from Cherríe Moraga and Gloria Anzaldúa, eds., *This Bridge Called My Back: Writings by Radical Women of Color* (Watertown, MA: Persephone Press, 1981) (reissued by Kitchen Table: Women of Color Press, Albany); Joan Nestle, *A Restricted Country* (Ithaca: Firebrand Books, 1987); Mab Segrest, *My Mama's Dead Squirrel: Lesbian Essays on Southern Culture* (Ithaca: Firebrand Books, 1985); excerpts from Elly Bulkin, Minnie Bruce Pratt, and Barbara Smith, *Yours in Struggle: Three Feminist Perspectives on Anti-Semitism and Racism* (Brooklyn, NY: Long Haul Press, 1984) (reissued by Firebrand Books); and Gloria Anzaldúa, *Borderlands/La Frontera: The New Mestiza* (San Francisco: Spinsters/Aunt Lute, 1987).

19. This point was made by Nancy Bereano, publisher of Firebrand Books, who contends that some lesbian/feminist presses consciously choose to publish mixed-genre works because they "understand that a mix of genres sometimes serves an author's purpose more than a single genre would. Women's presses understand that things don't happen in a linear way, so they're more willing to publish mixed-genre works than mainstream publishers are." (Bereano, the panel discussion, "A Look at Lesbian Writing: The Significance of a Lesbian Sensibility," Cornell University, March 14, 1990.)

20. As I discuss at greater length in chapter 6, there are significant similarities in the treatment of identity, subjectivity, and discourse between the autotheoretical texts and postmodern/poststructuralist feminist theory. These similar-

ities have been investigated by, among others, Katie King, Biddy Martin, Chandra Talpade Mohanty, and Norma Alarcón.

21. Each of these presses publishes, among other works, the kinds of feminist autotheoretical texts chapter 3 discusses. Chapter 2 analyzes the presses in terms of the publishers' understanding of their work, and how their political commitments inform their presses' activities.

22. In *Controversy and Coalition* (particularly the revised edition), Myra Marx Ferree and Beth B. Hess do consider what they call a distinction between "equal rights" and "real equality," the latter representing broad cultural changes as well as legal changes. In *Feminism and the Women's Movement*, Barbara Ryan makes a similar case. However, as I argue in chapter 4, they ultimately emphasize legal change over cultural transformation, both explicitly through such claims as "most feminist change must be legislative," and implicitly through their dismissal of feminist efforts at cultural change as having to do only with "personal transformation."

23. This argument is sometimes made by those valorizing from within them, not just those criticizing from without, as in Verta Taylor and Nancy E. Whittier, "Collective Identity in Social Movement Communities: Lesbian Feminist Mobilization," in Aldon D. Morris and Carol McClurg Mueller, eds., *Frontiers in Social Movement Theory* (New Haven: Yale University Press, 1992).

24. The studies are: Myra Marx Ferree and Beth B. Hess, *Controversy and Coalition: The New Feminist Movement* (Boston: G.K. Hall & Co.-Twayne, 1985); Ferree and Hess, *Controversy and Coalition: The New Feminist Movement Across Three Decades of Change*, revised ed. (New York: Twayne Publishers, 1994); Barbara Ryan, *Feminism and the Women's Movement: Dynamics of Change in Social Movement Ideology and Activism* (New York: Routledge, 1992); Jo Freeman, *The Politics of Women's Liberation: A Case Study of an Emerging Social Movement and its Relation to the Policy Process* (New York and London: Longman, 1975); Joyce Gelb, *Feminism and Politics: A Comparative Perspective* (Berkeley: University of California Press, 1989); and Ethel Klein, *Gender Politics: From Consciousness to Mass Politics* (Cambridge, MA: Harvard University Press, 1984).

25. I have taken as the collective subject of my critique five major, recent studies that claim to examine and evaluate the women's movement as a whole, with the goal of inquiring into the various aims and assessing the multiple strategies of the different segments of the movement. Because one of my criticisms of these studies is their implicit bias toward public policy as the appropriate arena for feminist struggle, I have omitted studies that explicitly promise and deliver an analysis of the effect of the women's movement on public policy: it would, after all, be tautological and unfair to critique such studies for doing what they say they will do. (For one example of this type of study, see Joyce Gelb and Marian Lief Palley, *Women and Public Policies* [Princeton, NJ: Princeton University Press, 1982]). I have also omitted studies which offer an overview of women's social, legal, and economic status in contemporary United States society. (For examples, see Jo Freeman,

Women: A Feminist Perspective, 2nd. ed., [Palo Alto, CA: Mayfield Publishing Co., 1979]; Paula Giddings, *When and Where I Enter . . . The Impact of Black Women on Race and Sex in America* [New York: William Morrow and Co., 1984]; Robin Morgan, ed., *Sisterhood is Global: The International Women's Movement Anthology* [Garden City, NY: Anchor-Doubleday, 1984]; and Sara E. Rix, ed., *The American Woman: A Status Report*, The Women's Research and Education Institute [New York: W.W. Norton & Co., 1990]). I have omitted as well historical overviews of women and/or feminism in the United States. (For examples, see Nancy F. Cott and Elizabeth H. Pleck, *A Heritage of Her Own: Toward a New Social History of American Women* [New York: Touchstone-Simon & Schuster, 1979]; Sara Evans, *Born for Liberty: A History of Women in America* [New York: The Free Press-Macmillan, 1989]; Mary Beth Norton, *Liberty's Daughters: The Revolutionary Experience of American Women, 1750–1800* [Boston: Little, Brown and Co., 1980]; Barbara Mayer Wertheimer, *We Were There: The Story of Working Women in America* [New York: Pantheon-Random House, 1977]; Nancy F. Cott's *The Grounding of Modern Feminism* [New Haven and London: Yale University Press, 1987]; and bell hooks, *Ain't I a Woman: black women and feminism* [Boston: South End Press, 1981]).

26. Nancy Fraser, *Unruly Practices*, 42.
27. Ferree and Hess, *Controversy and Coalition* (1985), xi.
28. Linda Nicholson, ed., *Feminism/Postmodernism* (New York: Routledge, 1990), 3.
29. They also counter the "universal" male subject by positing and then valorizing women's supposed emotionality and association with nature. Recently, some feminists have rejected the binarisms that underlie the association of women with nature and emotion, and of men with culture and reason. See, for example, Donna Haraway, "A Manifesto for Cyborgs: Science, Technology, and Socialist Feminism in the 1980s," *Socialist Review* 80, 1985.
30. Nicholson, *Feminism/Postmodernism*, 5.
31. Some of these theorists restrict their attention solely to resistance at the level of discourse, while others acknowledge that resistance is necessary in other arenas as well, including formal/juridical institutions.
32. Chris Weedon, *Feminist Practice and Poststructuralist Theory* (New York and Oxford: Basil Blackwell, 1987), 26.
33. Biddy Martin and Chandra Talpade Mohanty, "Feminist Politics: What's Home Got to Do With It?" in Teresa de Lauretis, ed., *Feminist Studies/Critical Studies* (Bloomington, Indiana: Indiana University Press, 1986), 191–212.
34. Katie King, "Audre Lorde's Lacquered Layerings: The Lesbian Bar as a Site of Literary Production" from *Cultural Studies* v.2 n.3 (Oct. 1988), 321–42.
35. Bonnie Zimmerman, "The Politics of Transliteration: Lesbian Personal Narratives," review essay in *The Lesbian Issue: Essays from Signs*, ed. Estelle B. Freedman, Barbara C. Gelpi, Susan L. Johnson, Kathleen M. Weston (Chicago: University of Chicago Press, 1985), 251–70.
36. Norma Alarcón, "The Theoretical Subject(s) of *This Bridge Called My Back*

and Anglo-American Feminism," in Gloria Anzaldúa, ed., *Making Face, Making Soul/Haciendo Caras: Creative and Critical Perspectives by Women of Color* (San Francisco: Aunt Lute Foundation, 1990), 356–69.

37. Bella Brodzki and Celeste Schenck, *Life/Lines: Theorizing Women's Autobiography* (Ithaca, NY: Cornell University Press, 1988).

38. My discussion also draws on Biddy Martin's presentation of these issues in several of her courses at Cornell University, particularly her course on post-structural theory and feminist autotheoretical texts (what she calls "autobiographical writings"). (Feminist Theory and the Politics of Experience, Society for the Humanities, Cornell University, Spring 1989.)

Chapter 2

1. Naiad Press, the oldest lesbian/feminist publishing company in the country, has published primarily lesbian novels, although it also has several nonfiction titles on its list, such as Susan E. Johnson's *Staying Power: Long Term Lesbian Couples* and Barbara Deming's *Remembering Who We Are*. Recently, it has begun to put more emphasis on video.

2. Firebrand published ten books per year for a while, but Bereano found that to be too much work for a press this size.

3. In 1995, Aunt Lute put out *Front Line Feminism*, a 500-page collection of articles from the twenty years that the feminist newspaper *Sojourner* has been in print. This project is the equivalent for Aunt Lute of two books.

4. Smith continues to act as a consultant to Kitchen Table.

5. The Union Institute Center for Women is an experimental university in Washington, D.C. that was formed in the 1960s to bring together academics and activists.

6. Grant sources have included Sisterfund, the Ottinger Foundation, Fund for a Compassionate Society, the Herb Alpert Foundation, the Ernie Reaugh Fund, the Haymarket Foundation (which has channeled consistent support from an anonymous donor), the Nathan Cummings Foundation, and the Seguaro Fund of the Funding Exchange.

7. Firebrand sold movie rights for Leslie Feinberg's *Stone Butch Blues* to Against the Tide Productions, an independent production company.

8. The staff structure at Aunt Lute includes two co-directors, a management team consisting of the heads of the three departments (production, marketing, and operations), other staff members, interns, and volunteers. When Aunt Lute's other co-director, Fabienne McPhail, left the press in the fall of 1994, Aunt Lute was losing money and was unable to hire another co-director to take McPhail's place. The press has interviewed for the position and selected someone to fill it, but is waiting until its financial situation stabilizes before hiring her.

9. After Aunt Lute received an Advancement Grant from the NEA in 1992, it

instituted a benefits plan for staff, but the benefits were rescinded when the press encountered financial problems.

10. Cynthia Peters, correspondence, July 1995.

11. Nancy Bereano, interview, September 1991.

12. Joan Pinkvoss, interview, January 1996.

13. Bereano, interview, July 1995.

14. Karin San Juan, interview, September 1991.

15. Carol Seajay, interview, October 1991.

16. Bereano also notes the "commodification of lesbian and gay" material. Nancy Bereano, interview, July 1995.

17. Joan Pinkvoss, interview, January 1996.

18. Nancy Bereano, panel discussion, "A Look at Lesbian Writing: The Significance of a Lesbian Sensibility," Cornell University, March 14, 1990.

19. Bereano, interview, September 1991.

20. Barbara Smith, interview, October 1991.

21. San Juan, interview, September 1991.

22. San Juan, interview, September 1991.

23. Cynthia Peters, correspondence, July 1995.

24. According to Cill Janeway at *Feminist Bookstore News*, there were approximately 105 feminist bookstores in the United States as of July 1992; Kathleen Moore at *FBN* reports that this number had increased slightly to 115 as of February 1996. The number varies slightly as some stores close and others open, but it generally remains roughly the same over time, according to Janeway and Moore.

25. Pinkvoss, interview, January 1996.

26. Bereano, interview, September 1991.

27. Pinkvoss, interview, September 27, 1991.

28. Barbara Smith, "A Press of Our Own: Kitchen Table: Women of Color Press," *Frontiers* vol. X, no. 3 (1989), 13.

29. Until recently, Kitchen Table devoted a lot of its energy to its distribution efforts. Over the years, Smith says, Kitchen Table has carried "hundreds" of books by and about women of color and/or racism published by other presses. Smith includes this practice of distributing other publishers' books that reflect Kitchen Table's political commitments among the distinctions she draws between Kitchen Table and white-owned feminist presses. Smith's successor, Andrea Lockett, says she would like to resume distributing other presses' books as a central activity of Kitchen Table, along with getting other presses to carry Kitchen Table's books, "which we haven't had as much of."

30. Andrea Lockett, interview, July 1995.

31. Pinkvoss, interview, September 1991.

32. Bereano, interview, September 1991.

33. Pinkvoss, interview, September 1991.

34. Pinkvoss, interview, July 1992.

35. Bereano, interview, September 1991.

36. Bereano, interview, July 1995.
37. Bereano, interview, July 1995.
38. Lockett, interview, July 1995.
39. Charlotte Ryan, *Prime Time Activism: Media Strategies for Grassroots Organizing* (Boston: South End Press, 1991).
40. San Juan, interview, September 1991.
41. Bereano, interview, September 1991.
42. Kesho Scott, Cherry Muhanji, Egyriba High, *Tight Spaces* (San Francisco: Aunt Lute Books, 1987).
43. Carmen de Monteflores, *Singing Softly/Cantando Bajito* (San Francisco: Aunt Lute Books, 1989).
44. Smith, interview, October 1991.
45. Bereano, interview, September 1991. Here Bereano refers to Audre Lorde's *Zami: A New Spelling of My Name, Sister/Outsider* and *A Burst of Light*; and Rosario Morales and Aurora Levins Morales, *Getting Home Alive*. Both *Zami* and *Getting Home Alive* are autotheoretical works, and Lorde's other two books contain some of that sort of writing along with more standard essays.
46. Pinkvoss, interview, September 1991.
47. Sara Levi Calderon, *Two Mujeres*, trans. Gina Kaufer (San Francisco: Aunt Lute Books, 1989).
48. Edna Escamill, *Daughter of the Mountain, Un Cuento* (San Francisco: Aunt Lute Books, 1991).
49. Pinkvoss, interview, September 1991.
50. Smith, interview, October 1991.
51. Smith, interview, October 1991.
52. Cherríe Moraga and Gloria Anzaldúa, eds., *This Bridge Called My Back: Writings By Radical Women of Color* (Watertown, MA: Persephone Press, 1983); later picked up by Kitchen Table: Women of Color Press when Persephone shut down.
53. Barbara Smith, ed., *Home Girls: A Black Feminist Anthology* (Albany, NY: Kitchen Table: Women of Color Press, 1985).
54. As of March 1996, the total number of copies in print of all of bell hooks's books that South End publishes is 106,974. By book, the breakdown is: *Ain't I a Woman* (1981), 12,000; *Feminist Theory: From Margin to Center* (1984), 9,916; *Black Looks* (1992), 9,490; *Sisters of the Yam* (1993), 18,000; *Talking Back* (1989), 28,702; *Yearning* (1990), 18,645; and *Breaking Bread* (with Cornel West, 1991), 9,508.
55. As of April 1995. (Conversation with Joan Pinkvoss, March 1996.)
56. San Juan, interview, September 1991.
57. Pinkvoss, interview, September 1991.
58. Barbara Grier, interview, September 1991.
59. Grier declined to offer any details about the circumstances under which she has lent money to feminist publishers and booksellers.
60. Grier, interview, September 1991.

61. Bereano, interview, September 1991.
62. Pinkvoss, interview, January 1996.
63. Bereano, interview, January 1992.
64. Smith, interview, October 1991.
65. San Juan, interview, September 1991.
66. San Juan, interview, September 1991.
67. San Juan invited a number of presses to participate in the aisle the first year: Monthly Review Press (one of whose members helped San Juan organize the reception that led to the establishment of the aisle), ILR Press, Graywolf, Kitchen Table: Women of Color Press, Milkweed, New Society Publishers, Press Gang, Publishers Feminist Cooperative, Sister Vision, Third World Press, Thunder's Mouth, University of Minnesota Press ("although they'll never join us," but were invited because they have a political bent), Verso, West End, and Zed Press. (Interview, September 1991.) Those that actually participated the first year included South End, Kitchen Table, Monthly Review, Syracuse Cultural Workers, Open Hand, and others. (San Juan, interview, September 1995.)
68. Pinkvoss notes that the cost of attending the ABA—including booth rental, equipment rental, and staff costs—is about $10,000 for a small press. (Interview, January 1996.)
69. San Juan, interview, September 1995.
70. Kitchen Table has not attended the last several conferences, but plans to resume attending following its recent reorganization.
71. Smith, interview, October 1991.
72. Bereano, interview, January 1992.
73. Bereano, interview, January 1992.
74. Bereano, interview, January 1992.
75. As far as opening up the aisle to incorporate South End and other progressive presses (including those owned by people of color), Bereano cites two difficulties. One of these is the political dilemma of what it means to invite new participants into something that is already underway and has been created on the basis of certain assumptions that newer participants might not share. The other concerns the physical layout of the ABA convention and the logistical limitations on the space to which the consortium has access. After its first few years, the feminist and lesbian/gay aisle established a cut-off point for the number of participants based on the number of booths on a row—a number that is dictated by the layout of convention centers and the way the ABA organizes that space. (Interview, January 1992.) However, the ABA convention is under new management (as of 1995) and has established a 28-booth minimum for aisles; if a group fails to fill the 28 booths, the convention management fills them without consulting the group. (Interview, July 1995.) San Juan hopes this new requirement will lead the "feminist/lesbian and gay" grouping to welcome the "political" presses as the former seeks to fill its quota with the latter. (Interview, September 1995.)

76. Grier, interview, September 1991.
77. Bereano, interview, January 1992.
78. Pinkvoss, interview, January 1996.

Chapter 3

1. They are: Cherríe Moraga, *Loving in the War Years: lo que nunca pasó por sus labios* (Boston: South End Press, 1983); and Minnie Bruce Pratt, *Rebellion: Essays 1980–1991* (Ithaca, NY: Firebrand Books, 1991). For titles of other autotheoretical texts, see endnote 18 in chapter 1.

   Certainly, the argument could be made that these and other autotheoretical texts and their authors are important to the women's movement. Many of these authors are longtime feminist activists; many find audiences for their work in movement publications as well as the texts under consideration here; and many enjoy sufficient notoriety to garner invitations to speak at universities and academic and political conferences. (In fact, the celebration of Audre Lorde's work was the occasion for a political/activist conference—the "I Am Your Sister" conference held in October, 1990 in Boston. Parts of both Minnie Bruce Pratt's and Cherríe Moraga's books have been presented as speeches and have appeared in movement publications.) Moreover, the ongoing teaching and activism of these authors have touched many lives. My concern here is to examine the ways that these texts and others like them, as well as the feminist presses, provide one "window" onto a form of politics that has come to have increasing importance in the women's movement in recent years.

2. Of course, film/video is another medium which lends itself to this kind of sustained analysis.

3. For example, as I have noted earlier, increased attention on the part of reproductive rights activists to women's differences, and in particular to the previously ignored needs of women of color and working-class women, has transformed the "abortion rights" agenda of the women's movement into a broader "reproductive rights" agenda, which also includes working against sterilization abuse.

4. Cherríe Moraga and Gloria Anzaldúa, eds., *This Bridge Called My Back: Writings By Radical Women of Color* (Watertown, MA: Persephone Press, 1981).

5. Evelyn Torton Beck, ed., *Nice Jewish Girls: A Lesbian Anthology* (Watertown, MA: Persephone Press, 1982).

6. Ann Snitow, Christine Stansell, and Sharon Thompson, eds., *Powers of Desire: The Politics of Sexuality* (New York: Monthly Review Press, 1983).

7. Carole S. Vance, ed., *Pleasure and Danger: Exploring Female Sexuality* (Boston: Routledge & Kegan Paul, 1984).

8. Thanks to Biddy Martin for her insights into the ways in which the supposedly exalted status of lesbianism placed the onus for creating liberatory mod-

els of relationship on lesbians. Martin raised the point in a course on "Feminist Theory and the Politics of Experience," taught at the Society for Humanities, Cornell University, Spring 1989.

9. Another way to "document" the evolution of these debates, and potentially to explore some of its impact, would be to examine movement publications, where these debates would be reflected in book reviews, conference coverage, and in the way that news articles and other pieces are framed, the questions they raise, their subject matter, and so forth.

10. Jon Wiener, "Law Profs Fight the Power," *The Nation*, September 4–11, 1989, 246.

11. Jon Wiener, "Law Profs Fight the Power," 248.

12. See especially *The Alchemy of Race and Rights: Diary of a Law Professor* (Cambridge: Harvard University Press, 1991).

13. Rosario Morales, "Concepts of Pollution," in Aurora Levins Morales and Rosario Morales, eds., *Getting Home Alive* (Ithaca, NY: Firebrand Books, 1985), 64–65.

14. Some would include "prediction" as one of the tasks of social/political science. However, it is in the search for ways to establish the predictability of certain sequences of events that our subjects of inquiry are most radically curtailed, in the interests of parsimony.

15. Eve Kosofsky Sedgwick, *Epistemology of the Closet* (Berkeley/Los Angeles: University of California Press 1990), 26.

16. Bonnie Zimmerman, "The Politics of Transliteration: Lesbian Personal Narratives," review essay in *The Lesbian Issue: Essays from Signs,* Estelle B. Freedman, Barbara C. Gelpi, Susan L. Johnson, Kathleen M. Weston, eds. (Chicago: University of Chicago Press, 1985), 251–70.

17. Biddy Martin, "Lesbian Identity and Autobiographical Difference[s]," in Bella Brodzki and Celeste Schenck, eds. *Life/Lines: Theorizing Women's Autobiography* (Ithaca, NY: Cornell University Press, 1988), 91.

18. Biddy Martin, "Lesbian Identity and Autobiographical Difference[s]," 95.

19. Toril Moi, *Sexual/Textual Politics: Feminist Literary Theory* (London and New York: Routledge, 1985).

20. There is a growing body of theoretical literature on particular women's autobiographies and on the genre as a whole. Some of the works that have influenced my approach to feminist autotheoretical texts are: Joanne M. Braxton, *Black Women Writing Autobiography: A Tradition Within a Tradition* (Philadelphia: Temple University Press, 1989); Chandra Talpade Mohanty, "Feminist Encounters: Locating the Politics of Experience,"in *copyright 1: Fin De Siecle 2000,* Fall 1987; Personal Narratives Group, eds. *Interpreting Women's Lives: Feminist Theory and Personal Narratives* (Bloomington and Indianapolis: Indiana University Press, 1989); Sidonie Smith, *A Poetics of Women's Autobiography: Marginality and the Fictions of Self-Representation* (Bloomington: Indiana University Press, 1987); Katie King, "Audre Lorde's Lacquered Layerings: The Lesbian Bar as a Site of Literary Production," *Cultural Studies* v. 2 n. 3, (October 1988): 321–42; Bonnie Zimmerman, "The Politics of Transliteration";

Bella Brodzki and Celeste Schenck, *Life/Lines: Theorizing Women's Autobiography* (Ithaca, NY: Cornell University Press, 1988); and Nancy K. Miller, *Getting Personal: Feminist Occasions and Other Autobiographical Acts* (New York: Routledge, 1991).

21. This insistence strikes at the heart of established academic prose style that insists on obscuring the agent behind the text—most evident in its absurdity, perhaps, when authors refer to themselves in the third person when citing their previous works.

22. Pratt, "My Mother's Question," *Rebellion*, 123.

23. Gelb, "Social Movement 'Success'," 273.

24. Biddy Martin and Chandra Talpade Mohanty, "Feminist Politics: What's Home Got to Do With It?" in Teresa de Lauretis, ed., *Feminist Studies/Critical Studies* (Bloomington: Indiana University Press, 1986).

25. Biddy Martin and Chandra Talpade Mohanty, "Feminist Politics," 192.

26. Pratt, "Identity: Skin Blood Heart," *Rebellion*, 36–37.

27. Pratt, "When the Words Open," *Rebellion*, 133.

28. Pratt, "The Maps in My Bible," *Rebellion*, 219.

29. Pratt, "Identity: Skin Blood Heart," *Rebellion*, 47–50.

30. Pratt, *Rebellion*, 34.

31. Pratt, *Rebellion*, 33.

32. Pratt, *Rebellion*, 34.

33. Martin, "Lesbian Identity," 95.

34. Pratt, "Identity," *Rebellion*, 49.

35. Pratt, "The Maps In My Bible," *Rebellion*, 221.

36. Pratt, *Rebellion*, 187.

37. Pratt, *Rebellion*, 188.

38. Pratt, "The Friends of My Secret Self," *Rebellion*, 142.

39. Pratt, *Rebellion*, 144.

40. Pratt, *Rebellion*, 189.

41. Pratt, *Rebellion*, 189.

42. Martin and Mohanty discuss this kind of shift in perspective in Pratt's work, specifically her essay "Identity: Skin Blood Heart," in their article, "Feminist Politics: What's Home Got to Do With It?" *op. cit.*

43. Pratt, *Rebellion*, 190.

44. Pratt, *Rebellion*, 182.

45. Pratt, *Rebellion*, 122.

46. Pratt, *Rebellion*, 85.

47. Pratt, "'I Plead Guilty to Being a Lesbian'," *Rebellion*, 87.

48. Pratt, *Rebellion*, 22–23.

49. Pratt, *Rebellion*, 24.

50. Pratt, *Rebellion*, 24.

51. Pratt, *Rebellion*, 24.

52. Pratt, *Rebellion,* 24–25.

53. Moraga, *Loving in the War Years*, 136–37.

54. Moraga, "It Is You, My Sister, Who Must Be Protected," *Loving in the War Years*, 8.
55. Moraga, *Loving in the War Years*, 11.
56. Moraga, *Loving in the War Years*, 94.
57. Moraga, "A Long Line of Vendidas," *Loving in the War Years*, 92.
58. Moraga, *Loving in the War Years*, 97.
59. Moraga, *Loving in the War Years*, 95.
60. Moraga, *Loving in the War Years*, 99.
61. Moraga, *Loving in the War Years*, 101.
62. Moraga, *Loving in the War Years*, 101–102.
63. Moraga, *Loving in the War Years*, vii.
64. Moraga, *Loving in the War Years*, iii.
65. Moraga, *Loving in the War Years*, ii–iii.
66. Moraga, *Loving in the War Years*, iii.
67. Moraga, *Loving in the War Years*, 136.
68. Moraga, *Loving in the War Years*, 118.
69. Moraga, *Loving in the War Years*, 120–21.
70. Moraga, *Loving in the War Years*, 101.
71. Moraga, *Loving in the War Years*, 125–26.
72. Moraga, *Loving in the War Years*, 126.
73. First published in Zillah Eisenstein, ed., *Capitalist Patriarchy and the Case for Socialist Feminism* (New York: Monthly Review Press, 1979); and later widely anthologized.
74. Moraga, *Loving in the War Years*, 133.
75. Moraga, *Loving in the War Years*, 113.
76. Moraga, *Loving in the War Years*, 133.
77. Moraga, *Loving in the War Years*, 53.
78. Moraga, *Loving in the War Years*, 73–76.
79. Moraga, *Loving in the War Years*, vi.
80. Moraga, *Loving in the War Years*, 141.
81. Moraga, *Loving in the War Years*, iii.
82. For a discussion of "heteroglossia" in Latina literature, see Diana Velez's introduction to the collection she edited, *Reclaiming Medusa: Short Stories by Contemporary Puerto Rican Women* (San Francisco: Aunt Lute Foundation, 1989).
83. Moraga, *Loving in the War Years*, 62–63.

Chapter 4

1. For a discussion of this strategy, see Ruth B. Mandel, "The Political Woman," in Sara E. Rix, ed., *The American Woman 1988-89: A Status Report*, (New York: Norton, 1988).
2. Freeman and Ferree and Hess assert the greater "studiability" of such barri-

ers. My argument is that other aspects of women's oppression are eminently studiable, but not necessarily within accepted social science methodology, which typically relies on traditional concepts of "evidence." Moreover, there is a vast difference between consciously narrowing one's focus to the more "studiable" aspects of a movement and acknowledging the concomitant limits of one's conclusions, on the one hand, and taking those aspects to be the whole of the movement, on the other. Despite efforts by some of them to the contrary, these studies—including Freeman's and Ferree and Hess's—ultimately follow the latter course.

3. While its title implies a policy focus, Freeman's book examines the women's movement and its effects more broadly—hence its inclusion here.

4. Myra Marx Ferree and Beth B. Hess, *Controversy and Coalition: The New Feminist Movement* (Boston: Twayne-G.K. Hall, 1985).

5. Myra Marx Ferree and Beth B. Hess, *Controversy and Coalition: The New Feminist Movement Across Three Decades of Change* (New York: Twayne, 1994).

6. Barbara Ryan, *Feminism and the Women's Movement: Dynamics of Change in Social Movement Ideology and Activism* (New York: Routledge, 1992).

7. Jo Freeman, *The Politics of Women's Liberation: A Case Study of an Emerging Social Movement and its Relation to the Policy Process* (New York: David McKay, 1975).

8. Ethel Klein, *Gender Politics: From Consciousness to Mass Politics* (Cambridge, MA: Harvard University Press, 1984).

9. Klein, *Gender Politics*, 34.

10. Joyce Gelb, "Social Movement 'Success': A Comparative Analysis of Feminism in the United States and the United Kingdom," in Mary Fainsod Katzenstein and Carol McClurg Mueller, eds., *The Women's Movements of the United States and Western Europe* (Philadelphia: Temple University Press, 1987).

11. Joyce Gelb, *Feminism and Politics: A Comparative Perspective* (Berkeley and Los Angeles: University of California Press, 1989).

12. The book also includes a brief section on the feminist movement and the state in Sweden.

13. Gelb, *Feminism and Politics*, 14.

14. Ferree and Hess, *Controversy and Coalition* (1985), ix; (1994), viii–ix.

15. Central to Ferree and Hess's first edition are four categories of feminism they identify as liberal (see pp.149–54), socialist (pp.154–60), radical (pp.160–65), and career feminism (pp.142–49). Many of the issues they associate with these forms of feminism are relevant, even central, to the lives of women of color, working-class women, and lesbians and bisexual women. None of these brands of feminism, however, places questions of race and/or sexuality at the center of their analysis, and only socialist feminism places class—and the needs of poor women—at the center of its analysis. While women from many different sets of circumstances stand to gain from the endeavors of any of these types of feminism, none of them profoundly disturbs the racism, for example, that accounts for the disproportionate representation of women of color at the bottom of class and social hierarchies; or the heterosexism and

homophobia that form the very fabric of lesbians' and bisexual women's lives. Class inequality is central only to socialist feminism, even though working-class women stand to gain from liberal and radical feminist agendas. There are feminist theories and activist agendas to which heterosexism, racism, and class inequalities are central. Without exploring those theories and agendas, Ferree and Hess's study falls short of their stated objective to represent the full spectrum of the New Feminism.

Moreover, the study's omission of these forms of feminism is particularly consequential, as it coincides precisely with the repression of the constituents of these feminisms that has been so fundamental to American society.

16. Ferree and Hess, *Controversy and Coalition* (1994), x.
17. Ferree and Hess, *Controversy and Coalition* (1994), 159.
18. Ferree and Hess, *Controversy and Coalition* (1994), 200.
19. Ferree and Hess, *Controversy and Coalition* (1994), 39.
20. Ferree and Hess, *Controversy and Coalition* (1994), ix.
21. Ferree and Hess, *Controversy and Coalition* (1994), 23.
22. Ferree and Hess, *Controversy and Coalition* (1994), 94.
23. Ferree and Hess, *Controversy and Coalition* (1994), 185–86.
24. Ferree and Hess, *Controversy and Coalition* (1994), 191.
25. Ferree and Hess, *Controversy and Coalition* (1994), 55.
26. See especially *Controversy and Coalition* (1994), 48, 209, 215.
27. Ferree and Hess, *Controversy and Coalition* (1985), 57; (1994), 67.
28. Ferree and Hess, *Controversy and Coalition* (1985), 104–11; (1994), 116–24.
29. Ferree and Hess, *Controversy and Coalition* (1994), 117.
30. Ryan, *Feminism and the Women's Movement*, 57.
31. Ryan, *Feminism and the Women's Movement*, 45.
32. Ryan, *Feminism and the Women's Movement*, 57.
33. Ryan, *Feminism and the Women's Movement*, 57.
34. Ryan, *Feminism and the Women's Movement*, 50–51.
35. Ryan, *Feminism and the Women's Movement*, 119.
36. As I have argued elsewhere, this lesbian chauvinism also caused a good deal of pain to bisexual women when it took the form of charges that bisexual women were duplicitous beneficiaries of the institution of heterosexuality. (See Young, "Breaking Silence About the 'B-Word': Bisexual Identity and Lesbian-Feminist Discourse," in Elizabeth Reba Weise, ed., *Closer to Home: Bisexuality and Feminism* ([Seattle: Seal Press, 1992], 75–87).
37. The AIDS Coalition to Unleash Power, a direct-action AIDS activist organization, was founded in New York City in 1987 and has chapters all over the world. ACT UP has been the single most effective direct action AIDS organization in securing policy changes favorable to people with AIDS as well as in educating the public at large about AIDS, and its connections to homophobia, racism, and sexism. See Marion Banzhaf, et al., The ACT UP/NY

Women and AIDS Book Group, *Women, AIDS and Activism* (Boston: South End Press, 1990).

38. Ryan, *Feminism and the Women's Movement*, 127.
39. Ryan, *Feminism and the Women's Movement*, 133.
40. Gloria T. Hull, Patricia Bell Scott, and Barbara Smith, the editors of *All the Women are White, All the Blacks are Men, But Some of Us Are Brave: Black Women's Studies* (Old Westbury, NY: The Feminist Press, 1982), an important early anthology on black women's studies.
41. Cherríe Moraga and Gloria Anzaldúa, eds., *This Bridge Called My Back: Writings by Radical Women of Color* (Watertown, MA: Persephone Press, 1981); later reissued by Kitchen Table: Women of Color Press.
42. Ryan, *Feminism and the Women's Movement*, 127.
43. Ryan, *Feminism and the Women's Movement*, 132.
44. Ryan, *Feminism and the Women's Movement*, 130.
45. Ryan, *Feminism and the Women's Movement*, 131.
46. Ryan, *Feminism and the Women's Movement*, 132.
47. Ryan, *Feminism and the Women's Movement*, 129.
48. Ryan, *Feminism and the Women's Movement*, 125.
49. Ryan, *Feminism and the Women's Movement*, 125.
50. Klein, *Gender Politics*, 61.
51. Klein, *Gender Politics*, 8.
52. Gelb, *Feminism and Politics*, 34.
53. Gelb, *Feminism and Politics*, 204.
54. Ferree and Hess, *Controversy and Coalition* (1985), 86.
55. Ferree and Hess, *Controversy and Coalition* (1994), 39.
56. Ferree and Hess, *Controversy and Coalition* (1994), 48.
57. Ferree and Hess, *Controversy and Coalition* (1994), 196.
58. Ferree and Hess, *Controversy and Coalition* (1994), 209.
59. Ferree and Hess, *Controversy and Coalition* (1994), 215.
60. Ryan, *Feminism and the Women's Movement*, 79–88.
61. This is perhaps due to her focus throughout her book on struggles within the women's movement over who qualifies as "radical," and on what grounds.
62. Ryan, *Feminism and the Women's Movement*, 161.
63. Freeman, *Politics of Women's Liberation*, 38.
64. Moreover, Freeman also neglects to seek out those barriers within the movement that discourage black and working-class women from participating. Rather than examining racism and the hegemony of women from middle-class backgrounds within the movement, Freeman limits her discussion to barriers that exist outside of it. In addition to her use of relative deprivation theory, for example, she also blames ideologies developed within the black community for black women's low rates of participation in feminism (40–41). She does not explore the ways that ideologies developed within the women's movement might repel black women.

It should be noted, however, that Freeman's study emerged from a very different political context than did the later studies, and it would be irrelevant to fault her for not responding to discourses concerning class, sexuality, and race that didn't emerge as such until well after she published her book. Discourses challenging ethnocentrism, heterosexism, racism, and other types of exclusions within feminism did, of course, exist at the time Freeman was writing. However, these challenges had not yet emerged as the diverse yet cohesive force that they were to become in the early 1980s. Thus, while it is symptomatic of the problems that these later discourses addressed, Freeman's relative inattention to these issues is easier to account for than similar inattention of Ferree and Hess, Gelb, and Klein to issues of race, sexuality, and class.

65. Freeman, *Politics of Women's Liberation*, 49–51.

66. Klein, *Gender Politics*, 124.

67. In their first edition, while Ferree and Hess explicitly set out to investigate a variety of forms of resistance—which indicates that they understand the workings of power and domination to be equally various—their partiality toward standard definitions of political activity (i.e., engagement with liberal institutions on their own terms) becomes evident all too soon. This results from their tendency to reduce feminist *political activity* to *organizational activity,* and then to evaluate this activity on the basis of whether or not those organizations successfully engage with liberal institutions.

68. This shift between the first and second editions' treatment of non-policy-oriented feminist activity coincides with—and can perhaps be attributed to—a similar shift within some strains of social movement theory toward taking more seriously the discursive aspects of movement activity.

69. Ferree and Hess, *Controversy and Coalition* (1994), 217–18.

70. Indeed, this tension in Ferree and Hess's revised edition—between their broader stated view of power and change and their restricted focus primarily on policy activity—underscores the need for social scientists to develop different methods, and definitions of "data" and "evidence," with which to fashion arguments that take power's complexity into account.

71. Evelyn Torton Beck, ed., *Nice Jewish Girls: A Lesbian Anthology* (Watertown, MA: Persephone Press, 1982); later reissued by Firebrand Books.

72. See, for example, Ferree and Hess, *Controversy and Coalition* (1985), 162; and Freeman, *Politics of Women's Liberation*.

73. Ryan, *Feminism and the Women's Movement*, 92.

74. Ryan, *Feminism and the Women's Movement*, 93.

75. Ryan, *Feminism and the Women's Movement*, 95.

76. Ryan, *Feminism and the Women's Movement*, 93.

77. Ryan, *Feminism and the Women's Movement*, 95.

78. Ryan, *Feminism and the Women's Movement*, 95.

79. Ryan, *Feminism and the Women's Movement*, 96.

80. Ryan, *Feminism and the Women's Movement*, 95.

81. Ryan, *Feminism and the Women's Movement*, 96.

82. Ryan, *Feminism and the Women's Movement*, 96.
83. Ryan, *Feminism and the Women's Movement*, 95.
84. Freeman, *Politics of Women's Liberation*, 97.
85. Freeman, *Politics of Women's Liberation*, 97–98.
86. Freeman, *Politics of Women's Liberation*, 99.
87. Freeman, *Politics of Women's Liberation*, 88.
88. Freeman, *Politics of Women's Liberation*, 72.
89. Freeman asserts that the older women tended to have had some success within institutions, whereas the younger feminists tended to come out of radical political organizing that took place outside of and in opposition to government and other formal institutions.
90. Klein, *Gender Politics*, 126.
91. Gelb, *Feminism and Politics*, 4.
92. Gelb, *Feminism and Politics*, 4.
93. Gelb, "Social Movement 'Success'," 273.
94. Ferree and Hess, *Controversy and Coalition* (1994), 115.
95. Ferree and Hess, *Controversy and Coalition* (1994), 130.
96. This is akin to Foucault's "juridical model of power."
97. Ferree and Hess, *Controversy and Coalition* (1994), 200.
98. Ryan, *Feminism and the Women's Movement*, 156.
99. Ryan, *Feminism and the Women's Movement*, 183.
100. Ryan, *Feminism and the Women's Movement*, 161.
101. Freeman, *Politics of Women's Liberation*, 145.
102. Freeman, *Politics of Women's Liberation*, 51.
103. Freeman, *Politics of Women's Liberation*, 145.
104. Klein, *Gender Politics*, 89.
105. Gelb, "Social Movement 'Success'," 283.
106. Gelb, *Feminism and Politics*, 180.
107. Gelb, "Social Movement 'Success'," 273.
108. Gelb, "Social Movement 'Success'," 283.
109. Gelb, *Feminism and Politics*, 182.
110. Ryan, *Feminism and the Women's Movement*, 5.
111. Ryan, *Feminism and the Women's Movement*, 6.
112. Freeman, *Politics of Women's Liberation*, 3–4.
113. Klein, *Gender Politics*, 10.
114. Klein, *Gender Politics*, 10.
115. Klein, *Gender Politics*, 10.
116. Klein, *Gender Politics*, 164.
117. Ferree and Hess, *Controversy and Coalition* (1994), 200.
118. Ferree and Hess, *Controversy and Coalition* (1994), ix.
119. Insofar as Gelb does examine changes in public attitudes, she does so apart from seeking the origins of such change in the women's movement, and by a method insufficient to capture the depth and breadth of cultural "sea changes."

Chapter 5

1. In this section, as elsewhere in this study, I use the term "social movements" broadly to denote activity aimed at transforming large-scale power imbalances. This can take the form of working for changes in laws and in other institutional policies, providing education and services to counteract the effects of oppression and discrimination, working to transform individual and group/societal consciousness, and so forth. Whereas much social movement theory dichotomizes policy-oriented activity and consciousness-centered activity (see, for example, Alberto Melucci's *Nomads of the Present*), this study works against that dichotomy, seeing them as two sides of the same process of creating social change through transforming power imbalances. Moreover, it challenges the notion that "social movement" always means collective/mass action, to the exclusion of individual acts that contribute to collective growth. As such, it implies an interdisciplinary approach, in order that political scientists may temper their policy/institutional fixation with attention to consciousness, world views, frames, ideology, and paradigms; and in order that sociologists and social psychologists may resist the temptation to psychologize social movement activity, particularly of "New Social Movements," whose emphasis on identity makes them especially vulnerable to being reduced to psychological motives and effects.

   The social movement theory I discuss in this chapter tends not to distinguish between different types of movements and movement activity: instead, it lumps together activity aimed at public policy and institutional arrangements; that aimed at effecting shifts in social consciousness; and movements launched on behalf of subjects who share a particular identity and claim to be discriminated against on the basis of that identity. Some theorists also include under the rubric of social movements "consensus movements," or those that enjoy almost universal support and encounter "little or no organized opposition," such as Mothers Against Drunk Driving (see Michael Schwartz and Shuva Paul, "Resource Mobilization versus the Mobilization of People: Why Consensus Movements Cannot Be Instruments of Social Change," in Aldon D. Morris and Carol McClurg Mueller, eds., *Frontiers in Social Movement Theory* [New Haven: Yale University Press, 1992], 205). Some, like Melucci, discuss fashions or cultural trends like punk rock and its fans alongside—and without distinction from—movements with more sophisticated social critiques and agendas for social transformation (1989). While these subcultures may be an indirect outgrowth of the social changes brought about by more directly political movements, they are not the subject of this study.

2. Mayer N. Zald, "Looking Backward to Look Forward: Reflections on the Past and Future of the Resource Mobilization Research Program," in Morris and Mueller, eds., *Frontiers*. Jo Freeman's *The Politics of Women's Liberation*, discussed in chapter 4, offers an application of deprivation theory to the women's movement.

3. Zald, "Looking Backward to Look Forward"; Carol McClurg Mueller, "Building Social Movement Theory," in Morris and Mueller, eds., *Frontiers.*

4. John D. McCarthy and Mayer N. Zald, "Resource Mobilization and Social Movements: A Partial Theory," in Zald and McCarthy, *Social Movements in an Organizational Society* (New Brunswick, NJ: Transaction Books, 1987).

5. Some RM theorists emphasize what they call the "political opportunity structure," or the set of institutions and actors that comprise the policy process. Changes in the political opportunity structure, they argue, can auger well or ill for social movements seeking to effect policy change. For example, a political opportunity structure characterized by a stable concentration of power is closed to new ideas and policies that would challenge that state of affairs, and is thus largely impervious to social movement efforts to effect policy change. Once the political opportunity structure "cracks," or becomes unstable as divisions between powerful institutions and individuals emerge, however, social movements are more likely to be successful if they are able to exploit those openings. (See Doug McAdam, *Political Process and the Development of Black Insurgency, 1930–1970* [Chicago: University of Chicago Press, 1982]; and Sidney Tarrow on protest cycles, especially *Struggle, Politics and Reform: Collective Action, Social Movements, and Cycles of Protest* [Ithaca, NY: Western Societies Program, Center for International Studies, Cornell University, Occasional Paper no. 21, 1989], and *Struggling to Reform: Social Movements and Policy Change During Cycles of Protest* [Ithaca, NY: Western Societies Program, Cornell University, 1983]). Cracks in the political opportunity structure can be created by economic or political crises, or by shifts in international or domestic political arenas that challenge the activities of established institutions and actors. In some cases, pressure from social movements or other interests within society is itself sufficient to create these cracks.

6. Zald, "Looking Backward."

7. Mueller, "Building Social Movement Theory."

8. Debra Friedman and Doug McAdam, "Collective Identity and Activism: Networks, Choices, and the Life of a Social Movement," in Morris and Mueller, eds., *Frontiers.*

9. Zald, "Looking Backward."

10. Many critics argue that RM theory still pays far too little attention to solidarity, relationships, and networks of obligation. See below.

11. See Myra Marx Ferree, "The Political Context of Rationality: Rational Choice Theory and Resource Mobilization," in Morris and Mueller, eds., *Frontiers.*

12. See Doug McAdam, *Political Process and the Development of Black Insurgency*; and Melucci, *Nomads.*

13. Tracy Morgan, member of ACT UP/New York (the AIDS Coalition to Unleash Power), quoted in *QW* magazine in the winter of 1990–1991. Morgan was referring to another long-time ACT UP/NY member, Mark Harrington, who went to dinner with Anthony Fauci, the director of AIDS research at the National Institutes of Health, the same day of the first feder-

ally-sponsored conference on women and HIV in December 1990, which Fauci did not attend. The conference on women and HIV was particularly contentious, as women activists from all over the country protested loudly against the government's virtual silence on the plight of women with HIV. In courting Fauci through "old-boy" networking tactics, Harrington, who was a very influential member of ACT UP's Treatment and Data committee, was seen by many women within ACT UP to be directly undermining their more direct-action confrontational stance toward Fauci as one of the key government officials responsible for the neglect of women with HIV. The event sparked the effort within ACT UP/NY to declare a six-month moratorium on the organization's meetings with government officials, signalling a shift back to the direct action activism that had always been its *forte*. (Private conversation, March 11, 1996.)

14. Of course, domination *is* often conscious. However, it also is often an unconscious performance of roles scripted by an overriding paradigm that sets out belief and value systems and corollary social and institutional practices that secure power divisions on a large scale, along lines of gender or race, for example. Neither Lukes nor Gaventa is primarily concerned with explicitly engaging these large-scale systems of domination. Although their work engages class divisions, it does so at local levels—in Gary, Indiana (Lukes) and the Cumberland Gap region (Gaventa)—and does not extrapolate to make claims about class divisions in general.

15. Steven Lukes, *Power: A Radical View* (London: Macmillan, 1974).

16. Many of NSM theory's limitations can be traced to its tendency to leap from legitimate claims about specific situations to broader but less well-founded claims. NSM theory has emerged within North American and European contexts, and as such, according to William Gamson, approaches the task of creating a theoretical paradigm for all contemporary political movements without giving sufficient attention to, for example, anti-apartheid activity in South Africa or the Palestinian intifada. What is needed is a refinement of the theory's global claims that do not hold in non-European/American contexts.

    Moreover, Gamson argues, the term "new social movements" may reify newness. One result is that recent social movements get lumped together, rather than explored for what they share and how they differ. This is particularly problematic when the result is a failure to distinguish between the non-confrontational status of consensus movements, the inward focus of subcultures, and the broad political and social agendas of identity-based movements and other movements that seek to effect broad transformation in consciousness and culture. William A. Gamson, "The Social Psychology of Collective Action," in Morris and Mueller, eds., *Frontiers*.

17. John Gaventa, *Power and Powerlessness: Quiescence and Rebellion in an Appalachian Valley* (Chicago: University of Illinois Press, 1980), 3.

18. Gaventa, *Power and Powerlessness*, 40–42.

19. Gaventa, *Power and Powerlessness*, 63–67.

20. Gaventa, *Power and Powerlessness*, 16–18.

21. Gaventa also begins to get at this issue in his discussions of the pleasures of compliance evident in, for example, mine workers' elaborate, public celebrations in honor of the very company that so thoroughly exploited them.
22. Mueller, "Building Social Movement Theory."
23. Mueller, "Building Social Movement Theory"; and Alberto Melucci, *Nomads of the Present*, ed., John Keane and Paul Mier (Philadelphia: Temple University Press, 1989). Other theorists—including Laraña, Johnston, and Gusfield, and Melucci himself at other times—cast actors as self-interested, but not so much in the material gains that attract RM theory's actors. Rather, NSM theory's actors seek a sense of self, a firm identity. Their quest remains individual and self-interested.
24. Alberto Melucci, "A Strange Kind of Newness: What's 'New' in New Social Movements?" in Enrique Laraña, Hank Johnston, Joseph R. Gusfield, eds., *New Social Movements: From Ideology to Identity* (Philadelphia: Temple University Press, 1994), 101–29; and Carol McClurg Mueller, "Conflict Networks and the Origins of Women's Liberation," in Laraña et al., *New Social Movements*. Mueller's work draws on both NSM and RM approaches.
25. Taylor and Whittier argue that this process of identity construction beyond public view is one of the primary functions of contemporary lesbian feminist communities. See Verta Taylor and Nancy E. Whittier, "Collective Identity in Social Movement Communities: Lesbian Feminist Mobilization," in Morris and Mueller, eds., *Frontiers*.
26. Interestingly, some New Social Movement theorists (such as Laraña, Gusfield, and Johnston) revive the notion of the self-interested environmentalist: s/he joins the movement seeking an identity in an increasingly anomic world. Laraña et al., "Identities, Grievances, and New Social Movements," in *New Social Movements*.
27. For example, Ron Eyerman and Andrew Jamison, *Social Movements: A Cognitive Approach* (University Park, PA: Pennsylvania State University Press, 1991); and Taylor and Whittier, "Collective Identity in Social Movement Communities."
28. Melucci, *Nomads*. Postmodern theorists of identity stress fragmentation of subjectivity/individual identity (see below). Their formulation goes even further than Melucci's in explaining why social movements are characterized by tension among their participants, in that they explore the sometimes conflicting identities and affinities or obligations individual participants experience. These conflicts can affect the contexts in which—and the degree to which—participants will experience themselves as being engaged by a social movement's agendas, goals, and strategies.
29. Mueller (in "Building Social Movement Theory") directly challenges Melucci's claim that collective identity is too contingent and unstable for movements to function as coherent actors. She concedes that movements' collective identities are fraught with tensions, even contradictions; yet, she argues, movements can operate as coherent actors under special circumstances. She offers the example of the women's movement in 1970, and public and governmental reaction to Women Strike for Equality Day that year.

Public support for women in nontraditional roles shot up, and the federal government sharply increased the number of pro-women bills it passed. These results, Mueller contends, have to do with a public perception of a unitary collective identity among women, one that may be illusory but that nonetheless had, for at least a short while, the role and impact of a historical actor. Despite conflict internal to the movement, its identity was constructed—both by the movement itself and by the mass media—in such a way that it was *seen* as a coherent actor and was thus *treated* as one—to its advantage—by its opponents in the political system.

30. Melucci, *Nomads*.
31. Gamson, "The Social Psychology of Collective Action."
32. Eyerman and Jamison, *Social Movements*, 80. See note 29.
33. Eyerman and Jamison, *Social Movements*, 166.
34. Two examples of NSM theorists who do this successfully are Aldon D. Morris, "Political Consciousness and Collective Action," in Morris and Mueller, eds., *Frontiers*; and Sylvia N. Tesh, "New Social Movements and New Ideas," paper presented at the Annual Meeting of the American Political Science Association, Washington, D.C., September 2–5, 1993.
35. Joseph R. Gusfield, "The Reflexivity of Social Movements: Collective Behavior and Mass Society Theory Revisited," in Laraña et al., *New Social Movements*, 64–65.
36. Gusfield, "The Reflexivity of Social Movements," 64–65.
37. Gusfield, "The Reflexivity of Social Movements," 69.
38. Melucci, "A Strange Kind of Newness," 101–102.
39. Melucci, *Nomads*, 208.
40. Melucci, "A Strange Kind of Newness," 102.
41. Melucci, *Nomads*, 112.
42. Melucci, *Nomads*, 113–14.
43. Melucci, *Nomads*, 119.
44. Melucci, *Nomads*, 121.
45. Melucci, "A Strange Kind of Newness," 125.
46. Taylor and Whittier, "Collective Identity," 109.
47. See Alice Echols, *Daring to Be Bad* (Minneapolis: University of Minnesota Press, 1989).
48. This problem is rooted in the authors' insistence on virtual unanimity among lesbians as to the meaning of lesbianism and its relation to gender politics: "Contemporary lesbian feminist consciousness is not monolithic. But its mainspring is the view that heterosexuality is an institution of patriarchal control and that lesbian relationships are a means of subverting male domination" (114). This formulation allows the authors neatly to sidestep a decade or more of heated debate among lesbians and feminists about sexuality, feminism, and related political struggles; it also requires that they ignore the myriad forms of lesbian feminist activism that have emerged from the various sides in these debates.
49. Laraña, Johnston, and Gusfield, "Identities, Grievances and New Social Movements."

50. Laraña, Johnston, and Gusfield, "Identities," 23.
51. Laraña, Johnston, and Gusfield, "Identities," 27.
52. Laraña, Johnston, and Gusfield, "Identities," 23–24.
53. Laraña, Johnston, and Gusfield, "Identities," 23–24.
54. Laraña, Johnston, and Gusfield, "Identities," 24.
55. Queer Nation is an example of anti-homophobia direct action activist orga-nization that has generally emphasized difference among queers rather than some ostensibly universal experience, identity, or behavior. See also Judith Butler's *Gender Trouble*.
56. Frigga Haug, et al., *Female Sexualization: A Collective Work of Memory*, trans. Erica Carter (London: Verso, 1987).
57. Morris, "Political Consciousness and Collective Action," 361.
58. Eyerman and Jamison, *Social Movements*, 166.
59. Eyerman and Jamison, *Social Movements*, 161.
60. David A. Snow and Robert D. Benford, "Master Frames and Cycles of Protest," in Morris and Mueller, eds., *Frontiers*, 137.
61. Morris, "Political Consciousness," 363.
62. Morris, "Political Consciousness," 361.

Chapter 6

1. Although there is no clear consensus about what constitutes postmodern theory, I find John McGowan's taxonomy useful. In *Postmodernism and Its Critics* (Ithaca: Cornell University Press, 1991), he cites as the four "most prominent variants of postmodern theory . . . poststructuralism, the new Marxism, neopragmatism, and feminism" (ix). McGowan restricts his focus to the first three of these four; I draw primarily on poststructuralism and feminism. Andreas Huyssen, in "Mapping the Postmodern," Linda J. Nichol-son, ed., *Feminism/Postmodernism* (New York: Routledge, 1990), presents a different view. He distinguishes postmodernism from poststructuralism, plac-ing them in very different relation to modernity.
2. David Couzens Hoy, "Foucault: Modern or Postmodern?" in Jonathan Arac, ed., *After Foucault: Humanistic Knowledge, Postmodern Challenges* (New Brunswick, NJ: Rutgers University Press, 1988).
3. Hoy, "Foucault," 13.
4. Michel Foucault, *The History of Sexuality, volume I: An Introduction* (New York: Vintage Books, 1980).
5. Foucault, *History of Sexuality*, 87.
6. Foucault, *History of Sexuality*, 86.
7. Foucault, *The History of Sexuality*, 89–90. It is also the representation still at work in social science analyses of the relationship of power to gender, race, and so on.
8. Although Foucault acknowledges "major dominations" (meaning hege-monic social divisions, such as those based on race, gender, or sexuality), he

does so in *The History of Sexuality* only in passing, maintaining his focus on local exercises of power and resistance. This emphasis has led some critics, including some feminists, to denounce feminist appropriations of Foucault's theories on the grounds that they obscure large-scale, systematic social dominations such as sexism, racism, and so forth.

9. Not everyone agrees that this is the case. See note 8 in this chapter.

10. Radical feminism shares with postmodern approaches the notion that power is exercised not just by a central, formal authority, but rather that power relationships permeate all levels of social organization. Where radical feminism and postmodernism diverge is in the former's conception of power as solely dominative, prohibitive, and Manichean in its distribution (i.e., people are either oppressors or oppressed), while the latter sees the exercise of power as being much more contingent, shifting, and nuanced.

11. Sandra Lee Bartky, "Foucault, Femininity, and the Modernization of Patriarchal Power," in Irene Diamond and Lee Quinby, eds., *Feminism & Foucault: Reflections on Resistance* (Boston: Northeastern University Press, 1988), 64.

12. Bartky focuses on three categories of discipline aimed at women's bodies: "those that aim to produce a body of a certain size and general configuration; those that bring forth from this body a specific repertoire of gestures, postures, and movements; and those that are directed toward the display of this body as an ornamented surface" (64).

13. Bartky, "Foucault," 66.

14. Bartky, "Foucault," 68.

15. Bartky, "Foucault," 75–76.

16. Bartky, "Foucault," 75.

17. Bartky, "Foucault," 76.

18. Radicalesbians, "woman-identified woman," (pamphlet) (Somerville, MA: New England Free Press, 1970). This piece also appeared in the leftist paper *Rat*.

19. This logic is not specific to feminism. It directly mirrors, for example, Marxist arguments that the working class, as a whole and by virtue of its position within the social structure, embodies the most revolutionary politics and is the inevitable vanguard of the revolution.

20. Margaret Small, "Lesbians and the Class Position of Women," in Nancy Myron and Charlotte Bunch, eds., *Lesbianism and the Women's Movement* (Baltimore: Diana Press, 1975), 59.

21. The Combahee River Collective, "A Black Feminist Statement," dated April 1977, in Gloria T. Hull, Patricia Bell Scott, and Barbara Smith, eds., *All the Women Are White, All the Blacks Are Men, But Some of Us Are Brave: Black Women's Studies* (Old Westbury, NY: The Feminist Press, 1982), 16.

22. Combahee River Collective, "A Black Feminist Statement," 22.

23. Chris Weedon, *Feminist Practice and Poststructuralist Theory* (Oxford and New York: Basil Blackwell Press, 1987).

24. Chandra Talpade Mohanty, "Feminist Encounters: Locating the Politics of Experience," in *copyright 1: Fin De Siecle 2000* (Cambridge, MA) Fall 1987.

25. Minnie Bruce Pratt, "Identity: Skin Blood Heart," in Elly Bulkin, Minnie

Bruce Pratt, and Barbara Smith, *Yours In Struggle: Three Feminist Perspectives on Anti-Semitism and Racism* (Brooklyn: Long Haul Press, 1984); and in Pratt, *Rebellion.* See chapter 3.

26. Biddy Martin and Chandra Talpade Mohanty, "Feminist Politics: What's Home Got to Do with It?" in Teresa de Lauretis, ed., *Feminist Studies/Critical Studies* (Bloomington: Indiana University Press, 1986), 209–10.

27. Frigga Haug, et al., *Female Sexualization: A Collective Work of Memory,* trans. Erica Carter (London: Verso, 1987). (German edition 1983.)

28. Haug et al., *Female Sexualization,* 46.

29. Haug et al., *Female Sexualization,* 24.

30. Haug, et al., *Female Sexualization,* 144–45.

31. Haug, et al., *Female Sexualization,* 142.

32. Nancy K. Miller, *Getting Personal: Feminist Occasions and Other Autobiographical Acts* (New York: Routledge, 1991), 126, 6.

33. Joanne M. Braxton, *Black Women Writing Autobiography: A Tradition Within a Tradition* (Philadelphia: Temple University Press, 1989), 208.

34. Braxton, *Black Women Writing Autobiography,* 206.

35. Personal Narratives Group, *Interpreting Women's Lives: Feminist Theory and Personal Narratives* (Bloomington and Indianapolis: Indiana University Press, 1989), 261–262.

36. Biddy Martin, "Lesbian Identity and Autobiographical Difference(s)," in Bella Brodzki and Celeste Schenck, eds., *Life/Lines: Theorizing Women's Autobiography* (Ithaca, NY: Cornell University Press, 1988), 95.

37. Martin, "Lesbian Identity," 98.

38. Diana Velez, ed., *Reclaiming Medusa: Short Stories by Contemporary Puerto Rican Women* (San Francisco: Aunt Lute Books, 1989).

39. Personal Narratives Group, *Interpreting Women's Lives,* 7.

40. Personal Narratives Group, *Interpreting Women's Lives,* 7.

41. Judith Butler, *Gender Trouble: Feminism and the Subversion of Identity* (New York: Routledge, Chapman & Hall, 1990).

42. Nancy Hartsock, "Foucault on Power: A Theory for Women?" in Nicholson, ed., *Feminism/Postmodernism,* 163.

43. Christine Di Stefano, "Dilemmas of Difference: Feminism, Modernity and Postmodernism," in Nicholson, ed., *Feminism/Postmodernism,* 76.

44. Di Stefano, "Dilemmas," 76.

45. Some of these theorists working on issues of identity in relation to autotheoretical texts include Biddy Martin and Chandra Talpade Mohanty, "Feminist Politics: What's Home Got to Do With It?" in Teresa de Lauretis, ed., *Feminist Studies/Critical Studies* (Bloomington: Indiana University Press, 1986), 191–212; Katie King, "Audre Lorde's Lacquered Layerings: The Lesbian Bar as a Site of Literary Production," *Cultural Studies,* v. 2 n. 3 (Oct. 1988), 321–42; Bonnie Zimmerman, "The Politics of Transliteration: Lesbian Personal Narratives," review essay in *The Lesbian Issue: Essays from Signs,* eds., Estelle B. Freedman, Barbara C. Gelpi, Susan L. Johnson, Kathleen M.

Weston (Chicago: University of Chicago Press, 1985), 251–70; Norma Alarcón, "The Theoretical Subject(s) of This Bridge Called My Back and Anglo-American Feminism," in Gloria Anzaldúa, ed., *Making Face, Making Soul/Haciendo Caras: Creative and Critical Perspectives by Women of Color* (San Francisco: Aunt Lute Foundation, 1990), 356–69; and Bella Brodzki and Celeste Schenck, *Life/Lines: Theorizing Women's Autobiography* (Ithaca, NY: Cornell University Press, 1988).

46. Martin and Mohanty, "Feminist Politics," 209.
47. Nancy Fraser and Linda J. Nicholson, "Social Criticism without Philosophy: An Encounter between Feminism and Postmodernism," in Nicholson, ed., *Feminism/Postmodernism*, 33.
48. Bartky, "Foucault," 79.
49. Bartky, "Foucault," 82.
50. Butler, *Gender Trouble*, 5.
51. Anonymous, "S/M Aesthetic," *OUT/LOOK: National Lesbian & Gay Quarterly*, Winter 1989: 42.
52. Fraser and Nicholson, "Social Criticism," 61.
53. Fraser and Nicholson, "Social Criticism," 35.
54. Butler, *Gender Trouble*, 5.
55. Butler, *Gender Trouble*, 143.
56. Butler, *Gender Trouble*, 147.
57. Butler, *Gender Trouble*, 145.
58. Butler, *Gender Trouble*, 14–15.
59. In some instances, postmodern discussions of the fluidity of subjectivity, if overstated, can obscure the ways some identities, in certain contexts and/or for certain individuals, are to some degree fixed. For this and other reasons, it is important not to embrace wholesale and uncritically postmodern or any other theoretical strain, but rather to draw selectively from its insights, always measuring them against the very practices that are supposed to ground the theories.

Chapter 7

1. Linda Alcoff, "Justifying Feminist Social Science," in Nancy Tuana, ed., *Feminism and Science* (Bloomington: Indiana University Press, 1989) 87.
2. Alcoff, "Justifying Feminist Social Science," 95.
3. David Snow and Robert Benford, "Ideology, Frame Resonance and Participant Mobilization," in Bert Klandermans, Hanspeter Kriesi, and Sidney Tarrow, eds., *From Structure to Action: Comparing Movement Participation Across Cultures* (Greenwich, CT: JAI Press, 1988).
4. Of course, telling my readers simply that I am white, a feminist, etc. is not sufficient in this regard. Such sketchy information seems adequate only if one subscribes to the crudest notions of static, essential determinism with regard

to such broad categories. The information I provide in chapter 8 begins to get more specific.

Chapter 8

1. That is, radical feminism in the tradition of Mary Daly, Andrea Dworkin, Susan Griffin, Robin Morgan, Shulamith Firestone, Ti-Grace Atkinson, and other writers who saw gender oppression as the root and primary form of oppression, and who emphasized in their writings direct male control over women's bodies and minds.

2 Joan Cocks, *The Oppositional Imagination: Feminism, Critique and Political Theory* (New York: Routledge, 1989), 8.

3. Thanks to Alexandra Carter for this gem.

4. Coming out later as bisexual, and embracing that identity, was in some ways more difficult, as I have written in "Breaking Silence About the 'B-word': Bisexual identity and lesbian-feminist discourse," in Elizabeth Reba Weise, ed., *Closer to Home: Bisexuality and Feminism* (Seattle: Seal Press, 1992). As it happens, the day I decided I could call myself bisexual (after wrestling with the term and its apolitical connotations for several years) was the day I heard a woman (whose name I have forgotten) speak about Rosario Morales and Aurora Levins Morales's book, *Getting Home Alive*, in which the authors write about their mixed cultural backgrounds and identities that don't fit neatly into any of the established categories. What I got from that talk, and from reading the book soon after, was the conviction that by embracing my "problematic" sexuality rather than trying to force it to fit rigid categories I could challenge the terms by which those categories come to be seen as the only available ones, just as the Moraleses had done with regard to the available ethnic categories which their ethnicities did not easily fit. I could work to make "bisexual" mean something different from all the stereotypes I had so thoroughly internalized, about bisexuals sitting on the fence, ripping off queer communities while basking in the warm glow of heterosexual privilege, and so forth. It was a truly liberating moment.

5. According to a 1989 study first commissioned and then squelched by the Bush administration's Department of Health and Human Services, lesbian, bisexual, and gay teens commit suicide at three times the rate of straight teens, accounting for 30 percent of all teen suicides. Suicide is the leading cause of death among gay teens, according to another study, published in *Pediatrics* magazine in June 1991. Shira Maguen, "Teen Suicide: The Government's Cover-up And America's Lost Children," *The Advocate* (September 24, 1991): 40–47.

References

Alarcón, Norma, "The Theoretical Subject(s) of This Bridge Called My Back and Anglo-American Feminism," in Gloria Anzaldúa, ed. *Making Face, Making Soul/Haciendo Caras: Creative and Critical Perspectives by Women of Color* (San Francisco: Aunt Lute Foundation) 1990.

Alcoff, Linda, "Justifying Feminist Social Science" in Nancy Tuana, ed. *Feminism and Science* (Bloomington: Indiana University Press) 1989.

Anderson, Benedict R. O'G., *Imagined Communities: Reflections on the Origin and Spread of Nationalism* (London: Verso) 1983.

Anderson, Benedict R. O'G., *Imagined Communities: Reflections on the Origin and Spread of Nationalism*, revised edition (London: Verso) 1991.

Anonymous, "S/M Aesthetic," *OUT/LOOK: National Lesbian & Gay Quarterly* Winter 1989.

Anzaldúa, Gloria, *Borderlands/La Frontera: The New Mestiza* (San Francisco: Spinsters/Aunt Lute) 1987.

Bader, Eleanor J., "Court Gives Kids To Abusive Dads," *New Directions for Women* 17; 1, 20.

Bartky, Sandra Lee, "Foucault, Femininity, and the Modernization of Patriarchal Power," in Irene Diamond and Lee Quinby, eds. *Feminism & Foucault: Reflections on Resistance* (Boston: Northeastern University Press) 1988.

Beck, Evelyn Torton, ed. *Nice Jewish Girls: A Lesbian Anthology* (Watertown, MA: Persephone Press, Inc.) 1982.

Braxton, Joanne M., *Black Women Writing Autobiography: A Tradition Within a Tradition* (Philadelphia: Temple University Press) 1989.

Brodzki, Bella and Celeste Schenck, eds. *Life/Lines: Theorizing Women's Autobiography* (Ithaca, NY: Cornell University Press) 1988.

Bulkin, Elly, Minnie Bruce Pratt, and Barbara Smith, *Yours in Struggle: Three Feminist Perspectives on Anti-Semitism and Racism* (Brooklyn, NY: Long Haul Press) 1984. (Reissued by Firebrand Books, Ithaca, NY).

Butler, Judith, *Gender Trouble: Feminism and the Subversion of Identity* (New York: Routledge, Chapman & Hall) 1990.

Calderon, Sara Levi, *Two Mujeres*, trans. Gina Kaufer (San Francisco: Aunt Lute Books) 1989.

Cocks, Joan, *The Oppositional Imagination: Feminism, Critique and Political Theory* (New York: Routledge) 1989.

Combahee River Collective, "A Black Feminist Statement" dated April 1977, in Gloria T. Hull, Patricia Bell Scott, and Barbara Smith, eds. *All the Women Are White, All the Blacks Are Men, But Some of Us Are Brave: Black Women's Studies* (Old Westbury, NY: The Feminist Press) 1982.

Cott, Nancy F. *The Grounding of Modern Feminism* (New Haven and London: Yale University Press) 1987.

Cott, Nancy F. and Elizabeth H. Pleck, *A Heritage of Her Own: Toward a New Social History of American Women* (New York: Touchstone-Simon & Schuster) 1979.

Di Stefano, Christine, "Dilemmas of Difference: Feminism, Modernity and Postmodernism" in Linda J. Nicholson, ed., *Feminism/Postmodernism* (New York: Routledge Chapman & Hall) 1990.

Eisenstein, Zillah, ed. *Capitalist Patriarchy and the Case for Socialist Feminism* (New York: Monthly Review Press) 1979.

Escamill, Edna, *Daughter of the Mountain: Un Cuento* (San Francisco: Aunt Lute Books) 1991.

Evans, Sara, *Born for Liberty: A History of Women in America* (New York: The Free Press-Macmillan, Inc.) 1989.

Eyerman, Ron and Andrew Jamison, *Social Movements: A Cognitive Approach* (University Park: The Pennsylvania State University Press) 1991.

Ferree, Myra Marx and Beth B. Hess, *Controversy and Coalition: The New Feminist Movement* (Boston: Twayne-G. K. Hall & Company) 1985.

Ferree, Myra Marx and Beth B. Hess, *Controversy and Coalition: The New Feminist Movement Across Three Decades of Change* (revised edition) (New York: Twayne) 1994.

Ferree, Myra Marx, "The Political Context of Rationality: Rational Choice Theory and Resource Mobilization," in Aldon D. Morris and Carol McClurg Mueller, eds. *Frontiers in Social Movement Theory* (New Haven: Yale University Press) 1992.

Foucault, Michel, *The History of Sexuality, volume I: An Introduction* trans. Robert Hurley. (New York: Vintage-Random House) 1980. English translation copyright 1978 by Random House, Inc.

Fraser, Nancy, *Unruly Practices: Power, Discourse and Gender in Contemporary Social Theory* (Minneapolis: University of Minnesota Press) 1989.

Fraser, Nancy and Linda J. Nicholson, "Social Criticism Without Philosophy: An Encounter between Feminism and Postmodernism," in Linda J. Nicholson, ed. *Feminism/Postmodernism* (New York: Routledge, Chapman & Hall) 1990.

Freeman, Jo, *The Politics of Women's Liberation: A Case Study of an Emerging Social Movement and its Relation to the Policy Process* (New York and London: Longman) 1975.

Freeman, Jo, *Women: A Feminist Perspective*, 2nd. ed (Palo Alto, CA: Mayfield Publishing Company) 1979.

Friedman, Debra and Doug McAdam, "Collective Identity and Activism: Networks, Choices, and the Life of a Social Movement," in Aldon D. Morris and Carol McClurg Mueller, eds., *Frontiers in Social Movement Theory* (New Haven: Yale University Press) 1992.

Gamson, William A., "The Social Psychology of Collective Action," in Aldon D. Morris and Carol McClurg Mueller, eds., *Frontiers in Social Movement Theory* (New Haven: Yale University Press) 1992.

Gaventa, John, *Power and Powerlessness: Quiescence and Rebellion in an Appalachian Valley* (Chicago: University of Illinois Press) 1980.

Gelb, Joyce, *Feminism and Politics: A Comparative Perspective* (Berkeley, Los Angeles, London: University of California Press) 1989.

Gelb, Joyce, "Social Movement 'Success': A Comparative Analysis of Feminism in the United States and the United Kingdom," in Mary Fainsod Katzenstein and Carol McClurg Mueller, eds. *The Women's Movements of the United States and Western Europe* (Philadelphia: Temple University Press) 1987.

Gelb, Joyce and Marian Lief Palley, *Women and Public Policies* (Princeton, NJ: Princeton University Press) 1982.

Giddings, Paula, *When and Where I Enter . . . The Impact of Black Women on Race and Sex in America* (New York: William Morrow and Company Inc.) 1984.

Gusfield, Joseph R., "The Reflexivity of Social Movements: Collective Behavior and Mass Society Theory Revisited," in Enrique Laraña et al., *New Social Movements: From Ideology to Identity* (Philadelphia: Temple University Press) 1994.

Haraway, Donna, "A Manifesto for Cyborgs: Science, Technology, and Socialist Feminism in the 1980s," *Socialist Review* No. 80, 1985.

Hartsock, Nancy, "Foucault on Power: A Theory for Women?" in Linda J.

Nicholson, ed. *Feminism/Postmodernism* (New York: Routledge, Chapman & Hall) 1990.

Haug, Frigga, et al., *Female Sexualization: A Collective Work of Memory*, trans. Erica Carter (London: Verso) 1987. (German ed. 1983)

hooks, bell, *Ain't I a Woman: black women and feminism* (Boston: South End Press) 1981.

hooks, bell, *Feminist Theory: From Margin to Center* (Boston: South End Press) 1984.

hooks, bell, *Talking Back: Thinking Feminist, Thinking Black* (South End Press) 1984.

hooks, bell, *Yearning: Race, Gender and Cultural Politics* (Boston: South End Press) 1990.

hooks, bell and Cornel West, *Breaking Bread: Insurgent Black Intellectual Life* (Boston: South End Press) 1991.

hooks, bell, *Black Looks: Race and Representation* (Boston: South End Press) 1992.

hooks, bell, *Sisters of the Yam: Black Women and Self Recovery* (Boston: South End Press) 1993.

Hoy, David Couzens, "Foucault: Modern or Postmodern?" in Jonathan Arac, ed. *After Foucault: Humanistic Knowledge, Postmodern Challenges* (New Brunswick, NJ: Rutgers University Press) 1988.

Huyssen, Andreas, "Mapping the Postmodern," in Linda J. Nicholson, ed., *Feminism/Postmodernism* (New York: Routledge, Chapman & Hall) 1990.

King, Katie, "Audre Lorde's Lacquered Layerings: The Lesbian Bar as a Site of Literary Production" from *Cultural Studies* v. 2 n. 3, Oct. 1988: 321–42.

Kitzinger, Celia, *The Social Construction of Lesbianism* (London; Newbury Park, CA; Beverly Hills, CA; New Delhi: Sage Publications) 1987.

Klein, Ethel, *Gender Politics: From Consciousness to Mass Politics* (Cambridge, MA and London: Harvard University Press) 1984.

Laraña, Enrique, Hank Johnston, and Joseph R. Gusfield, eds., *New Social Movements: from Ideology to Identity* (Philadelphia: Temple University Press) 1994.

Laraña, Enrique, et al., "Identities, Grievances, and New Social Movements," in Enrique Laraña et al., *New Social Movements: From Ideology to Identity* (Philadelphia: Temple University Press) 1994.

Lorde, Audre, *Sister/Outsider* (Ithaca, NY: Firebrand Books) 1984.

Lorde, Audre, *A Burst of Light* (Trumansburg, NY: Crossing Press) 1988.

Lorde, Audre, *Zami: A New Spelling of My Name* (Trumansburg, NY: Crossing Press) 1982. (Originally published by Persephone Press.)

Lukes, Steven, *Power: A Radical View* (London: Macmillan Press Ltd.) 1974.

Macdonell, Diane, *Theories of Discourse: An Introduction* (Oxford and New York: Basil Blackwell) 1986.

Maguen, Shira, "Teen Suicide: The Government's Cover-up And America's Lost Children," *The Advocate* (September 24, 1991): 40–47.

Mandel, Ruth B., "The Political Woman" in Sara E. Rix, ed., *The American Woman 1988–89: A Status Report* New York: W.W. Norton and Company) 1988.

Martin, Biddy, "Lesbian Identity and Autobiographical Difference[s]," in Bella Brodzki and Celeste Schenck, eds., *Life/Lines: Theorizing Women's Autobiography* (Ithaca, NY: Cornell University Press) 1988.

Martin, Biddy and Chandra Talpade Mohanty, "Feminist Politics: What's Home Got to Do with It?" in Teresa de Lauretis, ed. *Feminist Studies/Critical Studies* (Bloomington: Indiana University Press) 1986.

McAdam, Doug, *Political Process and the Development of Black Insurgency, 1930–1970* (Chicago: University of Chicago Press) 1982.

McCarthy, John D. and Mayer N. Zald, "Resource Mobilization and Social Movements: a partial theory" in Mayer N. Zald and John D. McCarthy, *Social Movements in an Organizational Society* (New Brunswick, NJ: Transaction Books) 1987.

McGowan, John, *Postmodernism and Its Critics* (Ithaca: Cornell University Press) 1991.

Mehta, Uday S., "Liberal Strategies of Exclusion," *Politics and Society* Dec.1990.

Melucci, Alberto, "A Strange Kind of Newness: What's 'New' in New Social Movements?" in Enrique Laraña et al., *New Social Movements: From Ideology to Identity* (Philadelphia: Temple University Press) 1994.

Melucci, Alberto, *Nomads of the Present*, eds., John Keane and Paul Mier (Philadelphia: Temple University Press) 1989.

Miller, Nancy K., *Getting Personal: Feminist Occasions and Other Autobiographical Acts* (New York: Routledge) 1991.

Mohanty, Chandra Talpade, "Feminist Encounters: Locating the Politics of Experience," in *copyright 1: Fin De Siecle 2000* (Cambridge, MA) Fall 1987.

Moi, Toril, *Sexual/Textual Politics: Feminist Literary Theory* (London: Routledge) 1985.

Monteflores, Carmen de, *Singing Softly/Cantando Bajito* (San Francisco: Aunt Lute Books) 1989.

Moraga, Cherríe, *Loving in the War Years: lo que nunca pasó por sus labios* (Boston: South End Press) 1983.

Cherríe Moraga and Gloria Anzaldúa, eds. *This Bridge Called My Back: Writings by Radical Women of Color.* (Watertown, MA: Persephone Press) 1981. (Reissued by Kitchen Table: Women of Color Press, Albany, NY.)

Morales, Aurora Levins and Rosario Morales, *Getting Home Alive* (Ithaca, NY: Firebrand Books) 1986.

Morgan, Robin, ed., *Sisterhood is Global: The International Women's Movement Anthology* (Garden City, NY: Anchor-Doubleday) 1984.

Morris, Aldon D. and Carol McClurg Mueller, eds. *Frontiers in Social Movement Theory* (New Haven: Yale University Press) 1992.

Morris, Aldon D., "Political Consciousness and Collective Action," in Aldon D. Morris and Carol McClurg Mueller, eds. *Frontiers in Social Movement Theory* (New Haven: Yale University Press) 1992.

Mueller, Carol McClurg, "Building Social Movement Theory," in Aldon D. Morris and Carol McClurg Mueller, eds. *Frontiers in Social Movement Theory* (New Haven: Yale University Press) 1992.

Mueller, Carol McClurg, "Conflict Networks and the Origins of Women's Liberation," in Enrique Laraña et al. *New Social Movements: From Ideology to Identity* (Philadelphia: Temple University Press) 1994.

Myron, Nancy and Charlotte Bunch, eds. *Lesbianism and the Women's Movement* (Baltimore: Diana Press) 1975.

Nestle, Joan, *A Restricted Country* (Ithaca, NY: Firebrand Books) 1987.

Nicholson, Linda, ed. *Feminism/Postmodernism* (New York: Routledge) 1990.

Norton, Mary Beth, *Liberty's Daughters: The Revolutionary Experience of American Women, 1750–1800* (Boston: Little, Brown and Company) 1980.

Personal Narratives Group, eds., *Interpreting Women's Lives: Feminist Theory and Personal Narratives* (Bloomington and Indianapolis: Indiana University Press) 1989.

Powell, Supreme Court Justice Lewis, *Regents of the University of California v. Bakke*, in Toby Kleban Levine, et. al, eds., *Eyes on the Prize: America's Civil Rights Years: A Reader and Guide* (New York: Penguin) 1987.

Pratt, Minnie Bruce, *Rebellion: Essays 1980–1991* (Ithaca, NY: Firebrand Books) 1991.

Pratt, Minnie Bruce, "Identity: Skin Blood Heart" in Elly Bulkin, Minnie Bruce Pratt, and Barbara Smith, *Yours In Struggle: Three Feminist Perspectives on Anti-Semitism and Racism* (Brooklyn, NY: Long Haul Press) 1984.

Radicalesbians, "woman-identified woman" (pamphlet) (Somerville, MA: New England Free Press) 1970.

Rix, Sara E., ed., *The American Woman: A Status Report*, The Women's Research and Education Institute 3. (New York: W.W. Norton) 1990.

Ryan, Barbara, *Feminism and the Women's Movement: Dynamics of Change in Social Movement Ideology and Activism* (New York: Routledge) 1992.

Ryan, Charlotte, *Prime Time Activism: Media Strategies for Grassroots Organizing* (Boston: South End Press) 1991.

Scott, Kesho, Cherry Muhanji and Egyriba High, *Tight Spaces* (San Francisco: Aunt Lute Books) 1987.

Sedgwick, Eve Kosofsky, *Epistemology of the Closet* (Berkeley/Los Angeles: University of California Press) 1990.

Segrest, Mab, *My Mama's Dead Squirrel: Lesbian Essays on Southern Culture* (Ithaca, NY: Firebrand Books) 1985.

Small, Margaret, "Lesbians and the Class Position of Women," in Nancy Myron and Charlotte Bunch, eds. *Lesbianism and the Women's Movement* (Baltimore: Diana Press) 1975.

Smith, Barbara, "A Press of Our Own: Kitchen Table: Women of Color Press," *Frontiers* vol. X, no. 3, 1989, 11–13.

Smith, Barbara, ed. *Home Girls: A Black Feminist Anthology* (Albany, NY: Kitchen Table: Women of Color Press) 1985.

Smith, Sidonie, *A Poetics of Women's Autobiography: Marginality and the Fictions of Self-Representation* (Bloomington: Indiana University Press) 1987.

Snitow, Ann, Christine Stansell, and Sharon Thompson, eds., *Powers of Desire: The Politics of Sexuality* (New York: Monthly Review Press) 1983.

Snow, David A. and Robert D. Benford, "Master Frames and Cycles of Protest," in Aldon D. Morris and Carol McClurg Mueller, eds. *Frontiers in Social Movement Theory* (New Haven: Yale University Press) 1992.

Snow, David and Robert Benford, "Ideology, Frame Resonance and Participant Mobilization" in Bert Klandermans, Hanspeter Kriesi, and Sidney Tarrow, eds., *From Structure to Action: Comparing Movement Participation Across Cultures* (Greenwich, Connecticut: JAI Press) 1988.

Solomon, Barbara, "Taking the Bullshit By the Horns," in Myron and Bunch, eds., *Lesbianism and the Women's Movement* (Baltimore: Diana Press) 1975.

Tarrow, Sidney, *Struggle, Politics and Reform: Collective Action, Social Movements, and Cycles of Protest* (Ithaca, NY: Western Societies Program, Center for International Studies, Cornell University), Occasional Paper no. 21, 1989.

Tarrow, Sidney, *Struggling to Reform: Social Movements and Policy Change During Cycles of Protest* (Ithaca, NY: Western Societies Program, Cornell University) 1983.

Taylor, Verta and Nancy E. Whittier, "Collective Identity in Social Movement Communities: Lesbian Feminist Mobilization," in Aldon D.

Morris and Carol McClurg Mueller, eds., *Frontiers in Social Movement Theory* (New Haven: Yale University Press) 1992.

Tesh, Sylvia N., "New Social Movements and New Ideas," Paper presented at the Annual Meeting of the American Political Science Association, Washington, D.C., September 2–5, 1993

Vance, Carole S., ed., *Pleasure and Danger: Exploring Female Sexuality* (Boston: Routledge & Kegan Paul) 1984.

Velez, Diana, ed., *Reclaiming Medusa: Short Stories by Contemporary Puerto Rican Women* (San Francisco: Aunt Lute Foundation) 1989.

Weedon, Chris, *Feminist Practice and Poststructuralist Theory.* (New York and Oxford: Basil Blackwell, Inc.), 1987.

Wiener, Jon, "Law Profs Fight the Power," *The Nation*, September 4–11, 1989; 246–48.

Wertheimer, Barbara Mayer, *We Were There: The Story of Working Women in America* (New York: Pantheon-Random House) 1977.

Williams, Patricia J., *The Alchemy of Race and Rights: Diary of a Law Professor* (Cambridge: Harvard University Press) 1991.

Willis, Ellen, *No More Nice Girls: Countercultural Essays* (Hanover, NH: Wesleyan University Press) 1992.

Young, Stacey, "Breaking Silence About the 'B-word': Bisexuality and Lesbian Feminist Discourse," in Elizabeth Reba Weise, ed., *Closer to Home: Bisexuality and Feminism* (Seattle: Seal Press) 1992.

Zimmerman, Bonnie, "The Politics of Transliteration: Lesbian Personal Narratives" review essay in *The Lesbian Issue: Essays from Signs* eds., Estelle B. Freedman, Barbara C. Gelpi, Susan L. Johnson, Kathleen M. Weston (Chicago: University of Chicago Press) 1985.

Zald, Mayer N., "Looking Backward to Look Forward: Reflections on the Past and Future of the Resource Mobilization Research Program," in Aldon D. Morris and Carol McClurg Mueller, eds., *Frontiers in Social Movement Theory* (New Haven: Yale University Press) 1992.

Index